11/8

Two week loan

Please return on or before the last
date stamped below.
Charges are made for late return.

CARDIFF UNIVERSITY LIBRARIES, PO BOX 430, CARDIFF CF1 3XT

LF 114/0796

D1338148

READING 'THE PROSTITUTE'

Reading 'The Prostitute'

Appearance, Place and Time in British and Irish Press
Stories of Prostitution

LORNA RYAN
Department of Sociology and Social Anthropology,
University of Kent and Department of Social Studies,
Trinity College, Dublin

Ashgate

Aldershot • Brookfield USA • Singapore • Sydney

Published by
Ashgate Publishing Limited
Gower House
Croft Road
Aldershot
Hants GU11 3HR
England

Ashgate Publishing Company
Old Post Road
Brookfield
Vermont 05036
USA

British Library Cataloguing in Publication Data
Ryan, Lorna
  Reading 'the prostitute' : appearance, place and time in
  British and Irish press stories of prostitution
  1.Prostitution in the press - Great Britain 2.Prostitution
  in the press - Ireland
  I.Title
  306.7'4'0941

Library of Congress Catalog Card Number: 97-70892

ISBN 1 85972 539 2

Printed and bound by Athenaeum Press, Ltd.,
Gateshead, Tyne & Wear.

Contents

Tables   ix
Acknowledgements   xi
Preface   xiii

Chapter One: Introduction and background to the research   1

1.1   Introduction   1
1.2   Background to the study   2
1.3   Initial problems and the reformulation of the research   5
1.4   The content of the book: An outline   8

Chapter Two: Discourses of prostitution   13

2.1   Introduction   13
2.2   Approaches to prostitution: An initial characterisation   15
2.3   Religious and moral discourses on prostitution   18
2.4   Medical discourses   21
      2.4.1 Psychopathological discourses   26
2.5   Sociological discourses   29
      2.5.1 Functionalist approaches within sociological discourse   30
2.6   Legal discourses   32
      2.6.1 Prosecutions for activities relating to prostitution   38
2.7   Feminist discourses   42
      2.7.1 Feminist approaches to legal discourses   46
2.8   Practitioners' discourses   47
2.9   Conclusion   49

Chapter Three: Selection of materials and findings from a content analysis   57

3.1   Introduction   57
     3.1.1   The research design: Selecting materials   58
     3.1.2   Data collection procedures   62
     3.1.3   Reliability and validity: Sample size   65
     3.1.4   Descriptive account of the materials:
             Findings from a content analysis   69
     3.1.5   Coding press content   75
     3.1.6   Conclusion   81
3.2   Analysing media products   82
     3.2.1   Introduction   82
     3.2.2   Models of media processes   82
     3.2.3   Language in the media: Expressions of ideology   88
     3.2.4   Studies of 'bias' in the media   89
3.3   Conclusion   92

Chapter Four: Methodology and methods of analysis   97

4.1   Introduction   97
4.2   Starting points: Qualitative research design   98
4.3   Starting points: Preliminary analysis   100
4.4   Ethnomethodological approaches   107
4.5   Ethnomethodological approaches to reading   109
4.6   Machineries of description   111
     4.6.1   Category bound activities   113
4.7   Ethnomethodological indifference   117
4.8   The Goffman additive   119
4.9   Conclusion   120

Chapter Five: Identifying 'the prostitute': Information signs   125

5.1   Introduction   125
5.2   Formulating categories: Physical appearance   128
5.3   Body gestures   134
5.4   Sartorial style   136
5.5   Conclusion   143

Chapter Six: Zones of prostitution and localised times: Formulating identity by place and time   147

6.1 Introduction   147
6.2 Spaces of prostitution   148
     6.2.1 Place formulations   149
     6.2.2 Inmates of the underworld   155
     6.2.3 Conclusion   160
6.3 Timed displays of prostitution   160
     6.3.1 Temporal formulations   162
     6.3.2 Timed events and events in time   163
     6.3.3 Prostitution time   165
     6.3.4 Conclusion   166
6.4 Evidence of intent: Identifying prostitutes   167
     6.4.1 Pre-prostitution: Visible presence as predictive 168
6.5 Conclusion   177

Chapter Seven: The photographic dimension: Visual images in the press   181

7.1   Introduction   181
7.2   Images: Written and visual   185
7.3   Description of the data   186
7.4   Attributions of news photographs   187
7.5   Approaching the visual data and finding a method
      of analysis   188
7.6   Classifying the photographs   189
7.7   Classification 1: Journalists as subjects   190
7.8   Classifications 2 and 3: The different 'ofs' of photographs
      and the different types of photographs   192
7.9   An uncaptioned image   193
7.10 Captioned images   194
7.11 Reading photographs: Inter and intra-textuality   198
7.12 Profiling the cast of players: Photographs 'of' pimps,
      clients and prostitutes   201
7.13 Unequivocal views: Evidencing the presence of a prostitute 204
7.14 Action sequences and synoptic visions: Photographs
      'of' prostitution   208
7.15 Photographing the subject of prostitution   213
7.16 Historically and culturally specific visions   214
7.17 Conclusion   216

Chapter Eight: The contextual web: Finding the connections   221

8.1 Introduction   221
8.2 Inter-discursive relations   223
     8.2.1 Interdiscursivity: The discourse of rape   227
8.3 Social control in social context   228
8.4 Social control: The role of the press   231
8.5 Evidence: Some final comments   231
8.6 Concluding remarks   232

Appendix I   *Definitions in the discourses of prostitution*   237

Appendix II   *Listing of newspaper stories of prostitution*
                in the British and Irish press: 1987 - 1991   241

Appendix III   *Newspaper photographs*   247

Bibliography   257

Tables

Table 2.1   List of publications on prostitution by discipline   16

Table 2.2   Literature on prostitution by area   16

Table 2.3   Prosecution figures for prostitution (1980-1994)
            Ireland   39

Table 2.4   Prosecutions: Offences by prostitutes (1983-1993) UK   41

Table 2.5   Cautions: Offences by prostitutes (1983-1993) UK   41

Table 3.1   Nationally available daily and Sunday newspapers
            in Britain and the Republic of Ireland   61

Table 3.2   Circulation figures for national newspapers in
            Britain and Ireland (1987, 1989, 1991)   62

Table 3.3   Distribution of newspaper articles by year and
            paper   64

Table 3.4   Distribution of newspaper stories by year (British
            and Irish press)   64

Table 3.5   Number of newspaper stories on prostitution:
            checking procedure   67

Table 3.6   Representations of AIDS in the Irish and British
            press (December 1986 – February 1987)   69

Table 3.7   Occurrence of story by month per year –
            British and Irish press (1987-1991)   72

Table 3.8   Distribution of stories by page numbers   73

Table 3.9   Genre of report by Irish and British newspapers   74

Table 3.10   Forms of prostitution: UK and Irish stories
           (1987-1991)   77

Table 3.11   Gender/age profile of prostitutes   77

Table 3.12   Reasons for entry into prostitution   78

Table 3.13   Violence and prostitution   80

Table 6.1   Places of prostitution   149

Table 6.2   Time periods of prostitution in the British and
           Irish press   162

Table 7.1   Distribution of photographs by year and newspaper   186

Table 7.2   Subject of photographs by newspaper   187

Acknowledgements

I would like to thank a number of people for their support, encouragement and critical commentaries over the course of carrying out this research. Staff of the Department of Sociology, Trinity College Dublin, have been interested in and encouraging of this work. Brian Torode, Trinity College Dublin, has, over the past decade, been especially unfailing in his support for and constructive criticism of the various research projects, including that reported here, which I have carried out. From him I have learned much about the rigorous and systematic nature of qualitative research. Howard Davis, University of Kent, provided support and constructive criticism of my work. Mary McIntosh, University of Essex, and Mary Evans, University of Kent, gave helpful comments. Jacqui Halson, University of Kent, combined much valued friendship and hospitality with sociological discussion.

Thanks to friends who acted, often involuntarily, as sounding boards for monologues about prostitution and other issues raised in this work. In particular I would like to thank Anne Keogh, Alison and John Lean, Stevie Tobin, Moirin Moynihan, Frankie Lynch and Ann Bond. I would also like to acknowledge the staff of the Lecky Library (Trinity College Dublin), including Paul, Seán, Sinéad, Eileen, Tony and Claire. Thanks to Jacqui Akkouh and staff at Avebury. Anne O'Neill rescued me from the horrors of typesetting and I extend my heartfelt thanks to her for efficiency and speed in preparing this manuscript.

Copyright permission was obtained for the photographs reproduced (Appendix III):
1. © Guardian Newspapers Limited, 1989
2. © James Stracham, 1990
3. © David Rooney, 1987

Preface

Prostitution, particularly the prostitution of women, has long been the concern of thousands of writers worldwide. This book is about broadsheet newspaper stories of prostitution. It was a project which began with a specific concern to document what the Irish and British press were saying about prostitutes and prostitution. There is a paucity of empirical research on this topic and the study is thus an exploratory one. My interest in the subject of prostitution stemmed from a more general interest in the area of sexuality and also from an interest in the divisive debates amongst feminists about the role of prostitution in contemporary Western societies. I was also interested in the role of the medium of the press and in media discourses generally.

When I started collecting broadsheet press articles about prostitution I was struck by how they did not conform to my expectations – there were no overt instances of sexist language, the 'whore image' to which feminists referred was not readily identifiable. The absence of what I would have seen as 'negative language' sent me back to the literature, a corpus dealing with historical, medical, psychopathological, and sociological aspects of prostitution. However, even armed with these diverse knowledges gave me no immediate handle on my textual materials. My sense of puzzlement cannot be understated - why were my materials, ever increasing in number, taken from the broadsheet press in two countries, so unremarkable? My attempt to find an answer to this question led me to a number of different methods of textual analysis, to further forays into the enormous literature on prostitution, on women's sexuality, on language or discourse. But to no avail. My initial aim of writing about the broadsheet press' coverage of prostitution seemed at that juncture to be misguided. One aim of this book is to provide a naturalistic account of a research study. In this sense it follows John Maxwell Atkinson's seminal work, *Suicide: Studies in the Social Organisation of Sudden Death* (1982) and the initial problems Atkinson encountered were those I was to later engage with in this study. I was able to make sense of the problems I encountered through an engagement with the work of the ethnomethodologists.

The ethnomethodological enterprise, pioneered by Harold Garfinkel and Harvey Sacks, claims to reorientate sociological enquiries, a reorientation which is based upon a shift from 'why' to 'how' questions about the social order. Crucially, at least for this study, one of its central features is its exhortation to sociologists to view the obvious, mundane and commonplace features of social life as 'anthropologically strange'. The research question about press articles on prostitution (and prostitutes) was radically reformulated along the lines suggested by ethno-methodology. What was said about prostitutes was no longer of prime interest, rather, how the newspaper texts could be said to be about prostitution/prostitutes at all became the central research question. In this way, I was concerned to explicate common sense methods of reasoning which I as analyst had initially unthinkingly relied upon. In short, it meant that I followed the ethnomethodological injunction to treat resource as topic, to be truly reflexive in relation to my analysis of my materials.

The analysis employed demonstrates that the press accounts of the activities of prostitutes and of the prostitutes themselves use descriptions of appearance, place and time in providing for, in ethnomethodological terms, 'recognisably correct' categorisations. Questions of motive and intent are central to the unequivocal categorisation of women as 'prostitutes'. This categorisation is based upon culturally specific understandings of types of women and types of activities which are used by both journalists and readers, including analysts. Reading is thus dialogical. The title of this book, *Reading 'The Prostitute'*, aims to encapsulate this process, and it involves both the textual and the visual. In regard to the latter, press pictures have been overlooked by many theorists of the press, a neglect which this study aims to rectify.

An overview of the study is provided in Chapter One and the developments and revisions made over the course of the study are elaborated throughout the book.

1 Introduction and background to the research

1.1 Introduction

This book documents an investigation of the construction of 'the prostitute' *
in the British and Irish broadsheet press over a five year period (1987-
1991). It aims to forge connections between three broad fields of research;
namely, prostitution, the study of media processes and the study of
discourse in everyday life. The issues of social categorisation and
classification emerged over the course of the research as central to the
question of the discursive construction of 'the prostitute'. The study is
concerned primarily with female prostitution. This is so because of two
factors; firstly, the newspaper stories which served as the data for this
study were 'about' female prostitution; secondly, my interest was focused
on questions relating to the social control of women.

Over the course of the study, the issue of description became central.
With the emergence of this aspect, the ethnomethodological enterprise,
with its focus upon procedures of category production, became
increasingly relevant to my concerns. However, this is not an
ethnomethodological study per se; rather, it uses the insights of this
approach in an instrumental manner consistent with my objective of
investigating a particular discourse site, that of the press, with a view to
promoting an understanding of its role in the social control of women.

In this chapter I am concerned to explicate the background to the
research; a retrospective re-construction of a process which is pertinent
here because the refinement of the initial (broad) research question,
concerning the representations of prostitutes in press discourse, occurred
some time into this study. It aims to specify the reasons why my focus
shifted in the way that it did and the methodological implications of this.

The chapter concludes with an outline of the study. As the research questions were generated over the course of the study and involved a re-thinking about methodology and, relatedly, methods to be applied to the data, I have attempted to convey this in a step-by-step manner. The discussion of the background to the research is here given cursory treatment as it is further elaborated as the thesis proceeds.

1.2 Background to the study

This study originated as an exploratory study of representations of prostitutes in the print media. It followed from an earlier, brief study of British and Irish newspaper coverage of a specific event – the World Whores Congress, which was held in Brussels in 1986 (Ryan, 1987). In this study, the dominant representation of the prostitute was that of a woman forced into prostitution. Over the course of this study, I was struck by the paucity of published research relating to media representations of prostitutes. If, as has been argued (e.g., Perkins, 1991), prostitution affects all women, this neglect is especially surprising. Some work does exist however: Nead (1988) has examined representations of female sexuality in nineteenth century paintings, with a particular focus on paintings of prostitutes; Clarke (1987) similarly has examined painting, specifically Monet's *Olympia*, and Perkins (1989) has focused upon screen realism vis-à-vis images of prostitutes. Other studies of images of women, for example, Butcher et al. (1974), refer to images of 'whores' as part of a wider concern to document public imagery of women. A basic aim, therefore, was to contribute to this small corpus of work.

A secondary focus, which also emerged from this earlier study, related to formal/linguistic discourse analysis and the rather ambitious aim to develop a method of discourse analysis which would counter John Thompson's assertion that

> However rigorous and systematic the methods of discourse analysis may be, they can never abolish the need for a creative construction of meaning, that is, for an interpretative explication of what is said … Interpretative explication always goes beyond the methods of formal analysis, projecting a possible meaning which is always risky and open to dispute (1984, p. 137).

Thompson's assertion seemed to me to deny the validity of close micro-analysis of textual data; 'risky', 'open to dispute' meaning/s of one's data, denying the possibility of replication (and hence validity) of

2

research findings. This question of validation of discourse analytic research findings was one with which I was particularly concerned, and ~3~ my adoption of the methodological procedures prescribed by 4 ethnomethodology, including the injunctions that theorising must be grounded in empirical data; that data extracts be supplied so that readers can judge for themselves the adequacy of the interpretation offered, was, given these concerns, not surprising (cf. Cicourel, 1964; Sacks, 1984).

In formulating the initial research problem I privileged the methodological problems raised by Thompson (above) and the substantive topic of prostitution was accorded a secondary role. By the *argument* completion of the research, however, this imbalance was rectified; I argue that press discourses of prostitution use descriptions of appearance, place and time in providing for the recognition of a woman as 'a prostitute'. This argument is premised upon an understanding of language, or discourse, as language in use. Language does not simply reflect objects to which it refers, it constitutes them. The work of Austin, Searle and Wittgenstein is centrally concerned with the performative nature of language (cf. Turner, 1971). 'Discourse', as language in use, is a problematic term in the social sciences, and has been defined in a variety of ways; van Dijk (1985) defines discourse as a communicative event, Schegloff, an ethnomethodological conversation analyst, simply defines discourse as a sequence of sentences (1982). The conception of discourse used in this study is taken from Nead who understands it as a particular form of language with its own rules and conventions (1988, p. 4). Discourses embody assumptions about the nature of social phenomena, and about social reality itself.

Different approaches to the analysis of discourse exist; for example, Fairclough (1985) distinguishes between critical and descriptive discourse analysis. The former aims to explicate the ways in which asymmetrical power relations are reproduced in and through discursive practices, while the latter, into which ethnomethodological conversation analysis falls, is concerned to describe features of texts (that is sequences of spoken or written utterances). In short, the latter approach is 'text-bound' while the former attempts to tie the processes of discursivity to wider social processes. My approach drew particularly upon the descriptive approach. However, I would reject claims that it remained 'text-bound'; rather the rationale for this approach was the detailed explication of textual processes and a consideration of the reading process involved vis-à-vis newspaper texts.

The broadsheet newspapers were selected as the data source for a variety of reasons. Firstly, as noted, there exists a paucity of work on the media representations of prostitutes. In particular, no published work exists on representations of prostitutes in the press. Also, given my interests in methods of discourse analysis and their application to written texts, newspapers as a specific site of public discourse, with a relatively stable structure (van Dijk, 1988) were appropriate to this end. The ready availability of newspapers was also a factor in my decision to focus upon the press, albeit a minor one. The selection rationale and procedure are further discussed in Chapter Three.

One of the main changes which occurred over this study was my realisation that my focus upon written discourse in the press had overlooked what is a mundane, unremarkable feature of newspapers, namely the press photographs. In the fashion of many discourse analysts who focus upon newspaper discourse (e.g., Lupton, 1994), I had been 'blind' to their existence. Initially, however, I was not interested in visual images, although in the preliminary analysis attempted, that of a newspaper story which reviewed a book on prostitution, I broached the question of authorship by reference to the *photograph* of the author.

Initially, a comparative approach was not entertained. However due to the paucity of reports on prostitution in the Irish broadsheet press and the changing focus of the research as it progressed, the study changed from being a study of Irish newspaper reports on prostitution to one which included the British broadsheet press. This comparative focus enables me to consider whether the findings of this study are 'culture-bound' or whether (as it turned out) they hold for both the British and Irish press.

Analysis of discourse, as Fairclough points out, aims to link the local with the broader context of its occurrence:

> … 'micro' actions or events … can in no sense be regarded as of purely 'local' significance to the situations in which they occur, for any and every action contributes to the reproduction of 'macro' [social] structures (1985, p. 746).

Discourses do not exist in a vacuum; social life is characterised by division. Ethnomethodology, as Rustin (1993) points out offers a quietist view of social life, in opposition to critical discourse analysts who seek to identify ideologies which reproduce inequalities along the lines of (especially) class, gender, race. However, in approaching the texts from an ethnomethodological perspective, the aim is firstly to identify what discourse processes are occurring, and how they are operating, before invoking extra-textual context. Fairclough's statement points to how the findings from analysis are to be interpreted, not to the starting point of analysis.

4

1.3 Initial problems and the reformulation of the research

The following resembles the 'confessional tales' of ethnography, as described by van Maanen (1988) and briefly details the initial problems I encountered. In another sense, however, it simply points to how research does not generally proceed in a clear cut, linear manner, a point a number of researchers have pointed out (e.g., Herbert, 1989) and 'messiness' is, Marshall and Gossman (1995) say, a feature of qualitative research. This 'confessional' is necessary and its purpose is to highlight how the research underwent a transformation.

The first problem encountered was in the course of carrying out a preliminary analysis of an Irish newspaper article. I describe this fully in Chapter Four and the current aim is to sketch out what occurred. The analysis was based upon Zellig Harris's (1952a, 1952b) distributional method which claims to be presuppositionless. Michel Pecheux's (1982) work on the relative clause and ideology in discourse was also used. Briefly, the aim of analysis was to identify discourse structure, identified by lexical cohesion. The problem of valency arose and rendered the analysis, which claimed to be 'presuppositionless', invalid. My way around this was to draw upon Berger and Luckmann's (1966) work on the social construction of reality. In particular, the theme of the everyday world at the margins of which the 'nightside' or 'twilight' world is located and the cultural anxiety about the perceived encroachment upon this everyday world was central. However, this analysis was directed by the interpretative framework supplied by Berger and Luckmann, it was not derived from the formal analysis of the text.

What this analysis demonstrated was that the role of interpretation was central, as was the issue how I, as a reader, read the texts. Further, and moving to consider the corpus as a whole, the stories were unremarkable, there were no overt instances of 'ideology'. The reports were measured in tone (although the double entendres contained in the headlines were noted, see Appendix II). I then turned to consider conversation analytic approaches with a view to attempting to apply such work to written texts. This yielded some success in terms of such devices as 'back-channels', 'recipient-design' and could be linked to the work of media scholars regarding the structure of the news report. However, the relevance of this work to my study of press discourses of prostitution was far from clear. Concurrently, I was, in the style of grounded theory (Glaser & Strauss, 1967), engaging in relevant reading on the substantive topic of prostitution and the media studies literature. The former literature constitutes a vast corpus, and as Allen has remarked

5

... the theme of prostitution reoccurs through the histories of women's work, welfare and poverty, class relations, sexuality, public health, crime and policing, leisure and popular culture (1986, p. 185).

In addressing this literature I was inconsistent in my approach because I was (initially) not conceptualising it in the same way as the newspapers, namely (as it was later conceptualised) as comprising different discourses articulated from a range of sites, from the academic to the legal. One option open to me was to attempt to specify the themes in the different discourses. However, this was problematic; for example, while in my earlier study (Ryan, 1987) the issue of women being 'driven into' prostitution was central, this was a minor topic in terms of the data considered in their entirety. Analysis by theme (such as prostitution and disease) was thus not a viable research strategy.

In addition, like Kathy Davis (1988), I could sense, intuitively, that there was 'something going on' in and across the newspaper stories (which by the end of the data collection phase totalled 86). In my introduction to ethnomethodology I noted one of the key methodological strategies advanced, that of the analyst becoming 'anthropologically strange' which means that the analyst cannot produce a 'gloss', e.g., that the stories are 'about 'prostitution or prostitutes. This strategy was adopted by me and the result was a problematising of the stories as stories of prostitution. How was I reading these stories, what was 'in' them to warrant my description of them as 'stories of prostitution'? In short, I took a step back, after the fashion of ethnomethodologists such as John Maxwell Atkinson (1982), and asked, 'who is "the prostitute"?' And, more centrally, how is the category 'prostitute' produced over the course of an occasion of reading?

Zerubavel has remarked that the sociologist should

... direct [her] efforts towards discovering new analytical perspectives from which to view social reality and discover 'intellectual novelties' ... [It] is far more challenging and exciting intellectually to observe the mundane and familiar and to illuminate it from a novel analytic perspective (1979, p. xiv).

The 'mundane' and 'familiar' aspects of the newspaper stories of prostitution were the descriptions of 'the prostitute' in terms of physical and clothed appearance and her time and place of presence. In focusing upon the descriptions of 'the prostitute', or the formulations used to 'hint at' 'prostitute', I was departing from the mainstream approaches to prostitution as a substantive topic. I was no longer primarily interested in the content of the stories in respect of what they said about the prostitute, rather I wanted to see how it could be said to be 'talking' about 'the prostitute' in the first place. I am therefore 'looking afresh' at the topic of prostitution.

I want to illustrate these points by reference to firstly an excerpt from a women's magazine story, and secondly, comments made by Peter Sutcliffe, which, although not data in this study, provide the most apposite examples which sum up what I experienced in the reformulation of the research question:

WOMEN TRUCKERS

Most women try to lay up in a truckstop lorry park because it's safer. But it has its own set of problems. Julie Thomas was asleep one night when a middle-aged woman in leopard-skin trousers, a boob tube, high heels and a scrap of a blouse knocked on the door of her cab. 'Anything I can do for you?' the woman said, and then her jaw dropped when Julie looked out. (Really she should have known better.) (*Marie Claire*, 1994, pp. 32-34).

When reading the story I read this excerpt and, immediately making a categorisation 'prostitute', carried on reading. It was only afterwards (that is, a number of paragraphs later) that I realised what had happened.

These four sentences raise the question of reader productivity and especially direct attention to appearance, place and time in the active 'assembly' (Sacks, 1974) of a category. It also reminded me of Garfinkel's comment about the operation of the 'et cetera' principle, namely that 'much ... of what is actually reported is not mentioned' (1967, p. 3). 'Prostitute' is not mentioned here (or anywhere else in the story), yet that it was a prostitute who knocked on the door of the cab is indisputable.

The second example comes from the transcripts of the court trial of Peter Sutcliffe, the so-called 'Yorkshire Ripper' (cf. Boulos, 1983). Peter Sutcliffe was on trial, in 1981, for the murder of thirteen women, most of whom were identified by the police as prostitutes, and the attempted murder of a further seven women. Wendy Hollway (1981) has considered the press reports of the trial in relation to the construction and reproduction of male sexuality and the 'normalising' of male violence against women which was effected in the construction of Sutcliffe as a pathological monster. Cameron and Frazer (1987) have also focused upon how prostitutes are, via discourses of sin, constructed as 'natural victims'. However, one feature of the transcripts which I want to focus attention on relates to Peter Sutcliffe's own statements about how he identified the women as 'prostitutes':

7

(1) I knew there were prostitutes operating in Manningham Lane, Bradford, because I'd seen them blatantly along the road.
(2) She was walking slowly along the kerb, looking across the road.
(3) She looked like a prostitute and she was walking slowly at a snail's pace. I killed her with no doubt. The voice shouted 'filthy prostitute' (from Boulos, 1983, pp. 7-13).

The issue of Sutcliffe's 'recognition' of a woman as a prostitute was not a central feature in the trial, the trial was more centrally concerned with his motivations (had he, as he said, 'just wanted to kill a woman' or was he following the directive of God, that is was he bad or mad?). That Sutcliffe 'could know' that a woman was a prostitute is of interest to current concerns, his reference to appearance and demeanour (3), to place (1) were not, in the trial, considered evidence of madness.

1.4 The content of the book: An outline

The foregoing has aimed to explicate some of the sources, and initial research experiences, which led me to the research question: how are women categorised as 'prostitutes' in the newspaper stories of prostitution, i.e., how are these descriptions organised? The nature of the data, newspaper stories, raised a second, related question: how are formulations of category membership read? These two questions together led to a third question concerning the functions of such descriptions, both within the text itself and within its broader context.

Atkinson (1982), in his work on the social organisation of suicide, commented that he had been unable to continue writing beyond the literature review until the reconceptualisation of his research endeavour had been achieved. Similarly, I grappled with the literature on prostitution for a considerable time, attempting first to structure my review according to theme and after that, according to chronological publication. There seemed to be a divergence between my materials and the content of the literature. This divergence was overcome by attending to Sacks' directive that

> ... nothing we take as subject can appear as part of our descriptive apparatus unless it itself has been described (1963, p. 2).

This statement meant that, strictly speaking, my attempt to focus upon categorisation procedures should include the literature, as discourses of prostitution, *as data*. This approach was not fully adopted. However, by understanding the corpus of literature as other discourses, which are to be set alongside those of the press, to be examined in the same way as I was examining newspaper discourse, I was able to proceed. Chapter Two, the opening chapter of the study proper, details the different discourses of prostitution which are in circulation (for example, in professional journals; throughout the various mass media). These discourses embody assumptions as to the nature of prostitution and journalists reproduce these assumptions in their stories of prostitution. This chapter thus lays the backcloth against which the data are to be considered. This chapter is followed by a discussion of the findings of content analysis which was carried out on the data (Chapter Three). This exercise provides an 'anatomy' of the corpus and indicates key themes present in the data over the five year period. It links back to the discussion of the different discourses by pointing to the continuities of themes between these and the press discourse. Content analysis, a quantitative method, is critiqued in terms of my aims of explicating textual process. Having introduced the reader to the data and my specific concerns with them, I move then to consider some of the current debates within the media studies field and indicate my position vis-à-vis the different approaches.

Chapter Four reviews the central (qualitative) methodological premises of this study, premises which did not change over the course of the reformulation or refinement of the research questions. I then discuss in detail the initial attempts to analyse the data and draw attention to the aspects of that initial analysis which emerged as central to later analyses of both the written and visual data. The search for structure in texts was abandoned as it was not consistent with my aims. The ethno-methodological approach provided the bases upon which the analysis could proceed and I discuss some of the key elements of this approach, which lays the methodological framework for the analysis of the data. My interpretative approach is also informed by the work of Erving Goffman (1959, 1961, 1963) and I suggest that his work can be legitimately used in conjunction with an ethnomethodological approach. Chapters Five, Six and Seven comprise the analytic sections of the study. These deal with descriptions of appearance, both physical and sartorial (Chapter Five), place and time (Chapter Six). Sacks' work on membership categorisation, and Schegloff's extension of that work, are used to analyse the descriptions of 'prostitutes' in the texts. These categorisations are used to formulate activities. The legal discourse of prostitution, described in Chapter Two, provides the framework within which to consider the stories of prostitution.

The concern of these stories is with visible presence, a central concern of the legal discourse. In this sense, Gerber's (1993) reference to 'media spectacles' is particularly apposite. Goffman's (1959) work on performances is also seen to hold relevance for the interpretation of the stories. I argue that the analysis of the descriptions of appearance, place and time are used not only to formulate category membership ('prostitute') but also provide for the warrantability of the category. Appearance(s), and presence in public places (streets) at specific times, function to infer evidence of intent to prostitute. Prostitution per se is not the concern of the press discourses, rather, as in the legal discourses, prostitution is inferred from loitering (and soliciting) 'for the purposes of prostitution'. In addition, as 'prostitution' is defined as sexual availability (in the sense of indiscriminate availability for sexual activities for money), the appearance, place and time of presence are selected and read as adequate descriptions of 'sexually available women' (that is, 'prostitutes').

I continue this focus upon the 'evidence of intent' theme, albeit less foregrounded, in the following chapter, which deals with the visual images of 'prostitutes'. Becker (1981) has considered the relative neglect of social scientists vis-à-vis the visual. This neglect is particularly apparent in work on press discourse. Press photography is an important area of investigation and I contend that my analysis of the selected photographs provides a much needed contribution to the analysis of press discourse. Given the neglect of this aspect of newspaper stories, this chapter is necessarily detailed. It aims to further emphasise and validate the findings from the analysis of the written texts.

That descriptions of 'prostitutes' are constructed on the basis of appearance, their time and place of presence; that these descriptions produce unequivocal readings of the women as 'prostitutes' and work to provide evidence of 'intent to prostitute', these are the findings of the analysis of both written and visual discourses. I have, to this point, remained 'true' to the ethnomethodological directive to produce my reading on the basis of the data. I have not imported extra-textual context into my analysis. However, at this stage, the question, and one which has been asked of ethnomethodological work (cf. Rustin, 1993), is 'so what?'

Chapter Eight, the final chapter, addresses this 'so what?' question raised by an in-depth focus upon texts. It attempts to consider the context of the newspaper stories of prostitution and the common-sense knowledge that readers draw upon in the occasion of reading. I use Fisher's (1986) heuristic device, 'the contextual web', to consider context. The issue of inter-discursivity is raised, that is, the relations between discourses. That women are categorised as 'prostitutes' (as sexually available) by way of descriptions of presence (appearance, time and place) has a wider relevance (cf. C. Wright Mills, 1959). It raises the issue of the social control of all women. If recognisable descriptions of 'the prostitute' are constructed on the basis of appearance, time and place of presence, then how are women to present themselves as not prostitutes, as not sexually available?

The concluding remarks consider what has been gained from this project of 'looking afresh' at the issue of prostitution; what issues have been raised over the course of analysis in respect of methods of discourse analysis and what the findings suggest about the role of the press in contemporary society.

The study as a whole aims to contribute to the three fields of discourse analysis, media processes and the substantive topic of prostitution. Ken Plummer (1981) has remarked à propos of the sociology of homosexuality that it is a 'necessary half-way house' on the road to understanding wider issues of social meaning, social order and social change. This study of press discourses of prostitution is similarly a 'half-way house' in the study of social categorisation and social control of women. It concludes with final remarks about possible areas for future research.

2 Discourses of prostitution

2.1 Introduction

Perkins' remark that 'if prostitution is the "oldest profession" (which is probably far from true), then it is also the oldest social debate' draws attention to the prolific outpourings of works on prostitution (1991, p. 1). A considerable literature exists on this subject, for example, Vern Bullough (1977) estimated that there were over 5,000 works, a figure updated by Perkins (1991) to over 6,500. In this chapter, I sketch out the backcloth against which the newspaper discourses of prostitution can be investigated, and consider a range of different approaches to the issue of prostitution. However, given the size of the existing literature, I have not attempted to provide an exhaustive review of all approaches.[1] Rather, it aims to delineate the key features of each of a selected corpus of work, from the sociological to the biographical/autobiographical literature which exists and this selective approach is guided by my concerns and interests for current purposes.

In approaching this vast corpus, I have been concerned to focus upon, in line with the theoretical and empirical focus of this study, the existence of different discourses on prostitution, that is, an 'economy' of discourses on prostitution, aiming to specify the dominant discourses and to examine their interrelationships. The term 'discourse' has many usages within the various fields in social science and broadly refers to language in use, which stresses the ways in which discourses do not reflect a pre-existing social reality but rather constructs that reality. Here, I am using Nead's conceptualisation of discourse, an approach which seeks to

> ... specify a particular form of language with its own rules and conventions and the institutions within which the discourse is produced

13

and circulated. In this way it is possible to speak of medical discourse ... which refers to the special language of medicine, the form of knowledge it produces and the professional institution and social spaces which it occupies (1988, p. 4).

In this approach to discourse (which is also conceptualised as a communicative event, following van Dijk (1988) involving the transmission and reception of information), the production of knowledge, specific to the different discourses, is highlighted. Different knowledges about prostitution (its nature, the causative factors associated with its existence) are produced from within different institutional sites and are articulated in discourse. Legal discourses, for instance, conceptualise prostitution as a public order problem and thereby legitimise police action in 'cleaning up' public places and indeed, inactivity à propos of more 'private' forms of prostitution, such as massage parlour prostitution.

The myriad of different discourses form what Fleck (1979) has termed 'thought-styles'. These are broadly similar to 'discourses' as they are produced in specific sites and articulate specific knowledges about, for example, the phenomenon of prostitution. Of particular interest to the current project are the ways in which different thought styles or discourses, from the psychopathological and medical to the legal and criminological, 'bleed into' (as Goffman, in a different context, puts it) the press discourses on prostitution.[2] A similar approach has been carried out by Perkins (1991, p. 63) but with a different objective; her consideration of the legal, moral, scientific and work perspectives aim to uncover an 'essential truth', a 'rational understanding':

> The essential truth highlights prostitutes as little more than 'sex workers', while the artificial devices seen [in the various disciplines' approaches] mark them permanently as 'scarlet women'.

Such an approach raises complex issues of epistemology and the 'truth claims' of the knowledges produced in different discourses, issues which are not addressed by Perkins but which, I contend, are critical in advancing particular knowledges as 'essentially true'. However, for current purposes, I am not concerned to privilege any one discourse over others but wish to detail the core assumptions of different discourses with a view to specifying the linkages between different discourses. In addition, the central aim, although implicit at this juncture, is to begin the process of considering journalistic appropriations, or adoption and reproduction, of different knowledges of prostitution regarding the nature of this phenomenon and of the women in prostitution in the stories they write. The availability of the discourses (medical, legal, sociological and feminist) is made possible through their circulation in and across different sites. These discourses have historical antecedents and have developed and evolved in different ways; a chronological approach to the different discourses, initially attempted, demonstrated the ways in which, for example, notions of psychopathology especially prevalent in the first half of the twentieth century have been largely discredited and displaced by competing explanations regarding the motivations to enter into prostitution. Again, however, space does not permit a detailed analysis of this aspect, other than to note that discourses do not simply exist, but are rather dynamic and changing, and further, that vestiges of understandings are identifiable in current discourses. Such issues are beyond the scope of the current work but they form a backcloth to contemporary knowledges of prostitution.

In addition, my consideration of the discourses of prostitution attempts to loosely follow Harvey Sacks' counsel that 'nothing we take as subject can appear as part of our descriptive apparatus unless it itself has been described' (1963, p. 2). This is the underlying rationale for considering the different frameworks within which prostitution has been treated and links this chapter to my overall thesis regarding the categorisation of some women as 'prostitutes'.

2.2 Approaches to prostitution: An initial characterisation

Various commentators (e.g., Benjamin & Masters, 1964; Perkins, 1991) begin their deliberations on the subject of prostitution by drawing attention to the enormous volume and outpourings of writings on prostitution. Judith Allen has remarked that the theme of prostitution recurs throughout the histories of women's work, welfare and poverty, class relations, sexuality, public health, crime and policing, leisure and popular culture (1986, p. 185). As noted, bibliographic sources (e.g., Vern Bullough, 1977) include almost 6,000 works, drawn from a range of disciplines. Tables 2.1 and 2.2 illustrate the contributions to this subject from a range of positions and also the cultural specificity of much of the writing. Whilst this list is taken from a bibliography which is somewhat dated, it is doubtful whether the general distribution has altered greatly.[3]

As is evident from Table 2.1, medical/public health approaches and legal publications relating to prostitution constitute over one third of the available literature with social science contributions amounting to 13% (Perkins, 1991, p. 33).

Table 2.1
List of publications on prostitution by discipline (in rank order)

1.	Medicine/Public health	1,130	(20.58%)
2.	Legal/police regulations	833	(15.17%)
3.	Area studies	787	(14.33%)
4.	History	540	(9.83%)
5.	Sociology	473	(8.61%)
6.	Fiction (English)	295	(5.37%)
7.	Biography/Autobiography	266	(4.84%)
8.	Anthropology	152	(2.77%)
9.	Religion/morality	133	(2.42%)
10.	Organisations publications	132	(2.40%)
11.	Business	112	(2.04%)
12.	General	108	(1.97%)
13.	Literature	88	(1.60%)
14.	Psychology	88	(1.60%)
15.	Juveniles	83	(1.51%)
16.	Psychiatry	77	(1.40%)
17.	War	72	(1.31%)
18.	Males (prostitutes/clients/pimps)	53	(0.97%)
19.	Guides/descriptive history	45	(0.82%)
20.	Bibliography	24	(0.44%)
	Total	5,491	(100.00%)

Source: Adapted from Bullough et al. (1977)/Perkins (1991).

Table 2.2
Literature on prostitution by area (10 – in rank order)

1.	United States of America	264	(33.55%)
2.	Japan	74	(9.40%)
3.	Latin America	60	(7.62%)
4.	France	51	(6.48%)
5.	*Great Britain & Ireland*	50	(6.35%)[4]
6.	India	44	(5.59%)
7.	Austria/Germany/Switzerland	42	(5.34%)
8.	Italy	30	(3.81%)
9.	USSR	24	(3.05%)
10.	Middle East	22	(2.80%)
	No area specified	10	(1.27%)
	Total	671	85.26% of total

Source: Adapted from Bullough et al. (1977)/Perkins (1991).

Further, psychiatry constitutes a small contribution, and although Perkins (1991) argues that it has probably had the most effective impact on the public consciousness, she does not comment further. I consider that this points perhaps to the process of medicalisation of women which Foucault (1976) has documented.

Table 2.2 indicates the concentration of works on prostitution in the United States. This is important to bear in mind, particularly given the different historical and legal contexts in which prostitution occurs. As Gagnon and Simon point out, the cultural and historical specificity of prostitution is masked by the very term 'prostitution' and they argue that to make temple prostitution in ancient Greece equivalent to contemporary prostitution is to 'rip [different forms of prostitution] from [their] historical context in some dubious search for cultural universals' (1973, p. 219). Indeed, this is a feature of various discourses of prostitution, for instance, Roberts (1993) begins her study with a detailed account of 'prostitution' in the Stone Age. The assumption of cultural universals is presented in discourses in which prostitution is conceptualised as a 'natural' feature of human organisation and this is expressed in the phrase 'the world's oldest profession'. Further, different knowledges and understandings about prostitution are, I suggest, culturally and historically specific, although tracing the genealogy of discourses has characterised approaches influenced by Foucault (1976). These approaches seek to uncover the 'historical present' (Weeks, 1985) and point to how different knowledges become sedimented within different perspectives, undergirding emergent knowledges.

It is instructive to consider the characterisations of the essential features of this corpus. Benjamin and Masters (1964, p. 19), commenting upon the diversity of the literature on prostitution, conclude that the plethora of arguments about this phenomenon can be condensed into a dichotomy: that in which prostitution is conceptualised as socially necessary and its obverse, in which it is presented as a social evil. This reflects only one dimension of the literature; a decade later, Atkinson and Bowles were to argue that:

> Most of research on prostitution has dealt with it either as a form of deviant behaviour or as one of the more extreme examples of occupational professionalisation. In the first instance, studies typically examine the social causes of prostitution or the personality characteristics of the participants ... In the second instance, the focus is on the patterns of recruitment, the socialisation process and the maintenance of occupational norms (1977, p. 219).

Forsyth and Furnet (1987) suggest that yet a further demarcation can be discerned in this corpus, that between the traditionalist interpretations and interactionist approaches, the former seemingly oblivious to the different forms which prostitution takes in contemporary society, an omission which the latter seeks to overcome. A further distinct instance in the history of the literature of prostitution relates to feminist analyses, themselves characterised by division, between prostitution as a social evil generated and perpetuated by patriarchy or as a valid occupational choice given women's limited economic choices in a society structured by patriarchy. The legal approach to prostitution has also changed over the 20th century and has itself been influenced by the different arguments and suppositions advanced by changing knowledges. All the above approaches, articulated in distinct discourses constitute available frameworks from which journalists can draw. The remainder of this chapter aims to sketch out a profile of the main discourses in which prostitution is conceptualised.

2.3   Religious and moral discourses on prostitution

Prostitution has been the subject of religious and moral discourses in the Western Christian tradition since 1 AD. Religious writing included a range of emphases, including deliberations on a range of issues, as Corrigan's summary of religious writing on clothing from the 3rd century AD onwards demonstrates (1988, chapter 1). These writings point to what was a key concern of many writers, namely their desire to ensure that clothing, as appearance, signalled the reality of a 'pure' or 'corrupt' [female] soul. The theological and philosophical questions relating to 'morality' and 'immorality' do not concern me here, rather, these approaches could, in my approach, be subject to analysis for their organising ideas.[5] A number of studies have commented upon the 'moral opprobrium' attached to behaviours identified as prostitution (cf. Perkins, 1991, Roberts, 1993). This section draws attention to the historical origins of the moral position which has been informed by the early Church fathers. The starting point is to note that the Judeo-Christian perspective sees sexuality as being sinful and dangerous outside of a strict set of boundaries (Ross & Ryan, 1995, p. 2). Lynda Nead, in her exploration of the discourses of sexuality in circulation in the late 19th century, refers to how:

> The language of Christianity lent authority to the definitions of sexuality proposed within other forms of public representation; the

uncertainties surrounding the contemporary adulteress could be partially displaced by invoking the biblical woman taken in adultery (1988, p. 56).

Religious discourse not only worked to define prostitution but also claimed the power to reform and control it. The anti-prostitution sentiments of the modern Christian Church derived from the Old Testament and the philosophies of the early Christian fathers and are intimately related to understandings about women and feminine nature as the writings indicate:[6]

> Do not profane your daughter by making her a harlot, lest the land fall into harlotry and the land become full of wickedness (*Book of Leviticus*, cited in Perkins, 1991, p. 18).

Fisher (in Roberts, 1993, p. 57) notes that:

> Christianity took the Jewish mistrust for women and added its own repressions, in a much stricter interpretation of Hebrew mores. Significant was the fact that the idealisation of chastity was transformed into a loathing for the body and a severe condemnation of sexual acts (1993, p. 57).

St Paul wrote:

> Do you not know that your bodies are members of Christ? Shall I therefore take the members of Christ and make them members of a prostitute? Never! Do you not know that he who joins himself to a prostitute becomes one with her? ... Shun immorality (ibid.).[7]

Connected with this denigration of prostitutes was the approach, documented by Brownmiller (1975, p. 330), of the veneration of chastity until marriage. However, a contradiction prevailed in the pronouncements of early writers. St Augustine (characterised by Perkins as 'the most ardent opponent of prostitution') who, while rejecting prostitutes, also spoke of how 'harlots' 'fill a most vile function under the laws of order', a theme which was expounded by Thomas Aquinas in the 12th century:

> Rid society of prostitutes and licentiousness will run riot throughout. Prostitutes in a city are like a sewer in a palace. If you get rid of the sewer, the whole place becomes filthy and foul (cited Roberts, 1991, p. 20).

This argument led to a 'peculiar tolerance' (Perkins, ibid., although see Roberts (1993) for a conflicting view) of prostitution by the Church from the fourth to the 16th century and the advent of the Reformation. This was followed again by a period of moral laxity until the 19th century, when, across Europe, prostitution became the subject of legal, social and religious concern. However, in this period, and especially in the 19th century, religious discourses also, while abhorring the 'prostitute', saw her as an object of redemption. The story of Mary Magdalene and her rescue from her 'evil ways' was to provide the impetus for the efforts of religious rescue work. Colin Jones provides a fascinating account of 'rescue' teams operating in eighteenth century Montpellier, noting how women who were involved in the management of the Bon Pasteur (a place for repentant prostitutes)

> ... appear to have run vigilante patrols, scouring the streets after dark and seizing wretched and harassed women out of the hands of carousing soldiers and lackeys, then carting them off to the Bon Pasteur. Once within the walls of the institution, these women would receive spiritual instruction ... (1986, p. 11).[8]

Religious writers in 1840s and 1850s England, such as William Tait and William Logan, who campaigned for temperance, argued that prostitution was a social evil which threatened the family as well as the social order.[9] The social purity movement in Britain following the Contagious Diseases Acts (1862, 1866, 1888) and the Criminal Law Amendment Act of 1885, articulated notions of morality and immorality based upon religious arguments (cf. Walkowitz, 1980).

Traditional Christian thought in which the prostitute is influenced by the devil and is therefore an enemy of Christ (although, of course, repentance and a reform of ways, as Mary Magdalene did, could lead to salvation), has been reformulated in many ways. However, it still persists: in the 1970s a prostitute, Theresa Maguire was told by a (Roman Catholic) priest that she was possessed by the devil and he suggested that she leave the country (Ireland).

Groups founded to save the souls of 'fallen women' still operate today and religious orders operate to 'rehabilitate' women who have engaged in prostitution.[10]

In conclusion, the religious/moral approach to prostitution is fundamentally influenced by Judeo-Christian dualistic thinking on sexuality: its high symbolism of sexual union in marriage versus its rhetoric of sin, of moral decay and corruption and of the breakdown of the moral order, provides its versatility for adoption by other discourses far removed from religious discourse.[11]

2.4 Medical discourses

As Vern Bullough's (1977) bibliography indicates, the category of medicine has constituted the greatest tranche in the overall corpus of literature on prostitution. The history of the medical profession has demonstrated its pervasiveness in regard to its 'traversing' and contributing to the formation of other discourses. This is particularly the case when medical knowledge has served as the rationale for the implementation of legislation. These two approaches (medical and legal), while developing within different frameworks have, historically, drawn upon the other in conceptualising prostitution and the prostitute.

The medical profession's involvement in the formulation of public health and legal strategies to deal with prostitution has a complex and lengthy history.[12] This history begins in the public health movement of the mid 1800s (cf. Brandt, 1988). The historical present, which indicates the continuities between past and current approaches to prostitution is especially evident in the legal and medical approach to the contemporary HIV pandemic. Medical knowledge was used as a basis for the formulation of *legal* approaches, that is legal discourses claimed legitimacy on the basis of medical knowledge.

Some of the earliest investigations of prostitution were carried out by physicians: Parent-Duchatelet (Perkins, 1991, p. 16) in the 1830s surveyed 5,200 Parisian prostitutes. His findings, that the women he investigated were in dire poverty, served as a reference point for subsequent studies, although as Walkowitz (1980) notes, successive British social investigators selectively drew on the results of this pioneering study, emphasising the prostitute's sterility, frigidity, dissolute habits and physical deterioration as William Acton's and William Tait's remarks (below) illustrate.[13]

In England in the second part of the 1800s, social investigators had begun to focus upon prostitution and various writers have documented the ways in which the approaches to this 'social evil' were infused with wider concerns about the moral health and military strength of the nation. A prime example of the deployment of medical knowledge by legal discourses is to be found in the Contagious Diseases Acts (1864, 1866, 1869). These were designed to control the spread of venereal disease amongst military and naval personnel, which was feared to have reached epidemic proportions. Estimates in 1862 of venereal disease amongst troops serving in the UK were: 291 per 1,000 (British Parliamentary Papers, 1866, p. 43). Walkowitz argues that while medical sources

... may have established a climate of medical concern over the incidence of syphilis in the general population ... it was the loss of man-hours and the mounting statistics on venereal disease among the troops that finally spurred legislation on the subject (1980, p. 72).

The Contagious Diseases Acts provided for the detention of women identified as 'common prostitutes', for them to undergo a medical examination ('sanitary inspection', Walkowitz, 1980, p. 124) and, if diagnosed as infected with venereal disease, to be detained in especially designated Lock Hospitals.[14] The first Act was passed in 1864 and the second, introduced in 1866, extended the power of police by introducing registration of prostitutes and fortnightly inspections. The final Act (1869) sought to extend the application of the Acts beyond garrison and sea port towns and it was with the passing of this Act that public reaction to the Acts was mobilised. The Acts were suspended in 1883. The nascent social purity campaigns of the 1870s flowered in the 1880s and their underlying rationale and rhetoric drew upon notions of cleanliness and hygiene in articulating deep seated concerns about prostitution and, more generally, women's sexuality.

A key figure in the drafting of the legislation was a medical doctor, William Acton, whose works include *The Functions and Disorders of the Reproductive Organs in Youth, in Adult Age, and in Advanced Life: Considered in their Physiological Relations* (1857) and *Prostitution, considered in its Moral, Social and Sanitary Aspects, In London and Other Large Cities: with Proposals for the Mitigation and Prevention* (1857). Acton was instrumental in pressing for the institution of the Contagious Diseases Acts and as such, his approach is taken as typical in examining the framework within which medical knowledge was produced.[15] Acton's perspective on prostitution is generally criticised by authors (Finnegan, 1979; Walkowitz, 1980) as exhibiting middle-class Victorian notions about female sexuality. However, as noted, such critiques are not my concern here; rather I wish to examine some of his arguments regarding the physiological or 'medical' features of prostitutes, which were given weight by legislators and consequently formed part of a common-sense about prostitutes. Acton considered that prostitutes were different from 'normal' women in having sexual desires and 'iron bodies'. His comments about the social issues associated with prostitution drew upon and were legitimated by his medical knowledge:

> I have every reason to believe, that by far the larger number of women who have resorted to prostitution for a livelihood, return sooner or later to a more or less regular course of life ... encumbrances rarely

attend the prostitute who flies from the horrors of her position. *We must recollect that she has a healthy frame, an excellent constitution, and is in the vigour of life* (cited in Finnegan, 1979, p. 5).

Acton's pronouncements on the physical state of 'the prostitute' were not consistent and he frequently contradicted himself in attempting to argue for one or other course of action. He described (in *Prostitution*) prostitutes as 'stupid from beer, or fractious from gin, they swear and chatter brainless stuff all day'. One in four prostitutes in London were, he estimated (op. cit.), diseased, with 'broken constitutions, sickly bodies and feeble minds':

> In a few words, then, prostitution consigns to a life of degradation thousands of our female population, ruining them utterly body and soul … it is the cause of disease, premature decay, ultimately death.[16,17]

While in these comments, the prostitute herself is not the source of deviation, rather the lifestyle of prostitution leads to 'decay' and so on, Acton in a later passage attributes a number of inherent features of prostitutes, features which demarcate them from other women:

> Natural desire. Natural sinfulness. The preferment of indolent ease to labour. Vicious inclinations strengthened and ingrained by early neglect. To this black list may be added love of drink, love of dress, love of amusement (op. cit., p. 7).

Such writings were influential in setting the terms upon which debate about the issue of prostitution were founded and were based upon the perceived epidemic of venereal disease, which had the infected prostitute as its identifiable source. However, the contradictions in Acton's remarks need to contextualised; Acton, in the course of arguing for the extension of the Contagious Disease Acts shifted his stance regarding the involvement of women in prostitution. Whereas, in his early writings he had proposed that prostitution was a transitory state, that women could enter and leave prostitution without 'damage', his later arguments were that once a woman engaged in prostitution she was doomed; there was no exit back into respectable society.

Another key figure in this period was William Tait, a physician active in the temperance movement. He spoke of how no law could recognise unbounded liberty:

> … the same rule of natural law which justifies the officer in shooting a plague stricken sufferer who breaks through a cordon sanitaire justifies him in arresting and confining the syphilitic prostitute, who,

if not arrested, would spread infection all around her (cited in Walkowitz, 1980, pp. 43-44).

The perceived public health threat of the prostitute provided the justification for detention of women arrested as prostitutes and detained in the local hospitals. This same justification is used in contemporary arguments about the control of the HIV infected prostitute. Its rationale was based upon three assumptions regarding the aetiology and epidemiology of syphilis; especially that which posited that it was spread through promiscuous sexual contact with diseased prostitutes (cf. Walkowitz, 1980, p. 48). The critical point here is that at the base of this assumption is the notion that prostitutes were readily identifiable.[18]

The history of the Contagious Diseases Acts is of interest in considering current medical understandings of prostitution as a public health issue. The wider history of medical knowledge draws attention to the range of causative theories of infection adopted; from the exogenous (including a miasmatic understanding of transmission) to the endogenous and retributionist theories in which ill health is a result (or manifestation) of moral transgression. Commentators, such as Nead (1988), have argued that the medical and social response to prostitutes in the 19th century find clear parallels in the contemporary HIV pandemic. While Nead notes this, she goes on to consider the response to gay men, *not* to prostitutes.

The medical response to AIDS has been exhaustively documented (e.g., Aggleton & Homans, 1987) and is not reproduced here.[19] Various theories regarding the causative agent of AIDS have been advanced. For current purposes, I want to consider an editorial in the *Lancet*[20] (1989), 'AIDS: Prevention, Policies, and Prostitutes', which is concerned with the education of prostitutes, providing 'rubbers for hookers' (p. 1112). The article begins by noting the 'disappointing' progress of prevention strategies and singles out prostitutes (individuals with multiple partners) for education in the use of condoms. Prostitutes are high-risk groups but,

> ... Nowhere has an orchestrated effort been instituted to improve the treatment of sexually transmitted diseases (STDs) among prostitutes, even though STDs are acknowledged risk factors for the acquisition and transmission of HIV infection (1989, p. 1111).

Further, given epidemiological trends of HIV infection amongst prostitutes in the developing world,

> ... From a public health viewpoint, it is prudent to assume that rapid spread of the type seen in Nairobi prostitutes ... will occur in many

24

groups with high-risk behaviours ... The fact that in most parts of the world HIV infection is still largely limited to high-risk groups presents a unique opportunity (p. 1112).

This discourse assumes that prostitution in Nairobi is the same as prostitution in the United States. Forms of prostitution are not considered culturally specific, but are rather cultural universals.

The role of the medical profession in the HIV pandemic is clearly stated: namely, it is given a 'lead role', especially in the realistic application of appropriate therapies (p. 1113). Some 'realistic' proposals include the provision of education, condom distribution, control and treatment of other STDs and facilities for clean needles for *all* risk groups (the cast includes urban prostitutes, gay men and intravenous drug users). Prostitutes, however, as the 'largest group' at risk of HIV infection must not be scapegoated; the editorial argues that 'many of them have been *driven* into their occupation by poverty and most *are mothers of children whom they love* and support '(ibid., emphasis added). Prostitution, as an involuntary activity, is carried out by women with children and the reason for their engagement in prostitution is because of their need to support their children. This assumption is taken from co-existing discourses in which the 'deviant' behaviours of women who prostitute is explained by reference to their mothering duties, namely, to feed their children.

Medical opinion is divided on the issue of prostitutes' risk behaviours. As Ward and Day note, reporting findings from a London study of prevalence rates of HIV amongst prostitutes, no evidence was found of especial risks amongst prostitutes:

> Their safety at work depends partly on the extent to which condoms protect against infection with HIV and also on the prevalence of HIV in the population of clients (1988, p. 1585).

This latter approach differs from that expressed in the *Lancet* (1989) in its focus upon different forms and practices of prostitution and highlights the divisions within the framework of medical approaches to prostitution. Prostitutes are variously considered 'high-risk groups' or not at risk given the adoption of safe sexual behaviours. The relevance of epidemiology is that the different interpretations placed on data lead to different health promotion strategies. One indication of this is the growing evidence that it is not prostitution but injecting drug practices amongst women who prostitute that is the relevant factor in terms of HIV infection. Medical knowledge about HIV transmission and its use to designate so-called 'risk groups' has real effects. One of the slogans, used in graffiti and in medical journals reads: 'AIDS: the price of prostitution just went up'. The assaults on and murders of prostitutes have been connected to this popular association between prostitution and HIV (ECP, 1988), an association legitimated by a dominant medical knowledge.[21]

In summary, the medical discourses of prostitution have drawn upon extra-medical assumptions in their approach to prostitution. They have been instrumental in the medicalisation of perceived social problems, such that the prostitution has been conceptualised as a public health problem, with the infected prostitute assuming a central position in these discourses (cf. Brandt, 1988). In addition, the *Lancet* editorial (1989) reproduces a popular (non-medical) understanding of the motivations for women's entry into prostitution, namely poverty but it also works against the understanding that prostitutes are 'unnatural women' by invoking 'motherly love'. Medical discourse has also been concerned to describe the physical condition of prostitutes, a concern which has persisted and has been taken up by the popular discourses of the press, as Chapter Five shows. In addition, the medical discourses of prostitution have historically been deployed by legal discourses in the attempt to control prostitution and women in prostitution. The medical discourses include psychiatry and one of its derivatives, psychopathology, and the construction of the prostitute as exhibiting identifiable psychopathological 'disturbances' has been a feature of medical discourses.

2.4.1 Psychopathological discourses

A variant of the medical discourse on prostitution includes psychiatry and psychopathology. The frameworks of psychopathology, of psychology and psychiatry have, as their starting point, the central question: *why do some women engage in prostitution?* The focus is upon the individual and psychological processes in seeking an explanation for research problems. The aim of such approaches is, in essence, to look under the skull (Garfinkel, 1963, p. 190). Reviews of psychoanalytic approaches to prostitution are available (cf. Smart, 1976; Perkins, 1991) and are not reproduced here. The psychoanalytic model attempts to provide an understanding of the existence of prostitution by reference to the psycho-pathology of the prostitute, and to a lesser extent, considers the client. One of the main contributors to this tradition was Edward Glover whose work provides an exemplar of the core assumptions of this discourse. His treatise on 'The psycho-pathology of prostitution' was prepared for the Institute for the Study and Treatment of Delinquency, London in 1943.

In this paper, Glover begins by noting the emotional difficulties which he considers inherent in the study of prostitution and aims to produce a 'scientific' approach to this subject. The core premise is that prostitutional activities fall within the rubric of delinquent behaviour and as a concomitant, that psycho-medical approaches are the proper domain in which solutions can be sought. One of the problems in the study of delinquent behaviour, at least for the psycho-analyst, is that mental pathology is not open to 'naked-eye inspection' (1943, p. 1). Glover presents an argument detailing the arrested sexual development of the prostitute (who is, in addition, a latent homosexual), an unconscious, unobservable state, and moves to consider the variety of prostitute 'types' which are observable.

Noting that it is 'absurd' to propose solutions to the prostitution problem without first 'establishing a reasonably exact classification of prostitutes' (p. 7), he argues that there is no such thing as a prostitute type, referring to the failure of the legal system to take into account the definition of individual psychology in its formulation of legislative measures, noting the existence of what he terms 'allied groups' who presumably also display features of retarded sexual development. These allied groups can include those 'individuals' [read women] who marry for money. Unfortunately, since such groups are so diverse, Glover restricts himself to those 'cases' coming within a legal definition, that is, engaged in loitering and soliciting.

His classification system includes three types of 'common prostitutes' which he has detected in his 'cursory' glances at police court cases: the drab streetwalker, the gay streetwalker and the flourishing professional. This scheme excludes, as he admits, those prostitutes who have escaped police surveillance. These points deserve attention because they point to a classification 'urge' and as a concomitant, an anxiety about boundaries between who is to be included or excluded. The *drab streetwalker* is apathetic, some are mentally disordered, others are mentally backward and they incline towards excessive use of alcohol. Most of the members of this type 'attribute their choice of profession to emotional disturbances in adolescence'; a second class, the *gay prostitute*, also termed the 'young' prostitute, are contrasted with the first group but included in their psychological attributes are border-line intelligence and irresponsibility. However these are readily amenable to social influences, suggesting that they can be 'cured'. The third class of prostitute is the *flourishing professional* who is restless, dissatisfied and given to excesses of various kinds.

27

Glover argues that this classification scheme is only one way to classify prostitutes, other ways include by age, social standing, degree of mental abnormality, to name but a few criteria. He acknowledges that his scheme is partial, that its fault lies in the problems of knowing the range and prevalence of different types of prostitutes and prostitutional behaviours. Given that Glover has been concerned to identify deviations from 'normal' sexual development, his points about the *impossibility of knowing all prostitutes* are used to forge a link between prostitutes and non-prostitutes:

> The most convenient test of the validity of these generalisations is that the pathological factors discovered should be present not only in groups of experienced prostitutes, but in what might be called 'larval' groups, i.e., the young groups from which experienced prostitutes are recruited (1943, p. 7).

'Experienced prostitutes', the neurotics, experience sexual frigidity, a 'condition' also common in what Glover terms *'apparently normal women'*(1943, p. 9, emphasis added). These comments establish commonality between prostitutes and 'normal women' and the reported parental characterisation of infant girls (three to five years) as 'little tarts' (p. 10) suggest that behaviours of prostitutes are to be found within the female population from a young age. They further suggest the appearances of 'non-prostitute' status may be misleading, and, while the three types outlined are the most 'obvious' they represent only the 'tip of the prostitute-type iceberg' implied by Glover. This concern with 'obviousness' has been taken up by popular discourses as I will discuss in the analytic chapters (Chapters Five, Six and Seven).

The causative factors of prostitution are not, in Glover's opinion, economic and he argues that this view has been propagated by members of the 'drab' prostitutes, a group which, he suggests, have alcohol problems, are mentally disordered and backward. The role of economic factors are deemed symbolic: money is equated with 'excretory products', and that the prostitute barters her body for 'filthy lucre' provides evidence, within this framework, of the primitive and regressive nature of prostitution. Hence, the argument of economic factors is misplaced, as is that relating to toleration of prostitution. Prevention of prostitution will require strategies targeting childhood patterns (remember the reference to 'little tarts' above) which 'predispose' to a choice of prostitution, although Glover argues that this may be problematic as such factors, being subjective, are not open to environmental influence.

Glover's approach echoes the perspective established within the discipline of criminology regarding the atavistic nature of the prostitute, proposed by Lombrosso and the early criminologists (cf. Smart, 1976). His focus upon psycho-pathology identifies the prostitute as diseased and links in with medical discourses. He further suggests that prostitution results from psychopathological disturbances, is an involuntary behaviour and thus cannot be considered as work. The psychopathological discourse appears in work dubbed as 'sociological' as is evident in one of the first UK empirical studies of prostitutes which was published in 1954, prior to both the Sexual Offences Act 1956 and the Street Offences Act 1959 and the 1957 Report of the Wolfenden Committee (the researcher of this study, Wilkinson, gave evidence to the Committee). This study[22] was funded by the British Social Biology Council and the orientation expressed may reflect this, although prevailing social opinion also viewed the prostitute through a psychopathological lens. It was conceived as a sociological study of prostitution (the title is *Women of the Streets: A Sociological Study of the Common Prostitute*). The book comprises 69 case histories and reviews current legislative and policing approaches. Wilkinson adopts a quasi-psychopathological perspective. Defining prostitution as

> ... a way of living ... consciously chosen because it suits a woman's personality in particular circumstances, and until a subjective experience in the woman's own life alters either the personality or the circumstances ... she will not be prepared to make the effort for change (1954, p. 107),

she, like Glover (1943) privileges individual personality (and the parent-child relationship), according economic factors merely one of a myriad of elements in accounting for reasons for entry into prostitution. She notes that while the economic factors are relevant in the individual's decision to enter prostitution, the causes of the existence of that trade are quite different.

The prostitute is deemed to inhabit a 'counter-society', to be outside 'ordinary society' and everyday life. She asks 'why are other women not prostitutes' and 'why are prostitutes not ordinary women', questions which are central to the psychopathological discourse.

2.5 Sociological discourses

Unlike the psychopathological or psychiatric approaches to prostitution which focus upon individual pathology and disease, the sociological approach aims to understand prostitution as a specific form of behaviour which exists within a wider system of institutions, not merely as Perkins' defines it as concerned with the external agents interacting with the person (1991, p. 38). Maggie O'Neill (1992) has pointed out that there are few published sociological works on prostitution. Sociological approaches to prostitution employ a range of theoretical frameworks which focus upon different aspects of prostitution, from a consideration of its inter-relation with other social institutions, as in the functionalist approach of Davis (1937) to sociological studies of deviance (Rock, 1973; Cohen, 1980) in which prostitution is considered as a form of sexual deviance, to the feminist sociological theories which consider prostitution within the context of a system of unequal gender relations (patriarchy), in articulation with a particular system of economic relations (capitalism), (Pateman, 1988). In addition, a critical sociological perspective considers medical and legal practices vis-à-vis prostitution, and relates these to social structure via considerations of power, ideology and domination. The sociological discourse on prostitution is not unitary, but is marked by divisions and different assumptions regarding the nature of prostitution.

In this section, I consider the functionalist approach of Davis. The feminist discourse is further considered in a separate section below, as it raises pertinent questions about the underlying assumptions characterising the different approaches considered here and also because feminist knowledge informs this study.

2.5.1 Functionalist approaches within sociological discourse

Kingsley Davis' 1937 paper is generally considered to be the first and best-known *sociological* treatise of prostitution. He argues that prostitution is related to the organisation of the family and particularly to the overall system of regulation of sexual contact in industrialised societies. Conceptualising a relation between prostitution and the family enables Davis to consider how a decline of prostitution and a decline of the power of the family à propos of the regulation of sexual contact are both linked with sexual freedom. Like others, he notes the definitional problems which confront theorists: prostitution cannot be defined simply as the use of sexual responses for ulterior purposes, as such a definition would immediately include 'a great portion of behaviour' particularly that of women, for example the employment of 'pretty girls' (1937, p. 476). He comments that:

> The basic element of what we actually call prostitution – the employment of sex for non-sexual ends within a competitive-authoritative system – characterises not simply prostitution itself but

all of our institutions in which sex is involved, notably courtship and wedlock (ibid.).

The definitional problems which are a constant source of trouble for theorists rest on precisely this feature of social organisation; that women employ sex for non-sexual ends but are not engaged in 'formal' prostitution. Consequently, Davis (p. 749) argues that prostitution (which he specifies as commercial prostitution) shares with other sexual institutions a basic feature, namely the employment of sex for an ulterior end in a system of differential advantages, but it differs from them in being mercenary, promiscuous and emotionally indifferent. However, this approach is problematic; prostitution is not merely for money; sex can be exchanged for privilege, power, food or clothing.[23]

The 'system of differential advantages' to which Davis refers is that based upon physical attractiveness: some members of society are born at the 'ugly' end of the scale and these persons 'must' and do use other means to obtain sexual fulfilment. Hence, economic factors alone cannot account for prostitution; rather prostitution performs a necessary function which is not performed by any other institution. It thus, in this framework, *complements* rather than erodes the institution of marriage. Perkins (1991, p. 38) argues that Davis' approach means that prostitution should not be regarded as 'deviant'. However, it is not clear that Davis does argue this; while he defines prostitution as an 'occupation' (1937, p. 754, footnote 24) he also argues that given the links between the family and prostitution, women are either part of the family or they are not. Prostitutes are members of a caste set apart and 'the harlot' is paid not (only) for her work, but for her 'loss of social standing' (1937, p. 750). This functionalist approach does not conceive of the institution of prostitution or of the family in terms of asymmetrical power relations and has been criticised by feminists such as Smart (1976). He, finally, reverts back to considerations of individual psychology in attempting to explain reasons for entry and reasons for buying sexual services.

The themes raised in Davis' approach:
- of the intrinsic links between prostitution and other institutions, especially the family;
- of the enduring character of prostitution, suggesting its naturalness and universality;
- of the presumed need for men to have access to sexual services outside of marriage, an institution which limits sexual 'variety';
- of the conceptualisation of women in terms of a caste system, with 'respectable' women located in the family and 'unrespectables' outside it;

31

- of the various factors mediating entry into prostitution, of which the economic is only one; and
- of the functional nature of prostitution;

together have formed the basic elements of sociological analyses of prostitution and are variously expanded or criticised depending upon the framework adopted. For example, Benjamin & Masters' functionalist approach posits the causes of prostitution in the social system which does not provide for the sexual needs of 'its members', that is men (1964, p. 24). Men are, in this hydraulic sexuality paradigm (Weeks, 1985) forced to pay prostitutes for sexual services denied them by their 'goody-goody wives' (1964, p. 8). Their adoption of a functionalist perspective means that prostitution is regarded as a metaphorical safety valve, echoing Davis' (1937, p. 755) assertion that prostitution is economical, providing a 'convenient outlet' for men. Drawing upon such formulations, they argue that

> ... the demand for sexual intercourse must be met one way or another. If enough promiscuous women are not available either, then the demand, frustrated, will result in sexual assaults and in an increase in the incidence of sexual deviations especially homosexual behaviour (1964, p. 96).

In this scheme, 'promiscuous' women could reduce the demand for prostitution, but either prostitutes or 'promiscuous' women must be available for sexual 'use' by men.

The approach taken in this examination of sociological discourses has been to separate the feminist contributions to this discourse; this decision has the unfortunate effect of presenting the sociological discourse as functionalist (in respect of prostitution existing to service men's sexual 'needs' and necessary for the maintenance of the family), whereas a more adequate description of this discourse would include feminist contributions.

The sociological discourse, thus far considered, raises the themes of the classification of women and of the social stigma associated with the 'caste' of women identified as 'prostitutes'. The foregoing postulates that prostitution is a necessary 'by-product' of the existence of the family.

2.6   Legal discourses

A law is defined (Giddens 1989, p. 742) as 'a rule of behaviour established by a political authority and backed by state power'. Focusing upon the legal perspective points to 'official discourses' and knowledges about what are deemed to be unacceptable behaviours in a society; that is behaviours which are formally proscribed. Legislation has related both to prostitution and to prostitutes, both directly and indirectly. Roberts (1993, p. 9) cites an Assyrian legal prescription on the dress codes of prostitutes in 1100 BC. However, de Marley (1986) points out that while sumptuary legislation in different periods has affected prostitutes, this legislation has not necessarily been explicitly targeted at prostitutes.

The legal approach to prostitution provides a context within which other discourses can be usefully considered. For example, Smart (1976) has noted the 'important influence' the legal code has had upon defining areas of study for criminologists; that it stakes out the terrain of study, determining what is to be studied. The application of legislation also impacts upon the organisation of prostitution (cf. Walkowitz's (1980) discussion of the effects of the Criminal Law Amendment Act, 1885) and hence its public form. Weeks (1979) argues that the legal approach to different social issues, whilst not creating public opinion, does shape and reinforce it. As will be demonstrated, the legal discourse on prostitution, and the knowledges it produces and reproduces, has assumed a dominance in respect of other discourses of prostitution, particularly in the press discourses.

As noted in the discussion of medical understandings of prostitution, the medical and legal approaches traverse and articulate with each other – public health legislation is a case in point. It has been premised upon medical knowledge and in turn, dominant notions about morality enter into and structure these knowledges. Perkins (1991, p. 29) cites Lord Devlin's (1959) argument that the law has a duty to protect the interests of the majority, and hence that morals should be, in a democratic society, enforced through legislation.

Reviewing the legislative approaches to prostitution, Perkins suggests that the historical backdrop to current legal contexts is essential, adding that while the laws on prostitution in western societies have reflected diverse systems of legal control, the 'present world-wide trend of prohibiting prostitution has its direct antecedence in 19th century morals and the changes of law in respect to that' (1991, p. 57). In respect of Britain and Ireland, much of the corpus of sexual offences legislation was instituted in the reign of Queen Victoria and few changes have been made (cf. Clarkson, 1992). This means that the historical legacy of prostitution legislation in both countries is one characterised by similarity (as the Republic of Ireland was under British rule until 1921).

There are essentially three approaches adopted by legislatures in western societies: *suppression*, characterised by the prohibition of all acts of prostitution, as well as those acts which foster or promote it, for example, legislation in New York, Britain and Ireland; *regulation*, characterised by registration systems, for example in Germany; and *abolition* (or decriminalisation) characterised by the revocation of laws licensing prostitutes, for example in Victoria, Australia (cf. McLeod, 1982).

For the purposes of clarity and for current aims, I want merely to consider the British and Irish legislation starting with the Criminal Law Amendment Act 1885 (previous legislation is discussed by Perkins, 1991, pp. 48ff and Roberts 1993).[24]

The Criminal Law Amendment Act (1885) was the legislative response to a culmination of a number of processes, relating to both homosexuality (cf. Weeks, 1979) and prostitution (cf. Walkowitz, 1980). In respect of the latter, the processes included the Maiden Tribute scandal which was instigated by W.T. Stead's newspaper article on the forced prostitution of young girls and the concurrent social purity campaigns which were in operation. The Act raised the age of (heterosexual) consent to sixteen and gave the police extensive power against procurers and brothel keepers. The effects of the Act on the structure or organisation of prostitution have been well documented (cf. Walkowitz, 1980; Perkins, 1991; Roberts, 1993).

The Vagrancy Act, 1924, was concerned with order in public places; this was to constitute the thrust of Wolfenden's Report (1957) on prostitution. Section three of this act provides that every 'common prostitute' wandering the public streets or public highways or any place of public resort and behaving in a riotous and indecent manner shall be deemed an idle and disorderly person. This provision articulates a presumption of ready identification.

In 1957, the *Report of the Committee on Homosexual Offences and Prostitution* was published, and its recommendations formed the basis of the Street Offences Act 1959. The Committee was explicitly concerned to define the scope of the criminal law in respect of prostitution. Noting the aims of criminal law (under which prostitution related offences are tried) as the preservation of public order and decency, and the protection of the citizen from what is offensive, the Committee averred that its function was as 'a guardian of the public good' (1957, p. 21). Acts which are committed in private are, then, not subject to the jurisdiction of criminal law; acts which come under the purview of the legal system are those which 'outrage public decency'. This legal discourse articulated a 'geography' of social life, explicitly defining the 'public' and 'private' spheres, and this division has implications for the identification of behaviours as prostitution.

The Wolfenden Committee maintained two central premises: that the law is not concerned with prostitution per se as an offence and argued that, given this, men (clients) cannot be arrested or punished (p. 80, p. 87). It further pronounced that the function of the law is as a safeguard for society, that is the public order. It is not concerned with immorality:

> If it were the law's intention to punish prostitution per se, on the ground that it is immoral conduct, then it would be right that it should provide for the punishment of the man as well as the woman (1957, p. 46).

These premises are expressed succinctly in the following passage:

> We are concerned not with prostitution itself, but with the manner in which the *activities of prostitutes* and those associated with them offend against public order and decency, *expose the ordinary citizen to what is offensive and injurious* (1957, p. 80, emphasis added).

It is the prostitute who is the object of the legal discourse, not prostitution, which is not defined, and the prostitute is deemed 'injurious' by her mere presence. Dealing with this presence is the core function of legislation.

The 'proper terms' for the focus of criminal law and the Committees' review of it, relate to offences in streets and public places generally. A further comment underlines the rationale behind limiting the jurisdiction of criminal law vis-à-vis prostitution:

> ... no case can be sustained for attempting to make prostitution in itself illegal. We recognise that we are ... on the border lines between law and morals ... But [prostitution] has persisted throughout many centuries and the failure of attempts to stamp it out by repressive legislation shows it cannot be eradicated through the agency of criminal law (1957, p. 79).

The presumption of the 'natural' existence of prostitution (cf. Gagnon and Simon, 1973) is clear here. The statement that prostitution cannot be 'stamped out' is a feature of contemporary police discourse.[25]

Loitering and solicitation for 'immoral purposes' in public places are the activities which are properly the law's concern vis-à-vis prostitution.

The activities of prostitutes refer to public activities; 'the presence, and the *visible and obvious* presence, of prostitutes in considerable numbers in the public streets', mean that the activities of loitering and soliciting are 'self-evidently public nuisances'. The essence of the Report is captured in the following comments:

> The problem of the prostitute is [as] a public nuisance; [prostitutes'] very presence [on the streets] would offend (pp. 89-104).

However, while considering male solicitation, the Committee confirms its gender-specific focus. The idea, the Committee states, of male importuning is unquestionably more 'repellent' to the general public than is the idea of female solicitation. However, male solicitation is not as offensive to public decency, an argument rationalised by noting that not simply are the numbers engaged in it smaller but because

> Males seldom importune other males who do not give them encouragement. Their activities are less obvious and more subtle and discreet than is the case with female solicitation (1957, p. 127).

The thrust of their recommendations, therefore, is to enable the 'ordinary citizen to go about his business without the constant affront to his sense of decency which the presence of these women affords'; the constant public parading of the prostitute's wares must be prevented by 'cleaning the streets' (pp. 96-7). The legal function is to, in effect, remove unsightly and offensive bodies from public places, to 'clean the streets'. This 'cleaning' aspect of the discourse has been adopted by others, most notably Peter Sutcliffe, the so-called Yorkshire Ripper, who attempted to rationalise the murders of women he identified as prostitutes:

> The women I killed were *filth*, bastard prostitutes who were just standing round *littering the streets*. I was just *cleaning the place up* a bit (in Roberts, 1993, p. 304, emphasis added).

The Committee notes that while prostitution is tolerated (because it is an 'unavoidable' feature of society), the prostitute must be allowed to carry on 'her business' somewhere, but not in a public place. It does not recommend the licensing of brothels but considers brothels something of a 'lesser evil'. Prostitution out of sight is thus deemed acceptable.

The Report of the Wolfenden Committee is of relevance to the current discussion as it indicates the adoption of approaches developed in different spheres; the definition of prostitution (as a way of living, and the prostitute's personality as involving unknown psychological elements) is taken from the psychopathological approach of Glover (1943) and Wilkinson's (1954) approach (both authors were witnesses to the Committee, along with the Roman Catholic Advisory Committee on Prostitution and Homosexual Offences and various other clergy). The recommendations that prostitutes should be counselled by 'moral workers' and a view of prostitution as resulting from 'human weakness' (of both clients *and* prostitutes) stem from moral understandings of prostitution, understandings which are incorporated into legal discourse.

The constant call for research into the psychological make-up of prostitutes reveals the influence of the psychoanalytic and psychiatric approaches. The Committee proposed that research (of a particular kind) into prostitution is urgently needed:

> Such research as has already been done in connection with female prostitution has been more often from the point of view of sociology and reform than from the point of view of deliberate scientific investigation. We still do not know at all precisely what it is in the total personality of a woman which results in her adopting a life of prostitution (1957, p. 98).

Research into this aspect would be expected to highlight a role for *psychiatric* social workers, revealing the assumption that women in prostitution are suffering from some form of mental ill-health.

Considering the explication of the criteria constituting loitering, the Committee raise the hypothetical issue of mistaken attributions of the behaviour of a woman, behaviour although innocent, may give rise to suspicion on the part of the police officer. Whilst the behaviour of 'innocent' women may be mistaken, this is unlikely to occur, and the Committee recommend the retention of the label 'common prostitute'. *Misidentification is deemed highly improbable.* This presumption is of crucial importance in respect of my current study, and relates to a persistent notion evident in the psychopathological and medical discourses that a 'prostitute' will not be mistaken for an 'innocent' woman and vice versa.

The rhetoric of the Wolfenden Committee is clearly evident in the Sexual Offences Act, 1959 (UK). This Act provides for the offences of loitering or soliciting in public places for the purpose of prostitution and for those guilty of certain offences in connection with refreshment houses and those who live on the earnings of or control prostitutes. Section 1 of the Act decrees that:

> It shall be an offence for a common prostitute to loiter or solicit in a street or public place for the purpose of prostitution ... A constable may arrest without warrant anyone he finds in a street or public place and *suspects, with reasonable cause*, to be committing an offence under this section (emphasis added).

The presence in a public place of a prostitute can be discerned by a constable who can, on the basis of 'reasonable' (that is reasonable to all) 'suspicion' caution a woman. This notion of 'reasonable cause' will become central to my later discussion of the press discourses on prostitution and it is of interest that the criteria for recognition are deemed commonsensical, that is available to all, by virtue of 'reasonable' inference.

The basic tenets of British (and Irish) legislation are to do with public[26] activities of prostitutes, with procurement, with brothel-keeping and pimping, 'living off the earnings of a prostitute'. These are not of concern at present and are therefore not discussed.[27]

Other relevant British legislation is the Sexual Offences Act (1985) which makes provision for the arrest of men who solicit women 'for sexual purposes', i.e., criminalises kerb-crawling. This Act continues its focus upon public places:

> A man commits an offence if he solicits a woman (or different women) for the purpose of prostitution –
> a] from a motor vehicle while it is in a street or public place; or
> b] in a street or public place while in the immediate vicinity of a motor vehicle that he has just got out of or off, persistently or ... in such a manner or in such circumstances as to be likely to cause annoyance to the woman (or any of the women) solicited, or nuisance to other persons in the neighbourhood.

The interpretative notes to the Act clarify that references to soliciting a woman for the purpose of prostitution are 'references to his soliciting her for the purpose of obtaining her services as a prostitute'. Behaviours are to be interpreted then by law enforcement agents and agencies by reference to the *purpose* or intent that they convey to 'reasonable' observers.

Prostitution is here defined as a 'service' and this definition holds in relevant Irish legislation also, suggesting traces of functionalist discourse. The main difference between British and Irish legislation is that in the former 'prostitute' refers to women only,[28] whereas in Irish legislation, following the 1993 Criminal Law (Sexual Offences) Act, 'prostitute' refers to men and women.[29,30]

2.6.1 Prosecutions for activities relating to prostitution

The legal framework criminalises behaviours relating to prostitution, not, as noted, prostitution itself. Legal proscriptions of various behaviours include details of fines and sentencing procedures. Court judgements represent the 'legal reality' and the application of the knowledge produced in legal discourse. This section presents prosecution figures relating to prostitution for both Britain and Ireland. The point of their inclusion is to return back to the reality in which 'real' women are sentenced and fined for activities relating to prostitution. Offences relating to prostitution are currently summary offences (meaning that they are not tried by jury), but are generally dealt with in district/magistrates courts.

In respect of the prosecution figures for Ireland, a problem with crime statistics is that offences classified as 'prostitution' are not disaggregated into separate offences, so for example, no data are available for prosecutions relating to soliciting. Table 2.3 presents data on prosecutions in Ireland and is presented in three columns to highlight the period with which this study is concerned (1987-1991), it includes figures for other periods to contextualise the study period and to indicate whether the study period was 'normal' or 'deviant' in respect of earlier and later prosecutions.

Table 2.3
Prosecution figures for prostitution (1980-1994) Ireland

1980	309	1987	–	1992	004
1981	661	1988	001	1993	001*
1982	399	1989	–	1994	013
1983	001	1990	003		
1984	001	1991	–		
1985	003				
1986	–				

* Criminal Law (Sexual Offences) Act passed
Source: Garda Annual Crime Reports/Crime Branch Garda Síochána.

These figures need to be interpreted in the context of the legal situation regarding the constitutionality of police activity. Following the decision of the Supreme Court in the case of *King v the Attorney General* in 1981, the offering of evidence which tended to indicate that a person had prior convictions was considered to be inconsistent with the Constitution. The proof that the Garda (police officer) knew the woman to be a 'common prostitute' was deemed unconstitutional. Hence from 1982 until the introduction of current legislation (Criminal Law (Sexual Offences) Act, 1993), prosecutions of women for loitering and soliciting were negligible. Hence, in the study period, the legal 'reality' of prostitutional activities in Ireland amounted to four cases.

In official legal discourse then, prostitution could be said to hardly exist in Ireland over this period, however, this 'reality' is not upheld by the press reports on prostitution as later chapters will demonstrate. Further, the 'reality' of crime is constructed in the legal discourse according to visibility, and visibility in public places as the following illustrates: Rosita Sweetman, interviewing a Garda spokesperson in 1979, raised the issue of the lack of police prosecution of massage parlours in (Catholic) Ireland:

RS: Do you think the State might be turning a blind eye to these premises since ostensibly they give no trouble?

Police: There is no policy of turning a blind eye, or ignoring a breach of the law. But our service is not to go rooting for offences ...

RS: Are there brothels operating? Or ... is prostitution carried on mostly in the streets?

Police: *Brothels as such are not known to us.* There have been no prosecutions in recent years so far as we are concerned none are operating. *Most prostitution is carried on in the streets*, or at least the soliciting or offering of the body is carried on in the streets, most of the women then take men to their flats. What goes on there is unknown (1979, pp. 183-4, emphasis added).

This official response indicates that the Irish police force's objectives are with the public offence caused by prostitution, indeed that prostitution is identified as prostitution only through public behaviour, as was argued by the Wolfenden Committee (1957).

In the UK, detailed figures for offences relating to prostitution are provided in the annual Home Office *Criminal Statistics: England and Wales* and in the *Supplementary Tables*. This source of information includes proceedings in magistrates courts (Vol. 1), in the Crown Court (Vol. 2), crime figures by police force areas and by convictions, cautions and appeals and court (Vols. 3, 4) and court proceedings by Petty Sessional Division (Vol. 5). The offences relating to prostitution include (the figures in brackets are the crime identification numbers, for tracking prostitution related crimes through the Court Proceedings):

- kerb crawling (165)
- offence by prostitutes (166)
- aiding and abetting offences by prostitutes (167)
- keeping a disorderly house (4)
- brothel keeping (107)
- soliciting by a man (27).

For current purposes we are concerned particularly with offences committed by prostitutes. Statistics relating to crime are also available in the Central Statistics' Office *Annual Abstract of Statistics*. Offences by prostitutes are included under summary offences. Table 2.4 provides figures relating to offences by prostitutes.

Table 2.4
Prosecutions: Offences by prostitutes (1983-1993) UK

1983	10.4	1987	8.5	1992	9.8
1984	8.6	1988	9.4	1993	8.2
1985	9.2	1989	11.1		
1986	9.3	1990	11.5		
		1991	10.9		

Source: Offenders (thousands) found guilty: by offence group, Magistrates' Courts and the Crown Court, all ages. CSO *Annual Abstract of Statistics* (1995, p. 70).

Table 2.5
Cautions: Offences by prostitutes (1983-1993) UK

1983	7.3	1987	4.9	1992	4.2
1984	4.9	1988	5.2	1993	4.0
1985	4.2	1989	5.3		
1986	5.0	1990	4.5		
		1991	4.1		

Source: Offenders (thousands) found guilty: by offence group, Magistrates' Courts and the Crown Court, all ages. From CSO *Annual Abstract of Statistics* (1995, p. 71).

These figures indicate, in contradistinction with those presented in Table 2.3, that prostitution is indeed a crime 'problem' in the UK. The enormous disjuncture between the 'legal reality', that is, the legal recognition (in the form of police activity and court sentencing) of the existence of prostitution in Britain and Ireland, over the period considered in this study (1987-1991), could not be more stark. It would be expected on the basis of these 'pictures' of prostitutional activity by women that the proportion of press coverage of prostitution would convey the differences in the two countries. However, as will be seen, this is not the case.

2.7 Feminist discourses

Carol Smart, reviewing the various sociological, criminological and psychoanalytic approaches to prostitution, states that the studies included

> ... do not meet even the basic requirement of a feminist perspective. The concentration on female prostitution and the concomitant neglect of male prostitution or the prostitute's client, the dependence on a pathology model or a presentation of analyses which merely serve to legitimate, justify or 'naturalise' unequal social and sexual relations signify a celebration of the status quo rather than an attempt at a rigorous analysis oriented towards the goal of liberating people from socio-culturally located common-sense perceptions of the nature of sexual relations (1976, p. 93).

Feminist approaches to the study of prostitution must be located within the wider feminist project. Developments and divisions within feminism, as a body of theory and as a social practice are reflected in writings spanning from the 1950s to the 1990s. Feminism is, in the definition provided by Linda Gordon, 'an analysis of women's subordination for the purpose of figuring out how to change it' (cited in Eisenstein, 1988, p. xii).

Feminism (in its different approaches) focuses upon how gender relations enter into and structure the everyday experiences of women and men and upon how other relations, based upon class and race, enter into and mediate gender structuring. Variants of feminist analyses begin with the social construction of gender and the ways in which women, as deBeauvoir (1953) suggested, 'become' and are 'not born'. The organisation of gender relations under a system of patriarchy is maintained and reproduced in discourses and social practices.[31]

Judith Walkowitz (1981) has pointed out that commercial sex is a 'hot and dangerous issue for feminists'.[32] It is so because, on the one hand, prostitution is viewed as the epitome of asymmetrical gender relations in which women are, given limited economic opportunities, *forced* to engage in prostitution in order to survive and on the other, because prostitution, with its flexible hours, enable women to facilitate domestic demands (see McLeod, 1982, for such an argument). Women can also earn more money 'on the game' than would be possible in 'traditional' women's employment. This pro-con statement brings to the fore some of the problems inherent in discussing prostitution from a feminist position/standpoint, simply because each argument is starting from a different position; Carol Pateman (1988) has suggested a way around this,

42

emphasising that an attack on the institution is not an attack on women in prostitution, a 'hate the sin, love the sinner' approach. Another issue raised is the notion of women involuntarily forced/driven into prostitution, a notion which is rejected by some feminists (e.g., James, 1980) and prostitutes themselves (see below).

An exemplar of this first approach is Kate Millett's *Sexual Politics* (1971). In this work, she argues that the oppression of women in capitalist societies is due to their dependence on men, a dependence maintained and reproduced by institutional arrangements and underpinned by, in particular, an ideology of romantic love. Prostitution occurs in the context of patriarchy. In the former, she follows Engels in his assertion that the institutions of marriage and the family are built on the ownership of women. The position of women generally illustrates the ways in which 'the prostitute's role is an *exaggeration* of patriarchal economic conditions where the majority of women are driven to live through some exchange of sexuality for support' (1971, p. 37). Hence, the prostitute's condition approximates that of all women. This theme, of the approximation of the prostitute with all women, is the main standpoint expressed by feminist analysis. Levine (1987) argued that *all* women exist within an atmosphere of prostitution and slogans, such as the English Collective of Prostitute's 'We are all bad girls', express this basic premise. Others, such as Dominelli (1986, p. 73), argue that women in prostitution, in their rationalisations of prostitution which draw upon notions of male sexual urges, are contributing to the maintenance of asymmetrical gender relations and reinforcing the ethos of a consumer society. Prostitution perpetuates 'sexuality as a matter of apolitical private concern' because it deals with men's sexual 'needs' on a privatised basis.

Posing a conceptual continuum, whore-madonna, rather than binary opposition of whore/madonna, enabled feminist researchers in a range of disciplines to consider the issue of prostitution, not in relation to what it yields in relation to prostitutes but rather, what the treatment of prostitutes means for all women[33] and how such treatment is central to the maintenance and reproduction of notions of 'normal' and 'deviant' sexuality.[34]

Feminist scholarship has documented the ways in which, for example, scientific, legal, medical, religious/moral, criminological knowledges have been constructed upon notions of female sexuality, notions which 'naturalise' unequal relations between men and women and such knowledge is used to formulate policy and hence practice, with concomitant material effects on women.[35] It has drawn attention to the operation of gender-blind theories and gender-based ideologies in traditional approaches to prostitution.

One of the first 'myths' that has been dismantled, is the notion that prostitution has always existed, in the same form, since time immemorial. The cultural and historical specificity (cf. Gagnon & Simon, 1973) of different forms of prostitution means that to refer to prostitution as the 'world's oldest profession' hides such specificity. Smart (1976, p. 93) argues that this gloss signals a celebration of the status quo and its adoption by theorists deflects rigorous analysis oriented towards liberating people from socio-culturally located common-sense perceptions of the nature of social relations. Research into prostitution should relate prostitution to wider cultural norms regarding female sexuality (cf. Dominelli, 1986; Nead, 1988).

The similarity of prostitution to marriage and all women's existence within Western patriarchal capitalist societies is, as noted above, a central tenet of feminist approaches to prostitution. As noted, June Levine (1987) has argued that all women exist in an atmosphere of prostitution and Karen Rosenblum, adopting an interactionist perspective, suggests that:

> ... the transition from non-deviance to deviance within prostitution requires only an exaggeration of the situation experienced by the non-deviant woman (1975, p. 169).

This is because a central aspect of the female sex role is, she suggests, the use of sex for non-sex purposes (as Kingsley Davis, 1937, pointed out). Women, then, who sell sex for monetary gain are operating within the female sex role, not outside or in contradiction to it. Dominelli (1986) reiterates this in her suggestion that as prostitution does not challenge existing social relations, it cannot be designated deviant behaviour.

Jennifer James (1978) however, argues that this is true only to a limited extent. She points out that prostitutes, especially street prostitutes, are considered to violate the female sex role in a number of ways; their place of business, the street, violates the sex role because they are unescorted by a man; the overt active sexual behaviour of the prostitute challenges notions of passive female sexuality.

The question which has divided feminists relates to why women enter into prostitution. One of the most recent books on prostitution is *The Prostitution of Sexuality: The Global Exploitation of Women* by Kathleen Barry (1995) who argues that women are forced into prostitution, that 'most' women in prostitution have been sexually abused and that prostitution is a crime against women; it is sexual slavery. This position was expressed by the 19th century feminist campaigners (cf. Walkowitz, 1980) and by Millett (1971, p. 123). The Gannons, writing about prostitution in Ireland, argue that the prostitute is one

> ... who, unless abnormal, must have gone through a fierce social, sexual and economic coercion to find herself in such a position (1979, p. 24).

However, unlike non-feminist approaches which also regard women in prostitution as forced into it (due to individual pathology, Glover, 1943), the feminist approach argues that women are driven into prostitution but the source of this is to be found in oppressive gender and class relations.[35]

The counter argument to this is expressed by James (1978) in her empirical study of prostitutes in the US. On the basis of interviews with women working as prostitutes, she argues that the traditional stereotype of prostitutes as wretched creatures, forced into prostitution by extreme economic deprivation is misplaced. She argues that the women she interviewed had chosen to enter into prostitution in order to have a better standard of living than would have been possible given the employment options open to them. This choice is a rational one, not a symptom of the immorality or deviance of the individual women.

This approach has been more recently argued by Perkins (1991) who, critiquing Carol Pateman's arguments in respect of the 'sexual contract', argues that women in prostitution are not powerless victims (cf. Sheehy (1979) for a view of prostitutes as victims). Pateman suggests that the contractual relation between prostitute and client cannot be compared to other employment contracts; rather the prostitution/sexual contract is one in which the 'law of the male sex right' is legitimated and the implication of this is that prostitutes sell their bodies, not sexual services:

> When women's bodies are on sale as commodities in the capitalist market, the terms of the original contract cannot be forgotten; the law of male sex-right is publicly affirmed, and men gain public acknowledgement as women's sexual masters – that is what is wrong with prostitution (1988, p. 208).

Perkins, in response, argues that the prostitutes in her study emphasised 'how different sexual interactions in prostitution are to ordinary (heterosexual) social sexual situations'. It may *appear* that prostitution is a 'public acknowledgement of the male sex right', but, Perkins avers, the *reality* is quite different. Indeed, Perkins' attack on what she considers to be 'unrealistic' appearances of a 'real' reality is graphically illustrated in her statement that cinematic representations of prostitutes are 'abortions of reality' (1989). Within a patriarchal-capitalist system, more women than men prostitute themselves and myths about masculinity perpetuate the objectification of women. In female prostitution women have, according to Perkins, more power over sexual interactions than in any other circumstance involving both sexes interacting.

She accuses Pateman of perpetuating the whore-stigma (cf. Pheterson, 1988) and suggests that a 'real' feminist approach to prostitution, instead of seeing prostitutes as misguided participants in patriarchy's sexual control of women, would illustrate how they are 'radical traditionalists' who turn 'tricks' to their sexual, social and economic advantage. Perkins thus considers prostitution as legitimate work, not as sexual oppression and in this approach, she is articulating the demands of prostitutes (ICPR, 1986).

2.7.1 Feminist approaches to legal discourses

Nowhere is the contradictory character of the law, as an oppressive instrument of a particular social interest as well as an immediately important area of struggle, more important than in the relationship in the law to women (Taylor, 1981; cited in Edwards, 1990).

Feminist research into the processing of women through the criminal justice system has suggested that sentencing policies are formulated on the bases of essentialist notions about 'women' and that the prostitution laws are archaic, sexist and destructive (Halft, 1978; James, 1978). The laws against prostitutes are considered (e.g., Smart, 1976) to provide a particularly clear instance of the operation of gender-based ideologies in their construction of prostitution as a sex-specific offence, although of course, legislation against kerb-crawling (UK Sexual Offences Act, 1985), does target male clients. Smart (1976) argues that the prevailing moral code is the reference point of legislative approaches to prostitution, a code which is historically specific. Walkowitz (1980, 1981) and Nead (1988) have focused upon the operation of ideologies about female sexuality in 19th century legal, moral and cultural responses to prostitution. The feminist analyses of the legal code (and the prevailing moral code) are concerned with the question of the social control of all women (Crites, 1978; Heidensohn, 1985; Edwards, 1987, 1990).

James suggests that 'rather than being the victims of prostitution itself, prostitutes may be the victims of the laws against prostitution and the ways in which they are enforced' (1978, p. 176). The focus of criminal law is on offences in the street and those which occur in the home are understood as 'private' and hence beyond the purview of the law. This explicit concern with public order (in the streets) has been documented in the section dealing with legal approaches to prostitution above (particularly the statements of the Wolfenden Committee, 1957).

Edwards (1987, p. 47), along with other theorists (McLeod, 1982; Heidensohn, 1985; Perkins, 1991; Roberts, 1993), notes that legislation (in Western societies) and policing practices have reflected a preoccupation with the streetwalker, endorsing prostitution as a covert activity. Acts such as the Sexual Offences Act (1959) place the burden of social invisibility onto the female prostitutes, not male clients. However, despite this extensive concern and legislative concentration with street prostitution, this form of prostitution is not the most prevalent form of prostitution. Perkins (1991) reports that the street prostitutes in her sample of prostitutes constitute 3.9%, a sample size consistent with the distribution of prostitute types in and employment location of the Sydney female prostitution population. Others have estimated street prostitution as constituting between 10 and 20% of all forms of prostitution. This is a significant point given that legal discourses are primarily concerned with street/public places and activities relating to prostitution.

2.8   Practitioners' discourses

An uneasy relationship exists between feminists and prostitutes, or sex workers, which includes all women in the sex industry (L. Bell, 1987; Edwards, 1990, p. 148). As the consideration of feminist approaches to the issue of prostitution illustrates, differing perceptions of prostitution and its relationship to the reproduction of unequal gender-power relations is an area fraught with conflict. The prostitutes' own understanding of prostitution represents an expanding contribution to the overall corpus. Kate Millett's *The Prostitution Papers* (1975) was one of the first collections of prostitutes' 'own words' stories about their lives. Other collections include Jaget (1982); Delacoste and Alexander (1988); the English Collective of Prostitutes (1988); and *Good Girls/Bad Girls: Sex Trade Workers and Feminists Face to Face* (ed. L. Bell, 1987). The International Committee for Prostitutes' Rights, COYOTE (Call Off Your Old Tired Ethics) in the US, the ECP (English Collective of Prostitutes) and PROS (Programme for the Reform of Laws on Soliciting), a UK organisation, and Prostitute Collective of Victoria, an Australian organisation, are all prostitutes' rights groups. The unifying argument of the different discourses is that women enter into prostitution for economic reasons; prostitution, the ECP declares, is a refusal of poverty.

The prostitutes interviewed by Millett (1975) argue that prostitution is slavery, reiterating Millett's earlier points (1971), for example, about the objectification of women and the degradation experienced by women in prostitution. This approach mirrored the feminist response to prostitution in the 1970s. However, since then prostitutes' rights organisations have argued that prostitution is a legitimate occupation, while retaining a focus upon the links between prostitutes and all women. Prostitutes (Valentino & Johnson in Jaget, 1980, p. 11; Perkins, 1991) have argued that they have control of their bodies, having power within the encounter with clients and that they are not unconscious victims. They further argue with feminists that the prostitution laws keep all women under control. The articulation of prostitutes' demands is found in various charters and statements issued.[36] These include the statements issued by the International Committee for Prostitutes' Rights at the Second World Whores Congress, which was held in the European Parliament, Brussels in 1986, focusing upon prostitution and human rights, prostitution and feminism, prostitution and health. Of particular concern is the ICPR demand that prostitution be accepted as legitimate work. It further proposes that the development of prostitution analyses and strategies within the women's movement must link the conditions of prostitutes to the condition of women in general.

Included in the ICPR collection was the European Parliament's *Resolution on Violence against Women* (1986) and the *World Charter for Prostitutes' Rights* (1985). The *World Charter* includes demands for the freedom of choice with regard to place of prostitution: 'There should be no law which implies systematic zoning of prostitution', rejecting attempts to 'contain' prostitution within specific places.

Prostitutes have attacked feminists for formulating analyses about prostitution 'knowing nothing about the *real lives* of sex trade workers' (L. Bell, 1987, p. 14). Arrington further argues that the feminist argument that all women on the streets are or have been sexually abused is 'not true', it is merely 'something that the academics use for their little statistics and their little studies' (in L. Bell, 1987, p. 176). A spokesperson for Canadian Organisation for the Rights of Prostitutes (CORP) argued against what is perceived as the feminist tendency to

> ... find it necessary to interpret prostitutes' experience of their lives and then fed it back to the prostitutes to tell them what is really happening, whereas they wouldn't dare to be so condescending or patronising to any other groups of women (in L. Bell, 1987, p. 213).

In the prostitutes' discourse, women enter prostitution because of poverty and because other employment open to them would not yield comparable monetary rewards. They reject medical, psychopathological and some feminist assumptions about prostitution, although some accept the functional nature of prostitution: regarding prostitution as operating as a 'safety valve' (Jaget, 1980, p. 134).

2.9   Conclusion

This chapter has aimed to describe the main features of the different perspectives on prostitution. Its purpose is to highlight the differing approaches to this issue and to lay the framework for a consideration of the ways such knowledges enter into and structure journalistic perspectives on prostitution as articulated in their stories of prostitution. It has also aimed to outline the key features of the different discourses of which a concern to build typologies of prostitutes is particularly evident. Problems of defining prostitution have been somewhat overlooked in this attempt but the confusion regarding definitions of what precisely prostitution is has been a noticeable feature of the different discourses (a range of the different definitions of prostitution are presented in Appendix I). While a confusion about what prostitution is exists, this is amplified in determining who is a prostitute. It is this concern about the identification of prostitutes which is the focus of this current project.

Much of the discussion has focused upon accounts of why women enter prostitution. In this regard, psychoanalytical and moral discourses, for instance, privilege individual pathology, whereas the practitioners identify poverty as the causative factor. Feminist approaches have directed attention to the importance of considering social structural factors, as opposed to individualising the issue of prostitution, and have focused on the operation of different discourses which articulate different assumptions about women and 'normal' female behaviour, particularly in regard to sexual behaviour (e.g., Finnegan, 1979; McIntosh, 1978; Walkowitz, 1980). One discourse which has been excluded relates to the popular cultural discourses on prostitution, however, given the lack of attention to this field, of which newspapers are an element, and given space constraints, this omission is justified.

Finally, the question of journalists' access to and take up of the different assumptions articulated in the various discourses needs to be addressed. One answer to this question relates to the role of the media as key information providers in society (cf. Ericson et al., 1987). Use of official sources in the presentation of events has been recognised as critical in the interpretation of events. As Ericson et al. note:

> ... news sources function as reporters in the sense that they prepare accounts already tailor made for both their purposes and the journalists' purpose of news communication (1987, p. 9).

The use of such sources reproduces particular discourses, for example, citing a medical doctor's 'opinion' (which is legitimated as 'fact' by her/ his institutional position) about high HIV prevalence rates amongst prostitutes reproduces a discourse of the infected prostitute. A second answer is to suggest that some of the discourses have, over time, achieved the status of 'common-sense' (or have, in Fairclough's (1985) terms, been 'naturalised') and are readily available in everyday conversation, for example the notion that street prostitution is the only form of prostitution, an approach which excludes other forms of prostitution. The responses to this question are superficial. However, for current purposes, they will suffice. I turn now to consider the press discourses of prostitution and to indicate, tentatively at this stage, the similarities and divergence of themes and concerns of the discourses described above with those in the press.

Notes

1   Reviews of different approaches to the study of prostitution are available and the reader is referred to these (e.g., Cohen 1980; Perkins, 1991; Smart, 1976).

2   Horton & Aggleton (1990) have considered the emergence of a modern thought-style of AIDS; this is a set of taken for granted assumptions about the nature and aetiology of AIDS, framing the kinds of questions which may be (legitimately) asked and the kinds of answers that can be regarded as 'legitimate'. Their work considers how discourses from outside medical science have informed the medical discourses on HIV aetiology.

3   The main increase in writings about prostitution from the mid-1980s to the present is most probably in the autobiographical category and also in the medical category, with the advent of the HIV pandemic in which prostitutes have been subjected to medical and social science surveillance.

4   The (Irish) Council for the Status of Women (now the National Women's Council of Ireland) commented, in 1993, in a policy

statement regarding the Criminal Law (Sexual Offences) Act 1993 that 'prostitution in Ireland is largely undocumented'. Indeed, only one 'sociological' treatise has been produced (I & J Gannon, 1979), the most recent popular feminist account of prostitution in Ireland being the story of Lyn Madden in *Lyn: A Story of Prostitution* (Levine & Madden, 1987). On-line catalogue searches did not disconfirm this assessment.

5 Perkins cites Ericson, a philosopher, in regard to the issue of the intrinsic immorality of prostitution:

> To say that prostitution is intrinsically immoral is in a way to refuse to give any argument. The moralist simply 'senses' or 'sees' its immorality. And this terminates rational discussion at the point where it should begin (1991, p. 26).

6 Roberts (1993) provides a detailed history of prostitution and the responses of the Christian Church.

7 Interestingly, while men were being directed to 'shun immorality' by not 'consorting with prostitutes', the directive to women was to 'shun the clothes of the immoral' (Saint Cyprian, 249, cited in Corrigan, 1988: 4).

8 Mary Cummins describes a more recent experience with the Legion of Mary (an Irish religious group founded by Frank Duff in 1923 and dedicated to the task of 'redeeming lost souls'); she joined up due to a curiosity about prostitutes and ended up talking to a woman [prostitute]:

> She was tall, had style, smoked non-stop and was furious with my friend and I for interfering with her. She walked up and down, refused to come for a cup of coffee and then, remained icily silent until we left (It goes on in Holy Ireland, *Irish Times*, 30.3.95).

9 See Nead (1988) for a discussion of early writings and the construction of the prostitute as a symbol of moral and social disorder; see also Walkowitz (1980, 1981) for a discussion of early religious writers.

10 The Council for the Status of Women's file on prostitution contains a report from a religious order (Roman Catholic) detailing their work with women in prostitution. One of the striking comments in this report relates to the order's understanding of the 'values' or rationale underpinning their work: 'each woman has the *potential* to

become fully human and beautiful', presumably however, only if she stops prostituting herself. The order further refer to a success they had in preventing a women entering into prostitution and their 'rehabilitation' efforts.

11   An obvious feature which may spring to mind, given the concern of this work, is any evidence of religious discourse, particularly in the Irish press, given the influence of Roman Catholic church in Ireland (and indeed the religious ethos which pervades the 1937 Constitution (Bunreacht na hÉireann). An explicit religious discourse was not discernible.

12   The history of medical and legal responses to homosexuality amply demonstrates this; cf. Weeks, 1985; Plummer 1981.

13   Nead (1988) argues that these attributes were critical in the construction of the dominant narrative of prostitution, a narrative which achieved closure with the physical decline and death of the 'fallen woman'.

14   The Contagious Diseases Acts were adopted in different degrees throughout England's colonies; in Ireland (the Lock Hospital was located in Dublin city, Westmoreland Street) and in Australia (cf. Perkins, Lovejoy & Marina, 1990).

15   Finnegan (1979: 2) notes that Acton has been regarded as the great authority on Victorian prostitution.

16   See Finnegan (1979) and Walkowitz (1980) for a discussion of the contradictions in Acton's arguments as he attempted to modify them to suit the purposes of proposed legislation.

17   The tone of anxiety about 'thousands of our female population' entering prostitution is not specific to the 19th century. An Irish press story reported a politician's concern about a similar state of affairs in late 20th century Ireland (No Job Girls 'Turn to Vice', *Irish Independent*, 10.8.90).

18   As Walkowitz (1988) has noted medical knowledge was fraught with seeming contradictions: the source of syphilitic infection was found also in 'virtuous women', that is women who were not prostitutes. This contradiction may be explained, in part, by reference to a general fear of female sexuality.

19   A search through the *Social Science Citation Index* (1994) indicates the shift in focus of medical-informed approaches. There is a preponderance of articles on HIV risk behaviours and prevalence amongst prostitutes across a range of journals, from *Addiction* (e.g.,

Gossop et al. (1994) focusing upon drug-using prostitutes and risks of HIV infection and hence transmission) to *Social Science and Medicine*. In addition, a range of specialist journals (e.g., *AIDS Care*) exist.

20   The *Lancet* is generally regarded, world-wide, as the official mouthpiece of the medical profession.

21   A continuity between the Contagious Diseases Acts and the HIV epidemic in the 1980s is evident in Australian public health legislation: Sharleen, a prostitute, who was HIV positive, was the target of the Public Health Act 1903 which provides for the incarceration of infectious persons for treatment. The rationale for this is the protection of the community. The Minister for Corrective Services argued that 'The full weight of the law must be used to stop her' (Perkins, Lovejoy & Marina, 1990).

22   The author of the book is Wilkinson, but it was Rolph who edited the book (and who refers to Mrs Wilkinson's 'perceptive feminine subjectiveness, which is seldom absent'). I therefore refer to the author as Wilkinson, although it is referenced under Rolph (1954).

23   Gossop et al. (1994) consider exchange of drugs for sex but encounter some problems in selecting a sample group and rely on traditional criteria (sale of specific sexual acts for money) for selecting respondents. Their work indicates how, if prostitution is defined as exchange of material (and indeed) non-goods, the criteria for identifying prostitutes (in the context of a society in which women, as feminists (e.g., Millett, 1971) have suggested, are dependent on men for economic survival), would yield an infinite population universe.

24   For a discussion of the American response to prostitution (and venereal disease), see Brandt, 1987.

25   This is expressed in comments such as the following: 'It's like standing on a half-inflated balloon, you crush prostitution in one area and it goes up in another place,' says the Chief Inspector (JUST WORKING GIRLS ..., *Plus Magazine*, June, 1991).

26   Public is generally understood as 'street' and legislation defines street as including:

> ... any bridge, road, lane, footway, square, court, alley or passage, whether a thoroughfare or not, which is for the time being open to the public; and the doorways and entrances of premises abutting on a street ... and any ground adjoining and open to a

street, shall be treated as forming part of the street' (Sexual Offences Act, 1985).

The Criminal Law (Sexual Offences) Act, 1993 (Ireland) provides a clarification to terms used as follows: street is defined in the same way as that prevailing in the UK legislation, adding 'car parks' to the list of areas defined as 'street'; solicits or importunes for the purposes of prostitution is where the person 'offers his or her services as a prostitute to another person'.

27 The Sexual Offences Act 1985 (UK) notes that 'words importing the masculine gender to include the feminine ... do not apply to this Act'.

28 The outcome of *DPP vs Bull* (1990) (UK) concerned the Street Offences Act, 1959, Section 1, and the term 'common prostitute' was deemed to be confined to female prostitutes, excluding the activities of male prostitutes. This Act was intended to 'remedy mischief created by women' and the term 'common prostitute' was ordinarily applied to women (Law Report, *The Times*, 1.6.94).

29 Interpretation note (4):

In this Act, and in any other enactment ... a reference to a prostitute includes a reference to a male person who is a prostitute and a reference to prostitution shall be constructed accordingly.

30 There is no one feminism, rather different approaches exist, for example, the essentialist understanding of women as innately good and the social constructionist understanding of women as socially constructed and of concepts of femininity as socially produced (cf. Eisenstein, 1988, for a full discussion of the various strands of feminism).

31 I am ignoring the feminist response to the Contagious Diseases Acts in the 1860s for reasons of space, Walkowitz (1980, 1981) provides detailed discussion of the feminist movement and the problems it encountered, including the ways in which its discourse was appropriated by social purity reformers.

32 Goode & Troiden (1974, p. 23) suggesting a linear view, rather than dichotomy, between deviance and conventionality, argue that every form of deviant behaviour is an exaggerated case of conventional behaviour.

33 The basic arguments of social constructionist approaches in the social sciences have been taken up and used by feminists in studies

of sexuality, and feminists have also reviewed the social science and other literature, pointing out the extent to which essentialist notions of femininity and masculinity were employed.

34   This approach has been particularly applied in the study of women's dealing with the various sectors of the medical profession (e.g., Murphy Lawless, in Torode, 1989).

35   The coincidence of feminist and non-feminist arguments in respect of women 'forced' into prostitution (an argument reached by different routes and premised upon different notions about female sexuality and the prevailing social relations) is of interest here. The anti-pornography campaign in the States has demonstrated how feminist discourses can be appropriated by 'the right' and used as the basis of anti-women strategies. Walkowitz draws attention to this in *The Politics of Prostitution* (1980) in which she considers the Victorian feminist campaign against prostitution.

36   The demands by prostitutes are often rejected by feminists; Edwards (1993, p. 89), noting the ICPR demand for the right of women to work as prostitutes, comments that this is rather like Plato's 'happy slave', it is a 'flimsy embourgeoisment and cannot alter the fundamental exploitation that exists, nor the indisputable fact of commodity exchange, nor the enduring fact of patriarchy, however improved are the work conditions or social status of prostitutes'.

3 Selection of materials and findings from a content analysis

3.1 Introduction

In the previous chapter, the discourses of prostitution, representing different frameworks of knowledge, were discussed. The question of the extent to which such assumptions (articulated in discourses) are in circulation across discourse sites was raised and I have suggested that the media are central sites in the reproduction of different discourses. The material effects of specific discourses are evident in respect of a consideration of, for example, the medical discourse in which prostitutes are identified as a 'high-risk group' in respect of HIV infection and transmission. In this chapter, which comprises two sections, I first detail the reasons for my choice of materials and then consider some of the wider aspects of the materials. The raw data are introduced by way of content analysis which aims to supply the reader with a broad overview of the key themes in these data. In reporting the findings of this exercise, attention will be drawn to the presence of the different approaches to prostitution already addressed in Chapter Two. These discourses are not immutable, rather, different discourses are drawn upon and approached from different angles, according to story topic. Further as regards categorisation of stories as stories of prostitution, the angle taken on a story can determine its inclusion in a category (cf. Glasgow Media Group, 1976, p. 44). Reports on prostitution are not necessarily filed by newspaper organisations as 'stories of prostitution', rather they may be filed under a 'sex-crime' category (as by the *Irish Times*).

In the second section, I address the issues raised by a content analytic method for handling the data and move from there to focus upon some of the contemporary debates about media discourse which are relevant for my purposes, in particular addressing questions of objectivity in respect of media content. This is done with a view to the following chapter, Chapter Four, which details the methodological issues raised over the course of this study. This second section serves to situate my work within the wider field of media studies.

3.1.1 The research design: Selecting materials

In their discussion of reliability and validity in qualitative research, Kirk and Miller write that the qualitative researcher must document the procedure adopted in the research, that is how the data are collected and analysed (1986, p. 72). In following this directive, I am at risk of providing extraneous detail. However, this detailed exposition of the data collection procedure forms the basis of my claim that the arguments presented are valid; that they are based upon representative data and relatedly, that they are not deductive but rather emerged inductively and that other researchers would arrive at the same conclusions.

As noted in the opening chapter, the research problem, that of the categorisation of women as prostitutes, emerged some time into the research. The initial research design was focused upon a broader question, namely, how is prostitution represented in the media, and it was the consideration of this question which led to the more specific research problem. My research interests in discourse analysis led me, at the start of this study, to consider media discourse as viable sources of data. The function of 'informal education of the population' by the media has been noted (Glasgow Media Group, 1976, p. 9), and their influence has been deemed 'profound' (Giddens, 1989, p. 79). Hebdige, discussing the sources of style, has suggested that media

> ... are crucial in defining our experience for us ... [providing] us with the most available categories for classifying out the social world (1979, pp. 84-5).

Hebdige's suggestion needs to be treated with caution; the media are not all-powerful and, as Chapter Two has attempted to indicate, there are other discourse sites in which the classification occurs (cf. Kitzinger & Miller, 1992). The media serve as sources of knowledge about events and persons in the world, beyond our everyday experience. They communicate particular knowledges, silencing, by omission, other knowledges, and it is in this respect that their relevance to the current project can be appreciated. The starting point was to consider how the assumptions about prostitution in the legal, sociological, medical and feminist discourses are adopted, to greater or lesser extents, by media producers, in short, which assumptions and discourses are dominant in the press reports of prostitution.

In approaching the research question, having decided that my focus would be upon mass mediated representations of 'prostitutes', I could have focused upon one of the range of media: film, television, radio, newspapers. I chose to investigate this issue through an examination of newspapers and this choice was dictated by my research interests in the role of the press in contemporary society, and my view that, despite the reported (relative) decline of press circulation, the press is deserving of sociological attention (Turnstall, 1983, p. 69). The circulation figures presented below testify to the 'importance' of newspapers, in terms of mass circulation. I was further interested in the press discourses as sources of knowledge about events and people in the world, knowledge which constructs the meaning of events and behaviours in particular ways. On a more mundane level, I considered the information role of the press important, this information (embodying knowledge) is drawn upon in everyday life, for example, the common *conversational* strategy to claim veracity is to state 'I read it in the papers' (cf. Kitzinger & Miller, 1992, p. 51).

In addition, the choice of press reports would enable me to carry out in-depth, micro-analysis of discourse structure of *written* texts, which was the initial aim of the study, and this data source was potentially infinite; after all, in Ireland, there were, during the data collection phase, thirteen daily, evening and Sunday newspapers available every week, excluding British newspapers which were also on sale. In Britain there were seven daily newspapers (excluding tabloids whose circulation rates outstrip quality newspaper sales) and six Sunday papers.

The ready availability of newspapers was thus an important consideration in the decision to select the press. I envisaged difficulties collecting audio and visual data, and suspected that had I selected radio programmes, television programmes or cinema I would have encountered problems with data collection due to the intermittent and relatively minor coverage of prostitution in these media.[1] In- addition, the fact that newspapers contain photographs meant that I would also be able to consider the visual discourses of prostitution. The overriding ground on which the decision to focus upon newspaper reports was that, despite the prolific outpourings on the subject of prostitution (cf. Bullough, 1977) and given the insistence of the central role of mass communication in the production and reproduction of culture (Thompson, 1988, 1990), the study of how prostitution is conceptualised and represented, across different discourse sites, and the relevance of such representations in the production and reproduction of cultural understandings of both prostitution and female sexuality, has been a neglected area of study. This study aims to focus in on one specific site and as such should be regarded as, to use a common metaphor, a piece in a larger puzzle.

Maio (1988) and Perkins (1989) have considered filmic representations of prostitutes; Nead (1984, 1988) has focused upon the construction of definitions of sexuality via an analysis of images of prostitutes in nineteenth century painting and religious/moral and medical discourse and Hollway (1981) has considered *The Guardian* press reports of the trial of Peter Sutcliffe. In addition, feminist analyses (e.g., Butcher et al., 1974) of images of women have included brief considerations of 'the prostitute'. However, whilst such studies exist, no specific study of the representation of prostitution over time and covering a range of issues has been undertaken. A study of press reports of prostitution thus contributes to the existing limited studies cited above, but goes beyond them in considering the ways in which prostitution has been reported across a range of reports dealing with different aspects of prostitution over a five year period. It also goes beyond existing studies in selecting British and Irish newspapers, introducing a comparative focus, although, as will be demonstrated, the variation between the British and Irish press stories on prostitution is not significant, a feature raising issues which are addressed later in the study.

I decided, following Hollway (1981), to focus upon the national broadsheet publications in preference to selecting the tabloid press. Hollway argues that this is a fruitful research strategy because, given the sensationalist and overtly sexist reporting in the tabloids,[2] arguments based upon data from the broadsheet press, which are generally considered to adopt a more measured approach to news events, will stand for both broadsheet and tabloid press approaches. A feature of contemporary broadsheet reportage which has been noted, is the increasing tendency towards tabloid style reportage, a feature which is tied to the institutional needs of the broadsheet newspaper industry to attract readers and which has produced the category 'broadloid' which refers to a new hybrid which wraps up the cheerful (gossip, sleaze) and the cerebral (politics, economics) in the same multi-sectioned package (Beckett, *Independent on Sunday*, 9.7.95, p. 4). This may account for some of the detailed descriptions of the physical appearance of 'the prostitute' and for the photographic images which accompany the newspaper stories (see Chapter Five, Chapter Seven). Taken together, there are a range of broadsheet newspapers (see Table 3.1) available over a weekly period in Britain and Ireland.

Table 3.1
Nationally available daily and Sunday newspapers in Britain and the Republic of Ireland[a]

	Daily	Sunday
IR:	*The Irish Times**	*Sunday Independent*
	The Irish Independent*	*Sunday Tribune**
	The Irish Press *	*Sunday Press**
	The Cork Examiner	*Sunday Business Post*
	The Evening Press*	
	The Evening Herald	
UK:	*The Guardian**	*Independent on Sunday**
	The Independent*	*The Observer**
	The Times*	*The Sunday Telegraph**
	The Financial Times	*The Sunday Times**
	The Daily Telegraph*	

* Reports selected from these newspapers.

[a] This table lists newspapers available at the time the data collection was carried out.

The circulation figures for these newspapers are reported in Table 3.2. I have only included three of the five years, as the purpose of this table is for background purposes only. The circulation figures, which have been compiled from monthly averages, hide the fluctuations in newspaper sales on a monthly basis. The table indicates the high circulation rates of tabloid newspapers as against the modest circulation rates of the 'quality' press or broadsheets. The inclusion of these figures points to the economic 'reality' of the newspaper industry: circulation figures are crucial in attracting the advertising revenue on which a newspaper depends. In addition, and more relevant for my purposes, the circulation figures and readership information or profiles of the different readership groups of the various newspapers are used in decisions about what stories a newspaper will run. The content of newspapers is not simply there, it is the result of a process in which considerations about circulation rates and perceived interests of the readership are central.

Table 3.2
Circulation figures for national newspapers in Britain and Ireland
(1987, 1989, 1991)

UK press	1987	1989	1991
The Sun	45,258,233*	49,141,249	44,165,451
Daily Telegraph	13,896,771	13,294,061	12,800,869
The Guardian	5,713,646	5,218,359	5,049.069
Independent	3,925,840	4,901,067	4,604,799
The Times	5,338,653	5,218,112	5,150,339
Observer	9,255,260	7,997,289	6,773,544
Sunday Times	14,793,732	15,404,681	24,112,608
Sunday Telegraph	8,760,666	7,727,205	6,868,760
Sunday Correspondent	—	929,672	—
Independent on Sunday	—	—	4,554,832

Irish press	1987	1989	1991
Irish Times	176,271	184,242	187,889
Irish Independent	302, 883	307,005	301,744
Irish Press	155,147	126,690	117,781
Evening Press	246,002	203,923	172,223
Sunday Tribune	193,008	197,976	181,540
Sunday Independent	438,217	461,801	466,808
Sunday World	549,499	518,977	481,667

*   The circulation figures for *The Sun* and *The Sunday World* are included to provide an indication of the phenomenal circulation rates that these tabloids have achieved.

Source: Compiled from the monthly averages of circulation, *Audit Bureau of Circulation* (1987-1991).

3.1.2 Data collection procedures

The data collection phase began when I started this study in October 1987. The articles included in the data pool were those whose subject matter was identified by me as being explicitly concerned with prostitution. In the course of carrying out a data check procedure in 1995, I accessed the *McCarthy Index* 1993-1995 (previous years were not available) a CD ROM facility which covers business news. Using the root 'prostit' and a wild card (*) I searched this database and the articles selected, from, for example, *The Guardian, Daily Telegraph, Financial Times, Evening Standard,* while not concerned with prostitution per se used 'prostitution' as a metaphor in descriptions of business activities. Such articles which used prostitution metaphorically were not included in the original data collection procedure. The selection criterion adopted in identifying stories of prostitution and the activities of prostitutes did not use headlines as a guide for selection, as often headlines to stories about prostitution did not include the search word 'prostitution' (see Appendix II). Different genres of newspaper articles were collected under the general heading of 'stories about prostitution' (cf. Bell, 1991, for a discussion of the different genres of newspaper articles and the distinction between 'hard' news genres and feature articles, which are journalists', not analysts', categories).

As my initial concern was with Irish newspaper reports on prostitution, the initial data collection phase, which was carried out over a three month period (October 1987-December 1987), focused on selected (on the basis of their availability) Irish daily and weekly broadsheet newspapers: *The Irish Times, The Irish Independent, The Evening Press, The Sunday Press, The Sunday Tribune* and *The Sunday Independent.* The results of this initial search were disappointing: only eight articles were collected over this three month period.[3] While I did not immediately turn to focus upon the British papers, I began collecting, in a somewhat less systematic way, articles about prostitution from *The Guardian* and *Observer.*

Ongoing monitoring of *The Irish Times* continued and, increasingly, given the small numbers of articles collected from the Irish newspapers, I began more systematic collection of articles from the British press. The period from November 1990 to September 1991 involved a monitoring of daily and Sunday British newspapers (a task which was part of another project I was involved in).[4] The relatively infrequent reporting on prostitution led me to include in the data pool any newspaper report I came across, a move which accounts for the three tabloid stories which I have included and one story from a local London paper. Their inclusion does not bias or skew the findings of this study as they relate to broadsheet press stories on prostitution.

Over a five year period, with continuous, but not totally systematic monitoring, the number of articles selected from the British and Irish press totalled 86. These form the 'core' data set. Table 3.3 details the spread of newspaper articles by newspaper and across the five year period. Women's magazines (such as *Marie Claire*) and other magazines (such as *New Statesman* and *Society*), proved to be a source of articles on prostitution and while the collection of these stories was not systematic, these stories were also included and drawn upon in my analysis. A further 64 reports on prostitution from Irish newspapers (1992-1995) were collected from the files of an Irish Government agency (Council for the Status of Women). These stories are drawn upon for argumentative purposes only. They are especially used in Chapter Seven which deals with the photographic images of prostitution. The focus on photographs as data marks a departure from discourse analysts' common strategy to accord them a minor role in analysis, if at all.

Table 3.3
Distribution of newspaper articles by year and paper

Irish press	1987	1988	1989	1990	1991	Total
Irish Times	9	8	5	1	1	24
Irish Independent	1	0	1	2	1	5
Irish Press	0	0	0	0	2	2
Evening Press	2	0	0	0	0	2
Sunday Independent	1	0	0	0	0	1
Sunday Tribune	0	6	1	0	0	7
Sunday World	1	0	0	0	0	1
Total	14	14	7	3	4	42

UK press	1987	1988	1989	1990	1991	Total
Guardian	0	2	3	10	2	17
Independent	1	1	0	1	6	9
The Times	0	0	0	0	1	1
Daily Telegraph	0	0	0	0	1	1
Daily Mail	0	0	1	0	0	1
Observer	2	2	1	1	2	8
Sunday Telegraph	0	0	0	1	1	2
Sunday Times	0	0	0	0	1	1
Mail on Sunday	0	0	1	0	0	1
Sunday Mirror	0	0	2	0	0	2
South London Press	1	0	0	0	0	1
Total	4	5	8	13	14	44

Table 3.4
Distribution of newspaper stories by year (British and Irish press)

Year	Stories	% of total	Year	Stories	% of Total
1987	18	(21%)	1990	16	(19%)
1988	19	(22%)	1991	16	(21%)
1989	15	(17%)	Total	86	(100%)

As Table 3.4 indicates, the spread of stories across 5 years was roughly similar across the five year period, with a slight drop in 1989 and 1990.

Table 3.3 indicates the different incidence of individual country reporting but totals for the five years are similar for the British and Irish press. As can be seen, there is something of an inverse relation holding between the numbers of press stories collected from the British and Irish press over this period, with more Irish stories collected for the years 1987, 1988 and more UK press stories collected in 1990, 1991. However, as my data checking procedure demonstrated, my sample was representative, so these figures reflect the general trends in newspaper reportage of events and persons associated with prostitution.

3.1.3 Reliability and validity: Sample size

The sampling procedure described above can be described as both purposive *and* representative; by this I mean that given systematic time sampling of both British and Irish newspapers, claims of representativeness can be claimed for identifiable periods, but not for the period as a whole.[5] The immediate questions which arise from this account of the methods of data collection employed in this study relate to sample size and reliability and validity of findings; how is the reader to know that the arguments presented are based on representative data?

The issue of sample size, like that of method employed, is directly contingent upon the research problem at hand. For example, van Dijk reports that he collected 250 newspapers from 100 counties concerned with one event (the assassination of Gemyal) on one day (1988, p. 31). He was concerned with whether and how different newspaper reports, produced in different ideological and political contexts, would report one single event. In terms of these research questions, his sampling procedure was critical to the arguments presented and in particular, to the findings of the content analysis applied to the data.

However, my initial concern, as noted, was with formal methods of discourse analysis, not with a theme based analysis. Discourse analysts (e.g., Kress, 1985; Fairclough, 1985, 1989; Thompson, 1984) focusing on newspaper reports in an attempt to explicate textual structure and meaning production are working closely with the materials. Their concern is not to produce percentages relating to the incidence of one or other feature of the materials being analysed; rather it is to consider, for example, the ways in which ideology works within a text; the textual processes involved in the production of meaning between text and reader. Such studies select a small number of texts which serve as data for analysis. To reiterate, the concern is not to produce statements about the frequency of a word or topic, although, as Silverman (1985, 1993) has suggested, simple statistical approaches have a limited place in qualitatively oriented research. That said, it is generally accepted in quantitative research that a minimum sample size of 30 can be adequate for performing statistical 'jobs' on data, although stronger cases regarding statistical associations or correlations must be made with larger sample sizes. My research problem, concerned with categorisation as a procedure, meant that a wide-ranging data collection exercise was not appropriate. I am concerned with the production of readings, with attempting to explicate how the stories are read as unproblematically stories of prostitution and with investigating how descriptions of women as prostitutes are produced/written and heard as *adequate* descriptions. My sample of 86 newspaper stories is, in this regard, an extremely large one for a qualitative study.

Procedures undertaken to ensure representativeness of sample To attempt to ensure that any charge of 'bias' against my sampling procedure was met and rendered invalid, I carried out a post-hoc data check exercise. The aim of this exercise was to ascertain the extent to which I had missed stories on prostitution. *The Irish Times* and other Irish newspapers do not have an on-line database facility, nor are indexes produced. However, I did (after much persuasion) gain access to the library files of the *Irish Times* and was able to check stories for the period 1987-1990 (there were no files available after this date). The data check for the *Irish Times* was confined to files compiled by newspaper staff and although their categorisation of stories of prostitution was under a general 'sex-crime' news category, 'biographical' stories of prostitutes were included in these files. This file category was generally concerned with rape, sexual abuse, legislative changes or recommendations for same. There were no stories of prostitution in the files for 1987. In 1988 there were three stories which were missed in the data collection phase. There were three stories in the files for 1989, all of which had been collected and a further story in the 1990 files about 'boy prostitutes'. Unfortunately, as noted, the files for 1991 were not available. I conducted a random four month check (February, April, June and September) of the *Irish Times* for this year on microfiche but no stories were recorded. I am justified therefore, in claiming a representative sample of the *Irish Times* reports on prostitution (1987-1991).

For the British papers, *The Times Index* (1987-1991) and the *British Humanities Index* (BHI, 1987-1991) were consulted for missing reports.

The BHI indexes *The Guardian, The Times, The Sunday Times* and the *Observer*. In 1988, *The Independent* was added to this index and in 1990, the *Independent on Sunday* was included. In the 1992 edition of the *Index*, a disclaimer to total coverage noted that the newspapers included were indexed selectively. This source is therefore not totally reliable but is adequate for current purposes. 'Prostitution' as an entry is subdivided into categories such as 'Prostitution: Europe: History' and articles relating to prostitution and AIDS are listed under the entry 'Acquired Immune Deficiency Syndrome'. Cross-references were followed up in this checking exercise.

Table 3.5
Number of newspaper stories on prostitution: checking procedure

Year	Newspaper	Number of stories
1987	*Guardian*	4
	The Times	2
	Sunday Times	1
	(*Times* Magazine	2)
1988	*Guardian*	1
	Sunday Times	2
	(*Observer* Magazine	1)
1989	*Independent*	4
	(*Observer* Magazine	1)
1990	*Financial Times*	1
	(*Independent on Sunday* Supplement	1)
	(*Observer* Magazine	3)
1991	*Guardian*	2
	Independent	2
	(*Independent* Magazine	3)
	(*Times* Supplement	1)
	(*Sunday Times* Supplement	1)

(The parentheses are used to indicate that these sources were not part of the data collection focus.)

A number of points can be made on the basis of the *British Humanities Index* relating to location of articles and number of articles. The data check confirmed that my UK newspaper sample is representative, both in terms of number of articles collected (see Tables 3.3 and 3.4 above) and in terms of the location of the reports in the newspapers included in the data set. The key difference is the absence of reports in the data set from the various supplements and magazines that accompany the Sunday papers. When I was carrying out the data collection, I purposely did not include lengthy newspaper features from outside of the 'main' newspaper, although I did collect these features as extra data which could be used as back up materials to my arguments. The reason for not including them in the data pool was their status as 'magazine articles' rather than 'news' articles, a distinction which is used by journalists. Only one magazine supplement article is included explicitly in the data set and that was a photojournalistic essay on prostitution (LIVING ON THE STREETS, *Sunday Correspondent*, 17.12.89) which was especially relevant to my analysis of the press photographs in Chapter Seven.

The Times Index was also consulted. The number of reports in *The Times* and the *Sunday Times* per year (1987-1991) are reported in brackets: 1987 (14); 1988 (18); 1989 (8); 1990 (11); 1991 (26), totalling 77. This is just slightly lower than the core sample (86) collected for this study for both British and Irish papers. However, *The Times Index* includes reports on homosexuality and the age of consent and such articles were not included in my data collection.

A further data check relating to the number of articles collected was conducted on the basis of another study I had been involved in which focused on the representations of AIDS, drugs and prostitution in the British, Irish and Dutch media.[6] A discourse 'identification' content analysis was carried out on the materials and the discourse category 'AIDS and prostitution' which included stories about and references to prostitutes and HIV/AIDS within wider stories about the HIV epidemic, indicates that even at the height of media reporting about HIV/AIDS, reports of prostitutes and their activities constitute a small percentage of wider reporting. Table 3.6 presents the distribution of references and stories by newspaper (British and Irish).

The figures presented in this table indicate that stories of prostitution, even in the context of the HIV pandemic and the perceived wide-spread attention given to prostitutes in relation to this issue (cf. Watney, 1987), are not significantly present in the press. The inclusion of these data serve to emphasise my claims that the number and frequency of reports about prostitution collected for the current project constitute a representative sample.

Table 3.6
Representations of AIDS in the Irish and British press
(December 1986 - February 1987)

Irish press

Newspaper	No. of articles	AIDS & prostitution
Irish Times	58	3
Irish Press	8	1
Sunday Independent	1	0
Sunday Tribune	6	1
Irish Independent	7	0
Cork Examiner	2	1
Total	82 (100%)	6 (7%)

UK press

Newspaper	No. of articles	AIDS & prostitutes
Daily Telegraph	5	2
Sunday Telegraph	1	0
Observer	5	1
Guardian	85	8
Sunday Times	3	0
Financial Times	3	0
The Times	14	2
Total	116 (100%)	13 (11%)

3.1.4 Descriptive account of the materials: Findings from a content analysis

As a preliminary introduction to the data used in this study a content analysis was carried out in order to sketch out the 'anatomy' of this corpus. This section reports findings from this method and concludes with a discussion of content analysis as a research method and its drawbacks for the current study.

Content analysis is one of the major tools used in the analysis of mass media content (Krippendorf, 1980; Bailey; 1987; van Dijk, 1988; Lemert, 1989). It developed alongside the survey method as the 'scientific' and 'objective' study of media content. One of its features, according to practitioners (Krippendorf, 1980, p. 29) is that it is unobtrusive and hence the question of 'bias' introduced by the researcher (a key concern in quantitative and, increasingly, qualitative methodologies, as Marshall & Rossman (1995) point out) does not arise. Krippendorf states that content analysis is potentially

... one of the most important research techniques in the social sciences, it seeks to understand data not as a collection of physical events but as symbolic phenomena and to approach their analysis unobtrusively (1980, p. 7).

This notion of 'unobtrusive' analysis relates only to the raw data and central criticism levelled against content analysis is that it rests upon an assumption that the categories selected would be recognised by both readers and communicators, that the meaning of terms is unproblematic (cf. Cicourel, 1964).

Content analysis is considered the equivalent in document analysis to survey research (and thus is subject to many of the same criticisms). There are a number of different definitions of content analysis which range from the vague to the specific: content analysis has been variously defined as

- some kind of systematic coding or categorising of mass media content (Lemert, 1989, p. 48);
- it is 'a research technique for the objective, systematic and quantitative description of the manifest content of communication' (Berelson, 1954, cited in Bailey, 1987, p. 300);
- it can be used 'interchangeably with "coding"' to refer to the objective, systematic and quantitative description of symbolic behaviour' (Cartwright, cited in Bailey, op. cit.); and
- it is any research technique for making references by systematically and objectively identifying specified characteristics within text (Stone, cited in Bailey, op. cit.).

The words 'systematic' and 'objective' are cornerstones of the content analytic technique and the issue of reliability and validity is central to assessments of the success of this method. The methodological assumptions of content analysis have been criticised because it is a priori – the researcher decides in advance of analysis what will be categorised and analysis starts with a specific hypothesis to be tested. Secondly, the analyst assumes, and has to assume in order to carry out the analysis, that the 'meanings' s/he ascribes to the content, by assigning it certain categories, are intersubjectively held. Further, it has been argued that content analysis studies ignore the changing cultural meaning of symbolic materials (Silverman, 1985, p. 153). As van Dijk remarks à propos of his content analysis of press reports

... what cannot be read from the statistics is the way events are covered and described and how actors are qualified (1988, p. 44).

70

However, for the purposes of providing an overall introduction to the corpus, while these points are accepted, their critical focus does not detract from the (limited) 'yields' that a content analysis can provide. Content analysis has specific aims which include the description of trends in media content, the identification of patterns in communication and the evaluation of communication content against standards. The third purpose has been a particular focus of content analysis, particularly in respect of the amount of coverage and the nature of portrayals of women in the various media (e.g., Butcher et al., 1974).[7] Content analysis, like the quantitative survey method, has its uses in terms of being able to analyse large amounts of data and allows comparisons to be made between the various documents.

In terms of this characterisation of research methodologies, content analysis, which is concerned with end products rather than with processes occurring within the text, is not an appropriate method for my purposes given that my concern is to gain access to the cultural categories and assumptions present in the press reports. Rather than imposing some a priori framework or grid through which I analyse the data, I am concerned to focus upon how the stories get constructed as stories about prostitutes.

Some analysts, like Silverman (1985, 1993), argue that the theoretical basis of content analysis is unclear and its conclusions can often be trite. Others, like van Dijk, while agreeing in principle that the findings of a content analysis are superficial and incomplete as regards the nature of media coverage, see a valuable role for content analysis in discourse analytic research of mass communications;

> ... the combination of qualitative and quantitative analysis, is the *only* adequate approach to the study of mass media messages' (1988, p. 66, emphasis added).

The use of a content analytic method here is to provide an overall picture of the raw data (cf. Silverman, 1993).

Bailey (1987, p. 301) describes content analysis as the transformation of a non-quantitative document into quantitative data. Asking 'how does one perform this marvellous social alchemy that can turn words into numbers?', he supplies the simple answer: mere word counting. Categories are, Bailey says, generally established after initial viewing of the raw data. I contend that these categories are not inductively derived – the research interests dictate which categories are, at least initially, constructed. After constructing the categories all that remains is to examine the documents from the viewpoints of all these categories and to classify each document by counting the categories it exhibits.

The categories I established were based upon my understanding of the different frameworks of assumptions regarding prostitution (outlined in Chapter Two) and, as this exercise was carried out at a late stage in the research, on my research interests. Questions relating to unit of analysis were not a core concern; whilst words were used as a basis of scoring, categories such as violence included references to threat of violence as well as reports of assault and murder of prostitutes. The criteria for inclusion in the categories are discussed as each is presented. The frequencies are generally disaggregated into separate British and Irish scores given the comparative focus of this study.

44 British and 42 Irish reports on prostitution formed the basis of the content analysis. An initial attempt to code the data enabled me to code the content as comprehensively as possible by noting difficult to code content and revising the coding scheme accordingly. The baseline data relate to date of newspaper report (see Table 3.3), the location of the article (page number), the type or genre of article. Tables 3.7, 3.8 and 3.9 present the frequencies for these features of the data.

Table 3.7
Occurrence of story by month per year – British and Irish press (1987-1991)

	Irish	UK	Total
January	7	4	11
February	10	3	13
March	6	2	8
April	1	3	4
May	1	2	3
June	0	3	3
July	4	4	8
August	2	6	8
September	1	5	6
October	7	0	7
November	0	9	9
December	3	3	6
Total	**42**	**44**	**86**

The rationale behind including this table is that I wanted to see whether newspaper reports were clustered in specific months.[8] As this shows, the data collected were spread over all months with the pattern being more consistent in the UK press than in the Irish press. The table indicates the ongoing flow of reports with specific months showing marked increases, probably due to a specific story being reported, for example, the Jimmy Swaggart case in America.

The location of an article is an indication of its importance as 'news'. Table 3.8 presents the figures for distribution of stories by page numbers. This table is, unfortunately, incomplete, as during the data collection phase, page numbers were frequently not recorded. However, it does indicate, in a broad manner, the concentration of reports on particular pages.

Table 3.8
Distribution of stories by page numbers

Page no.	UK	Irish	Total
1	0	3	3
2-5	14	4	18
6-9	4	4	8
10-14	4	8	11
15-19	2	1	3
20-53	6	1	7
Total	50 (58%)		

This distribution is presented in this way because it (broadly) represents the different parts of the newspaper; page one: front page news, pages 2 to 5 generally home news; pages 6 to 9 generally international news, including features and pages 10 to 14 would generally include analysis/ commentary sections of the paper. Pages 15 to 19 could include special feature articles and pages 20 onwards would generally refer to supplements in the Sunday papers.

Broadsheets are also divided according to 'Home News', 'World News', 'Comment/Analysis' pages. The distribution of stories across pages can be used to indicate their category as 'Home News' and so on. The distribution suggests that most of the stories are concentrated in the 'Home News' and the 'Commentary/Analysis' or 'features' categories (pages 2 to 5 and pages 10ff respectively). 'World News' generally follows 'Home News' (pages 6 to 9). This distribution accounts for 58% of the data and can be accepted as a valid indicator of location in reports.[9]

Prostitution is rarely front page news, perhaps because it is conceptualised as an endemic feature of society; a routine occurrence which does not meet the criteria of 'newsworthiness' (cf. Cohen & Young, 1973); despite this, stories of prostitution are in the 'news' sections of the press. The status of stories of prostitution relates to 'genre' of story (cf. Bell, 1991). Stories of prostitution are spread over different newspaper genres as Table 3.9 indicates. The criteria on which identifications of report type were made were taken from Bell (1991, p. 14).

Table 3.9
Genre of report by Irish and British newspapers

		UK	Irish
[1]	Feature [inc. comment and analysis]	55% (24)	31% (13)
[2]	News inc. AP/Reuters	30% (13)	45% (19)
[3]	Gossip [inc. personal columns]	2% (01)	10% (4)
[4]	Women's page [*Guardian*]	5% (02)	0% (0)
[5]	Law Report	2% (01)	2% (1)
[6]	Letters	7% (03)	2% (1)
[7]	Review of radio, TV	0% (0)	10% (4)
Total		44	42 (86)

The main differences between the genres of the reports in the British and Irish press is in relation to feature articles and news (that is, 'soft' and 'hard' news). The Irish press was more likely to include stories of prostitution as 'news' than was the British press, a tendency reversed in the 'feature' genre.[10]

Of the 86 stories of prostitution, 31 (36%) included a photograph (or, on occasion, more than one photograph). This figure excludes the photographs of journalists' accompanying feature articles. Press photographs have been, as I demonstrate in Chapter Seven, largely overlooked in the analysis of press discourse. Chapter Seven provides a more detailed discussion of the subject matter of selected photographs.

The tables above present 'baseline' data about the corpus. I have been referring to this corpus as 'stories of prostitution'. I use this as a shorthand as prostitution (the exchange of sexual 'services' for money, which is what I understand by the word) is rarely the subject of the press reports; rather they are concerned with activities relating to prostitution and with prostitutes. 'Stories of prostitution' thus covers activities / or events and persons. In addition, *my* classification of all the reports as 'stories of prostitution' is, in strict discourse analytic and linguistic terms, quite illegitimate. Brown and Yule (1983) point out that a story should properly include information about setting, theme, plot and resolution. The newspaper stories collected could be categorised in a variety of ways. I have already noted that *Irish Times* staff categorised stories in which prostitution or a prostitute was an important part of the text as 'sex-crime' stories. Whether this category holds across newspapers I cannot say. Indeed, one area for further investigation might include a consideration of how journalists categorise the various stories. Stories were categorised by me as 'stories of prostitution' if they were 'about' prostitutes' activities or those associated with prostitutes (for example, clients). This categorisation hides the variation in the press stories and is not ideal (for example, it could be disputed that the Jeffrey Archer libel case (1987) was 'about' prostitution; however, Monica Coghlan, the prostitute at the centre of this case and the activities of Archer with Coghlan were key topics and as such justified for inclusion as 'stories of prostitution').

3.1.5 Coding press content

A coding sheet was devised on the basis of my knowledge of what were the core themes across the 86 stories (based upon repeated re-reading). This coding sheet was produced by a ClarisWorks spread-sheet facility.

Baseline data (described above) regarding the location of the story, genre and so on were collected. Fourteen coding categories were established; these categories were my constructs. I identified, for instance, a theme of violence; even if the word was not mentioned in the report, I read – and coded – it as 'violence' (cf. Garfinkel, 1967, for a discussion of coders' work). The coding of the content of the materials was also dictated by my concern to identify themes relating prostitution in the press and to see if these themes were similar to the assumptions of the various discourses outlined in Chapter Two. The discussion of the different content categories is invariably disjointed but has, as its merit, the systematic (albeit brief) discussion of the core categories in the data.

Location of news event Stories about prostitution are, as noted, reported in both the 'Home News' and 'World News' pages of British and Irish papers, that is, are about prostitution both in Britain, Ireland and world-wide. In the UK press, 37 stories (84%) were concerned with the UK generally with specific mentions of London (15); Kent (1); Manchester (2); Hull (1); Cardiff (1); Southampton (1); Birmingham (1). In the Irish press, 23 stories (55%) were about prostitution in Ireland generally with specific mentions of Dublin (17); Tuam (1); Ballingarry, Co. Tipperary (3); Limerick (2); Cavan (1). The Irish press reported on prostitution in the UK (9 stories, of which London (8); Manchester (1)). For both the UK and Irish press collectively, 14 stories (16%) were about prostitution in Europe (3), the US (7) and internationally (4). This breakdown of specific references to location of prostitution activities indicates the concentration on major urban centres, specifically London and Dublin. Prostitution has been conceptualised historically as an urban problem (Wilson, 1991) and the focus on these urban centres needs to be contextualised in this context. Chapter Six further discusses the importance of place in the stories of prostitution.

Story topic The stories were identified by headline and my reading of 'main topic' of each story. This was a somewhat arbitrary decision as stories include different themes, for example a story about police activity can include legal approaches, threat of violence, different types of prostitution and discussion of clients of prostitutes. There are a range of stories covered by both the British and Irish press. The similarities between the Irish and British papers relate to murder and police activity. In the UK press there were 11 stories (25% of all stories), as opposed to 14 stories (33%) in the Irish press about murder of prostitutes, rape trials involving prostitutes, assault and threat of violence and a further four specifically concerned with police activity and legislative measures vis-à-vis activities relating to prostitution.

Forms of prostitution As noted in Chapter Two, legislative measures targeting activities associated with prostitution have been specifically concerned with street prostitution. I was interested in assessing the extent to which coverage specified the different forms of prostitution as various authors (e.g., Goode & Troiden, 1974, p. 106; Edwards, 1987, p. 47) have argued that as the streetwalker is more visible than other prostitutes, she is an easy target both for police action (i.e., arrest) and research. Table 3.10 presents summary figures on coverage relating to different forms of prostitution (cf. Perkins & Bennett, 1985, chapter 1). Street and brothel prostitution are the main forms of prostitution and the category 'clipper' is a UK specific activity associated with prostitution. Nine stories from the Irish press did not specify particular forms of prostitution as compared with five in the English press. The figures presented in this table illustrate the especial focus upon street prostitution, with Irish stories focusing on this form of prostitution more so than their UK counterparts. The relevance of these data is that street prostitution is a particular concern of the press stories, with brothel prostitution as a secondary concern.

Gender/age profile of prostitutes As noted in Chapter Two, prostitution has been treated as a gender-specific offence by the legal system (cf. Smart,

1976; Wolfenden, 1957). The sample of stories on prostitution reflect this general, common-sense assumption that the prostitute is a female. Child prostitution has, historically, served as a 'moral panic button' (cf. Walkowitz, 1980). The press reports do not give any indication of this being a 'newsworthy' story-topic. The only difference between the two countries is seen in the marginally more reports on male prostitution in Ireland, and with Irish reports on child prostitution. As I was not concerned with stories about rent-boys specifically, this result could be said to be an artefact of the sampling procedure.

Table 3.10
Forms of prostitution: UK and Irish stories (1987-1991)

Form	UK	Irish	Total
Street [outside]	15	21	36
Brothel [inside, includes hotels]	17	11	28
Sex industry	1	0	1
Clippers	3	0	3
'Good time girl'	1	0	1
Call boy/rentboy	1	1	2
Call girl	1	1	2
Phone sex	0	1	1

Table 3.11
Gender/age profile of prostitutes

Newspaper	Female	Male	Child	Not specified
UK	42	1	0	2
Irish	40	5	3	3

The figures amount to over 86 because some stories included more than one category.

Reasons for entry into prostitution Given that, as outlined in Chapter Two, the question 'why do some women become prostitutes?' (e.g., Rolph, 1954) has been a particularly central one in the legal, feminist and medical discourses of prostitution, I focused upon the reasons for entry given in the stories (either in journalistic opinion or as quoted by women identified as 'prostitutes'). Specific categories of 'poverty' and 'drug use' were also used. 18 of the 42 Irish reports (43%) did not mention reasons for entry as compared with 28 of the 44 UK reports (64%).

Table 3.12
Reasons for entry into prostitution

Reason	UK	Irish	Total
Survival	1	3	4
Needed money	5	9	14
Runaway/homeless	2	0	2
Money for drugs	3	2	5
Forced by pimps	1	3	4
Expelled from school	1	0	1
Nymphomania	1	0	1
Forced (no agent)	0	6	6
Sexual abuse (childhood)	0	4	4
Free choice	1	2	3

'*Needing money*' is the prime motivation. In this, the reports concur with the feminists' and prostitutes' argument that women enter prostitution for the money. Active choice (articulated in the practitioners' discourse) is not a factor in the decision to prostitute, rather survival, drug use, homelessness are key factors.[11] The psychopathological approach is present in the categories 'nymphomania' and child sexual abuse, the latter articulating a variant of feminist approaches (cf. Barry, 1995). Prostitution as a 'regular job' is mentioned only twice. It could be suggested that, given the focus upon involuntary engagement in prostitution, those reports which do not mention reasons for entry rely on this notion. As 'needing money' was a key reason for entry, the category 'poverty' was introduced. 2 (2.4%) of the 44 UK reports referred to 'no income' or 'no money'; 6 (14%) of the Irish reports used the word poverty and one spoke of prostitution in the context of poverty. The contradiction emerges of 'reasons for entry' being attributed to 'needing money' but the stories themselves do not focus upon the issue of poverty.

Pimps 'Forced by pimp' was one of the 'reasons for entry'. Pimping is prohibited by law and has been an object of the feminist discourse (e.g., Levine, 1987). The notion of the 'brutal pimp' is dismissed by Benjamin and Masters (1964) as a 'myth'. Similarly, Wilkinson suggests that it is no longer a feature of prostitution (Rolph, 1954), as has Jennifer James (1978, 1980, cf. Cohen, 1980, for a discussion of various approaches to the issue of pimping). 20% of the British reports and 30% of the Irish reports referred to pimps, with only one report (British papers) including a reference to the state as a pimp (which draws on the feminist and practitioners' discourse in which licensing of prostitution is considered to turn the state into a pimp, as the state would receive taxes from prostitution).

Clients Clients were also featured in the press stories, either in prostitutes' accounts of clients or in general accounts of prostitution. This is in contradistinction to, for example, the medical discourses. The clients of prostitutes are often ignored in approaches to prostitution, but are explicit objects in the feminist discourses. Clients were mentioned in 9 (20%) of the 44 UK press reports, with one story recounting the experience of a client who was 'hoodwinked' by a 'clip girl' (CLIENTS FLEECED BY CLIP AND RUN RIP-OFF, *Guardian*, 9.7.90). 12 (29%) of the Irish reports referred to clients. The context in which clients were mentioned were in relation to violent behaviour, soliciting behaviour, general views (of prostitutes) towards clients (for example in relation to safe sex behaviours, one woman (prostitute) commented that 'Some smack-heads [prostitutes] will do anything for gear. Some blokes carry heroin to persuade them not to insist on a rubber' (LYN'S GAME PLAN FOR SAFE SEX, *Observer*, 28.2.88). Other stories focused upon the sexual predilections of clients (e.g., PROSTITUTES AND THE LIVES THEY LEAD, *Irish Times*, 11.3.91; WHEN PROSTITUTION IS JUST ANOTHER JOB, *Irish Times*, 17.4.89). The kerb-crawling behaviours of clients was a particular feature in the UK press, possibly due to the passing of the Sexual Offences Act, 1985, which provided for the prosecution of men soliciting clients (Chapter Two).

Violence Violence has been termed an 'occupational hazard' of prostitution and the feminist and practitioners' discourses have been particularly concerned with this issue (see Chapter Two, practitioners' discourse). Violence against prostitutes is acceptable within, for example, moral/ religious discourses and the notion that women in prostitution cannot be raped is widespread.[12] The perceived vulnerability of prostitutes to violent clients is a feature of UK stories, and violent pimps constitute a distinct topic in Irish press stories, and to a lesser extent in the UK press. Table 3.13 details the sub-categories of 'violence'. In just over half (55%) of the UK press sample, there was no reference to violence, and a similar figure (50%) holds for the Irish sample. The main difference between the newspapers by country relates to the incidence of the category 'threat of violence', this was the topic of a far greater number of British reports (25%) than Irish reports (7%). Violence as a category was not present in over half of the entire sample, suggesting that it does not receive press attention. This conclusion would be misleading as murder and rape stories (of prostitutes) are identifiable 'types' of story.

Table 3.13
Violence and prostitution

Violence	UK	Irish
Murder	6	2
Assaults	4	7
Rapes	3	4
Threat of violence	11	3

Disease As outlined in Chapter Two, the medical approach to prostitution has been concerned with it as a form of behaviour which is epidemiologically significant in the spread of venereal disease. There were 13 (30%) references to HIV in the UK stories about prostitution. Some alluded to the disease (e.g., 'skeletal with illness'). Such references are not included given that content analysis looks only at 'manifest' or surface features of a text. In the Irish reports there were four references to HIV and one to sexually transmitted diseases as a general category (cf. Table 3.6).

Law enforcement This category included sub-categories of 'legislative situation', 'police activity' and 'court trials'. The stories refer to prostitutes in the courts and proposed legislation. However, and notably, trials in which a woman is labelled a 'common prostitute' are not reported. Nine of the UK reports were concerned with legislative changes, particularly relating to the legislation of brothels. This compared with 5 references to prostitution and the legal situation in the Irish press. Trials involving prostitutes accounted for 36% and 29% of the UK and Irish reports. Court issues related to rape, drug offences, fines and public order.

Police activity formed a distinct category: 12 (29%) of the 42 Irish reports were concerned with this (for example, police investigating a possible prostitution ring operating in Tuam, Co. Galway). This compared with 14 (32%) of stories in the UK papers. A qualitative difference between the accounts is that the British reports detailed police action and included statements from the police as key news actors.

Definitions of prostitution As noted in Chapter Two, definitional problems have been a feature of the different approaches (articulated in discourses) to prostitution (Benjamin & Masters, 1964; Bullough, 1977; Perkins, 1991; see Appendix I). Definitions were identified if, in the report, reference to what 'went on' was mentioned. Discussion of what precisely prostitution is, a concern in the discourses discussed in Chapter Two, is not a concern in the press reports. An array of definitions are used, the most popular being 'sex for money' (used in 11 (26%) of the 42 Irish reports and 4 (9%) of the 44 UK reports). Others included soliciting, 'selling favours'; 'turning tricks'.[13] The UK reports include references to buying sex, turning tricks; bargain with clients, business, operating, economic activity, working, prostitution as an occupation. The Irish papers include references to 'soliciting and loitering'; 'women selling themselves'; 'sleeping with men'; 'encounter with men'; 'sex with men' and 'making money'. There is a distinct ambivalence in the 'definitions' offered, references to 'work' serve to disclaim that it is work. However, there are no explicit statements that prostitution is a 'deviant' behaviour. Finally, I considered what words were used to refer to women identified as prostitutes; this lexicon of prostitution indicates that just under half of the stories used terms other than 'prostitute' or used them interchangeably. Other references included 'hooker' (3); 'whore' (3); 'working girl' (6); 'tart' (3) and individual reference to 'ladies of the night', 'slaves', 'regular ladies'. These euphemistic terms hint at the category 'prostitute'.

3.1.6 Conclusion

Silverman's (1985, 1993) comment that the results of content analysis are often trite is in contradiction to his argument that quantitative methods and simple statistics can be used profitably in qualitative research (that is they are trite only if the researcher stops at this point). The preceding descriptive account is included to provide the reader with an overview, necessarily sketchy, of the content of the materials on which this study is based. The 86 reports provide sufficient basis on which to argue about trends in content of the press reports on prostitution. The similarities between the British and Irish press are of relevance given the different cultural context of the production of these stories. This similarity in the British and Irish stories will assume a greater significance as the study proceeds. For the moment, however, it will suffice to note its occurrence.

Content analysis is merely one approach to the analysis of mass media products and its specific purposes, as outlined above, are intimately tied to the research question at hand. Other approaches to the analysis of media content have not been concerned with the counting/coding of words or themes or images, an approach which rips out these 'parts' of a text from its overall context. Rather they have focused upon the structure of media texts, the language used and its environment and, crucially, been concerned to theoretically and empirically work through issues relating to how to tie the content of media products to the wider issues of production, reception and use of these products in everyday life. It is to an overview of approaches to the study of mass communication that I now turn.

3.2 Analysing media products

3.2.1 Introduction

The content analysis of the newspaper stories of prostitution study poses a number of questions which need to be addressed before moving to discuss the methodological choices made in respect of the handling of these data. These questions are at the base of the media research endeavour and are focused upon the role of the media in the production and reproduction of culture; the importance of media languages in this process; the role of patterns of ownership and journalistic production routines and, in particular, the realisation of meanings by the recipient of media products. How these questions relate to my current study requires a (brief and superficial) examination of the issues. In addition, as the focus of attention in media studies has shifted, over the last decade, to the audience, with calls for audience research as the cornerstone of work on media products (e.g., Radway, 1984; Ang, 1990), one central objective of this part of the chapter is to meet such calls with a justification or rationalisation as to why I did not carry out ethnographic work with readers of the different newspapers which are used in this study. This rationalisation extends into the next chapter which continues the discussion of methodology used. The purpose of what follows is to lay down the framework within which the analysis of the newspaper reports on prostitution needs to be considered. General comments about objectivity, media products as texts and as symbolic cultural forms are raised within sections as they arise.

3.2.2 Models of media processes

The mass media are pervasive in contemporary Western societies[14]; average television viewing time of adults in the UK is estimated to be approximately 26 hours per week, a figure which excludes time spent listening to the radio, reading newspapers and magazines or going to the cinema (Central Statistics Office, 1995: 25).[15] This pervasiveness of the mass media means, on this point alone, that they are deserving of serious attention but the focus of attention has been, and continues to be contentious.

According to 'conventional' approaches to media analysis there are three 'moments' (Corner, 1983) in the communication circuit (Hall, 1980): the institutional and organisational conditions and practices of production, which are governed by legal and technological constraints, and include, for newspapers, the fact that as private enterprises they must generate advertising revenue in addition to sales of their product, a point made earlier regarding circulation figures; secondly, there is the text itself which is a symbolic construction resulting from cultural and technical practices and thirdly, there is the 'moment' of reception. Each of these moments takes place in a social context. However, this context has often been used to deductively, rather than inductively, build media theory and it is this 'context' which poses, I contend, the central problem across the different approaches to the theoretical models and analyses of the operation of the mass media. Further, each of these moments has occupied central places in media research; for example, the current focus upon media consumption has evolved from a dissatisfaction with text-bound notions of media products and it is 'in danger' of being displaced by more macro structural analytical approaches (Morley, 1993). The history of the field of media studies has yet to be written (Davis, 1991) but some brief reviews are available (e.g., Curran, 1990).

The analysis of the political economy of the mass media focuses upon the patterns of ownership and control of media institutions in terms of their operation within a capitalist system. These analyses are described by Davis (1991, p. 40) as reactions to the 'culturalist tendencies' of the 1970s, taking as their starting point the importance of the economic organisation and dynamics of media production and its determining influences. However, as Davis notes:

> In the absence of empirical investigation it is tempting to move from questions of economic organisation to questions of cultural content as if the logic were apparent (1991, p. 41).

A danger in the political economy approach is then that it is, a priori, the content of the media works to promote and reproduce the dominant modes of economic organisation. Of course, this dominance is not simply given but is, as Fairclough (1985, 1989) points out, *maintained*, which signals that conflict and tensions also exist. These contradictions are inherent both within capitalist forms of organisation and in their articulation with modes of gender organisation under patriarchy (cf. Turner, 1984).

Questions of ownership and control are important and find their expression in terms of diversity of views presented in the various media.

The political economy approach, exemplified by the work of Graham Murdock and Peter Golding, is explicitly part of the sociological enterprise with its focus upon the social structure and the workings of capitalism in the perpetuation of systematic social stratificatory systems. Gender divisions are not addressed in this model.

The second moment in the communication circuit is the symbolic form produced; the text itself. This aspect is explicitly concerned with language of the media and a variety of different approaches have been employed, for example, structuralism, semiotics, linguistic theory, discourse analysis and content analysis. The structure of the text (or rather texts, as different types of text forms and genres are present within the different media) has been subject to in-depth analysis, focusing upon internal coherence and contradiction, upon the lexicalisations employed, the grammar used, the subject positions available, to name but a few of the foci of approaches (cf. Tuchman, 1991). The findings from such work have been criticised for their lack of attention to the political and economic structures within which the media are located, that is for being 'too text-bound'.

The third moment, that of reception, has always been recognised, if only implicitly, within the approaches to the second moment, as crucial (cf. Morley, 1993). However, despite perfunctory references to 'real' audiences, much of the second approach has constructed what Holub (1984) termed a 'phenomenological' reader/viewer/listener whose reaction to the media texts mirrored that of the analyst. The focus on the audience has led to, in the extreme, the neglect of the prior two moments – it is claimed that the audience is all that needs to be attended to and the social context of reception is what determines how texts are received (Ang, 1990). Morley (1993) notes that the 'active audience' approach rests on two assumptions; that the audience is always 'active' and that media content is always polysemic (that is, is open to various interpretations). This has implications, both theoretical and methodological. On the theoretical level, it means that John Thompson's (1984, 1990) argument regarding the 'vulnerability' of interpretations stands. Texts are read in different ways by different people and this (post-structuralist) view of the 'unfixity' of meaning leads to a situation in which, in effect, nothing can be said with certainty about the meaning of a text. Methodologically, it requires that the different readings of differentiated audiences need to be investigated, the analyst's own reading cannot stand in for these other readings.

Janice Radway's (1984) argument that the 'meanings' of texts are produced by an audience interacting with the text, is similarly advanced by ethnomethodological approaches, discussed in the next chapter. This is my basic position regarding the production of textual meaning. However, it is another step to accept her argument that

> ... our own interpretation as analyst is an inevitable part of all mass cultural research, *it is nevertheless important and helpful to begin with a real audience's conscious surface interpretation of a given form if we wish to understand how that form functions within the larger culture* (1986, p. 99, emphasis added).

Here, she suggests that the analyst's reading comes after the readings of 'real' audiences (as if the analyst were not 'real'). What Radway does not discuss is how the analyst then 'reads' and interprets this 'real' audience's reading. Thompson (1987, 1990) endorses Radway's arguments arguing that analysis of symbolic forms (media products) must be related to their reception in specific socio-historical contexts. The 'active audience' draws attention to 'resistance' to a preferred meaning (a problematic concept given the presupposed polysemy of texts) and accords the audience a role in the production of meaning. As Morley succinctly comments, however,

> The power of viewers [or readers] to reinterpret meanings is hardly equivalent to the discursive power of centralised media institutions to construct the texts that the viewer then interprets, and to imagine otherwise is simply foolish (1993, p. 258).

The theme of audience 'work' is one which is central to an ethnomethodological approach to media discourses; the meaning of the text is realised over the course of reading as a course of social action. However, I do not accept that texts are open to multiple interpretations; while resistance to the preferred meaning is undoubtedly present, in order to read a text readers must firstly make sense of its presumed sense.[16] As Ros Coward (1980/1987) has argued à propos of advertising messages, both written and visual, we must first engage with the culturally dominant meanings of the advertisements *before* we reject them. In respect of the polysemy, of the many interpretations of texts, the question is thus how can we (that is, analysts of media discourses) argue that the meaning of the text is, for example, sexist, if many meanings and readings exist? How are we to adjudicate between the different readings?

These points are of particular relevance to this study because the question of why I did not interview different readers of the Irish and British newspapers needs to be addressed, especially given the active audience approach within media studies. An example of one piece of audience research (Kitzinger and Miller, 1992) enables me to specify my position vis-à-vis audience research, a position further elaborated in the next chapter.

Kitzinger and Miller comment that there is a paucity of research exploring how media reporting might actually relate to audience understandings. Their work is concerned with the role of the media in changing, reinforcing or contributing to ideas about AIDS, Africa and race (1992, p. 28). One of their conclusions is that people (audiences) draw upon pre-existing ideas about Africa. They conducted group interviews and the sample included, for example, older and young people, doctors, gay help-line workers (male), office cleaners and a group of women on a Glasgow estate. The problem I have with this piece of research, admittedly condensed for a contribution to a book, is that statements made by different occupational (e.g., doctors) and social (e.g., 'family') groups are presented, as if the different readings by these different groups signal something about structural position vis-à-vis the realisation of meaning of texts (although quite what, I cannot see). What is to be made of a 'group of women with children at a playground' who 'held up the photograph of black people as a visual symbol of Africa while declaring "This country [Britain] could be as badly affected as those abroad"' (1992, p. 37)?

How are readings on the basis of gender, race, social class, sexual orientation and so on to be dealt with? Kitzinger and Miller's paper details the ways in which personal experience structures the meaning of an event and the way such experience is held up to media accounts in a correspondence test.[17] They point out that audiences rejected media AIDS-Africa associations if, for example, they had access to alternative information; made links with their own experiences; had exposure to alternative media accounts and indeed, if they were black. They argue that their research 'shows' both media power and the pervasiveness of stock of white cultural images of black Africa (1992, p. 49). In relation to the materials used in this study, I could perhaps hypothesise that prostitutes themselves would resist the meanings of press messages, that feminists would resist meanings of the texts (those for example, which suggested a woman in prostitution cannot be raped) and so on. Further, Kitzinger and Miller (1992) point out that journalists draw on cultural assumptions (expressed by audience groups) when they produce stories, and thus reproduce and legitimise such assumptions. This point has been made by me in respect of the different discourses of prostitution.

However, given the resistance of audiences to various assumptions, this legitimising process is never given. The question then arises of where are these cultural assumptions articulated? I have attempted to overcome this by focusing upon the different discourses of prostitution which are in circulation, in journals, media and filtering down to everyday conversation. I decided not to carry out audience research because of my perceived difficulties with this approach for *my research question*. Given that the stories of prostitution contained different topics, such as legislative changes, audience interpretations/readings of these texts would have simply produced more texts. This approach is undeniably ethnomethodological and the tenets of this 'school' are discussed in the next chapter.

While the different moments of the 'communication circuit' provide the focus for different research endeavours, two broad models within which the media are approached are the Marxist inspired mass manipulative and the commercial laissez-faire or pluralist models. These models relate to the function of the media in the production and reproduction of existing social arrangements and it would be difficult to attempt to specify my study in terms of these models. While I understand the press as one discourse site in which the production and reproduction of assumptions, drawn from various competing discourses, and contributing to the reproduction of unequal gender and social class arrangements, an approach which would concur with the mass manipulative model, I would also draw upon the pluralist understanding of the existence of a range of sources of information, although not the argument that the audience does not necessarily adopt the meanings produced across media texts. This is an inadequate application of these models but aims to signal where I stand vis-à-vis traditional approaches. These models are somewhat dated and there is evidence (Curran, 1990) to suggest that the polarities which existed in the 1970s vis-à-vis analysis of media are crumbling in the face of new theoretical and methodological dilemmas.[18] However, despite this, Curran suggests that vestiges of these models persist under new guises.

To complicate this picture, the question of subject positionality, of interpellation, raised the question of ideology in psychoanalytic terms and 'desire', 'pleasure' and Oedipal movement of narratives became key words in (especially) analyses of film. The question of the 'pleasure of the text' emerged in response to notions of ongoing ideological subjugation of audiences, a response to the perceived weary and gloomy view that the audience in its 'meeting' with a text is simply overpowered by the dominant ideology which reproduces unequal class, gender, racial and so on, divisions (see Milne, 1987). Much, if not all of this work, has been concerned with women's 'consumption' of media products and an exemplar of such an approach is Radway's (1984, 1986) analysis of readers of romance stories (cf. van Zoonen, 1991). However, the question of 'pleasure' does not occur in relation to newspaper texts.

Criticisms levelled against studies of each of the three moments tend to converge into one main argument: that there is little empirical evidence to support the claims advanced. As Thompson, discussing the role of ideology in the media acting to sustain unequal social relations beyond the media, states:

> One of the problems with this perspective is that it tends to take for granted what needs to be shown, namely that the messages transmitted by mass communication do in fact serve to sustain the social order (1988, p. 360).

3.2.3 Language in the media: Expressions of ideology

Research into media discourses has been approached from a variety of perspectives: structuralist, semiotic and linguistic to name but a few. van Dijk (1985, p. v), surveying the historical development of mass communication research and discourse analysis (by which he means the study of language in use), states that despite areas of common interest, namely text, talk and communication generally, the links between the two fields are tenuous and slight. This lack of interdisciplinary communication is not surprising given the concern of media scholars to relate media products to relations of production, ownership patterns and wider social processes, a concern which has not been evident in much of the work of discourse analysts in the 1970s and early 1980s. The work of van Dijk (1988) and Thompson (1990) are particular examples of attempts to forge a link between the two fields. The application of the different perspectives to the analysis of newspaper texts raises as a central issue the nature of the discourses being analysed; the production imperatives of journalists and of the routines of newsmaking generally are relevant in considering media content, particularly as regards the issue of 'newsworthiness'.

Tuchman, reviewing qualitative approaches to the analysis of media institutions, refers to how the most interesting questions about news and news organisations concern the general relationship between news and ideology or the specific processes by which news reproduces or alters ideology (1991, p. 79). Media discourses are central to this examination (in addition to that which focuses on the routinised practices of news production, cf. Golding & Eliott, 1979).

The work of the Centre for Contemporary Cultural Studies throughout the 1970s emphasised the processes of meaning production in media discourses and the ideological nature of news discourse (cf. Hall et al., 1979).[19] The theme of 'ideology in the media' has been a particular focus of discourse analysts. The Glasgow Media Group defined ideology as the

> ... representation of sets of facts which consistently favours the perceptual framework of one group (1976, pp. 121-2).

Thompson (1984, 1987, 1990) discussing the different notions of ideology adopts a critical conception of ideology which posits as its fundamental characteristic its role in maintaining relations of power and domination. He argues that to 'study ideology is, in some part, to study language in the social world' (1987, p. 517). This is a similar position to Fairclough who defines ideology as the assumptions embedded in forms of language;

> ... if ideology is pervasively present in language, that fact ought to mean that the nature of language should be one of the major themes of modern social science (1989, p. 3).

Socio-linguists such as Fowler understand ideology as a system of shared beliefs about reality (1985, p. 65), and Kress (1986) suggests that ideology structures the linguistic presentation of the event, hence the task is to consider, for instance, the vocabulary used and grammatical devices such as transivity and modality. Identifying the ideological has not proved easy; the Glasgow University Media Group expressed this in their question, 'why does ideology prove so slippery and intractable when under study?' (1976, p. 13).

I follow Weedon in my understanding of ideology as the representation of social reality as 'natural', a formulation which draws upon common-sense. She suggests that

> Commonsense consists of a number of social meanings and the particular ways of understanding the world which guarantee them ... These meanings, which inevitably favour the interests of particular social groups, become fixed and widely accepted as true (1987, pp. 77-78).[20]

Discourse as a particular form of language (Nead, 1988) is ideological.

3.2.4 Studies of 'bias' in the media

The argument that the media present a distorted view of reality is a pervasive one. The distortion of an objective reality has been particularly investigated in relation to women and relates to a conceptualisation of ideology as a distortion of reality (e.g., Butcher et al., 1974; Root, 1984; Heidensohn, 1985; Bardsley, 1987). Perkins (1989) argues that cinematic representations of prostitutes are 'abortions of reality'. The coverage of crime is a particular area of interest in respect of the issue of bias. In 1983 Ditton & Duffy argued that analysis of media coverage of crime is important because 'the public' needs to know about the correspondence between 'real' crime rates and what is reported in the media.[21] Their argument is couched in terms of the impact of media coverage on public opinion and the near monopoly of press coverage of crime:

> Accordingly, it is important to monitor regularly the newspaper coverage of crime to assess whether or not the overall picture of crime which newspapers collectively produce is informative and balanced (1983, p. 159).

They assessed coverage in terms of column inches/space allotted and number of reports of crimes and court cases. These latter were compared with official records (the 'actual' incidence of crime). This method revealed, they argue, 'a high degree of selectivity' (1983, p. 161). It further demonstrated that newspapers 'over-report' crimes involving sex and are, by implication, abusing their information role by systematically misleading people. Questions of impartiality of the media, particularly television, have been investigated; for example, the Glasgow University Media Group (1983) examined performance against news producers' *own* standard of balance, neutrality and the like.

This question of bias, of impartiality, rests upon notions of objective facts which can be reported. The concept of objectivity is one on which journalistic practice rests. Lichtenberg notes that claims of bias and so on suggest that objectivity is possible, that there is a correspondence between media texts and an external (social) reality to which they refer. The central premise of the social constructionist approach (to the sociology of knowledge) is to reject a notion of objective reality; Lichtenberg (1991, p. 217) seems to takes this as saying (physical) reality itself is socially constructed, which is a crude reading of the social constructionists. Rather, I understand the social construction of reality as meaning that our *understanding* and knowledge of reality is socially constructed; it is not saying that reality as such does not exist. That discourse has material effects means that what is spoken about and the ways in which it is spoken (how it is spoken about) have real effects. Language thus constitutes our social reality. Lichtenberg argues that the social construction of the reality approach adds up to nothing:

> ... if we abandon the concept of a reality independent of news stories we undermine the very basis on which to criticise the media's constructions (1991, pp. 221-223).

In arguing her case she draws upon a number of 'facts'; for example that a particular individual is the President of the United States and suggests that the postmodernists and radical social constructionists would have a difficult time arguing against this. However, Graeme Turner emphasises in his analysis of Oliver North as a sign that his analysis of the cultural representation of North 'may have little to do with a *material* Oliver North you could call on the phone; this is a reading of the cultural construction of Oliver North' (1990, p. 34).

Positing a continuum of objectivity which in its centre is a truth, a 'right answer', Lichtenberg writes that

> ... we must ... proceed under the assumption that there is an objective truth, even if sometimes in the end we conclude that within a particular realm the concept of truth does not apply (1991, p. 228).

Discussing the journalistic practices to attain objectivity, she refers to 'a confusion between objectivity and the appearance of objectivity' (ibid). It would seem that she is suggesting that the job of the media critic/researcher is to distinguish between what is 'real' and what is 'appearance', a project which raises all the problems confronting theorists/analysts who attempt to find ideology lurking behind surface content. Lichtenberg finally, in her closing paragraph, states baldly that the question of objectivity is political not metaphysical. Noting that metaphysics has been rejected by philosophers because it assumes a naive ontological connection between knowledge and a reality conceived as a thing-in-itself, metaphysical arguments, as Alcoff (1988) comments, are those which concern factual claims about the world but which cannot be decided empirically.

Lichtenberg's argument that objectivity is a political matter means that questions of objectivity are political and suggests a standpoint argument which does not move the debate about objectivity beyond the point at which she started. The key point that I take from her argument, which I develop in Chapter Four, is that claims of facticity are central to the journalistic project and that such claims are monitored, depending upon the nature of the 'fact' being reported, by audiences. The claimed objectivity of the press and media generally has been subjected to criticism by researchers who, like Ditton & Duffy (1983) above, focused upon content categories. Other researchers have approached this issue via an analysis of media languages, for example, Jalbert (1983) considers the use of textual devices in the media presentation of events, suggesting, with socio-linguists such as Fowler (1991), that the grammar and syntax produce stories of events which are ideologically biased.

3.3 Conclusion

This brief review of some of the concerns of the media studies field highlights a number of concerns: firstly, the need to locate historically and socially the different media which use different technologies in their transmission of messages (and hence their reception, Thompson, 1990); secondly, the question of reception, especially reading, has revived concerns, characterising work in the late 1970s and early 1980s, with a concept of preferred meaning and how analysts are to forge a link between such a preferred meaning (if it can be identified) and the audience realisation of that meaning.[22] I have purposely not provided detailed reviews of different approaches to media discourse as these are touched upon in the following chapter. The aim of this section has been to provide a broad framework of the current approaches to the mass media, noting the key domains of study. The current project falls most immediately into the second 'moment' of the communication circuit, namely a concern with the texts themselves, but is also concerned with reception issues, that is the reading of the texts. I am also mindful of the nature of the newspapers as commercial enterprises with concerns about circulation figures and relatedly, revenue. The specific issues which my analyses of the texts gave rise to were not resolvable by reference to various approaches to the analysis of media discourses, as the following chapter details.

Notes

1 Certainly, films about prostitutes have been produced; at the time of the start of this study the Irish State Censor had banned the general release of *Working Girls* (see Perkins, 1989, for a discussion of the feminist orientation of this film) and it seemed that a focus on filmic representations would have presented problems in collecting data.

2 On the Gerry Ryan radio programme (RTÉ, 2FM, 22.6.95), reviewing 'what's in the papers,' Ryan started reading headlines. He read out 'How to be a sex pot,' stopped and said, 'oh this must be *The Star*' (an Irish tabloid).

3 In the course of carrying out a data check exercise, I contacted the *Irish Times* library (where files on different stories are maintained) for assistance. The response to my question about the possible existence of a file on prostitution and related stories was that 'The

Irish Times wouldn't cover stories of that nature' and I was referred to the *Sunday World* (a tabloid paper).

4   This was part of my job at the Association of Community Health Councils (England & Wales).

5   Time periods of systematic monitoring:

1987: October: (IR) *Irish Times, Irish Independent, Evening Press, Sunday Tribune, Sunday Independent, Sunday Press*; (BR) *Observer*.

November: (IR) *Irish Times, Irish Independent, Evening Press, Sunday Tribune, Sunday Independent, Sunday Press*; (BR) *Observer*.

December: (IR) *Irish Times, Irish Independent, Evening Press, Sunday Tribune, Sunday Independent*; (BR) *Observer*.

1988: January: (IR) *Irish Times, Irish Independent, Evening Press, Sunday Tribune, Sunday Independent*, (BR) *Observer*

February: (IR) *Irish Times, Sunday Tribune*, (BR) *Observer; Guardian*

March: (IR) *Irish Times, Sunday Tribune*; (BR) *Observer, Guardian*

April: (IR) *Irish Times*; (BR) *Observer, Guardian*

May-December: no systematic monitoring

1989-1990 January-December: no systematic monitoring;

1990: November-December: (IR) *Irish Times*; (BR) *Guardian, Independent, Times, Daily Telegraph, Sunday Times, Sunday Telegraph*

1991: January-September: (IR) *Irish Times*; (BR) *Guardian, Independent, Times, Daily Telegraph, Sunday Times, Sunday Telegraph*

That no systematic monitoring of particular newspapers occurred in different periods should not be taken to mean that data collection halted. As a daily and Sunday consumer of the broadsheet press (both British and Irish), reports were collected but not on a systematic basis and mainly were from the *Irish Times* and the *Guardian*. The representative nature of the materials was evidenced in a subsequent re-checking exercise described below.

6   The study title was 'Representations of AIDS, Drugs and Prostitutes in the British, Irish and Dutch press' (December 1986-February 1987). It was carried out in the Department of Sociology, Trinity College, Dublin and the Principal Investigator was Dr. Brian Torode. I was the research assistant. Findings from this study were not published.

7   The Irish submission to the UN Global Women and Media Project is a content analysis of press reports, detailing the frequency of

coverage. Content analysis is thus still a current method used to make general statements about media content.

8   I was also interested in seeing whether the incidence of reports on prostitution increased during the so called 'happy' or 'silly' season, i.e., when the Dáil and Houses of Commons and Lords are not sitting, thus 'freeing up' newspaper space.

9   At time of writing (July, 1995), the Hugh Grant story (about his arrest for indecent behaviour with a prostitute) 'hit' the headlines and was front page news. Beckett (*Independent on Sunday*, 9.7.95) provides a detailed account of this coverage in the UK broadsheet and tabloid press. The page one status that this story received was probably more to do with the key actor (Grant) than with prostitution per se.

10 I also carried out a content analysis of 'authorship' to ascertain whether the stories were predominantly written by male or female journalists. No differences emerged. I have not reported the percentages here because it would suggest, contrary to my view, that I was proposing that there is a style of 'male' and 'female' writing. Had the findings indicated that stories of prostitution were women journalists' preserve, this might indicate a delegation of human interest stories to these workers. However, for current purposes, this is not of interest.

11 In a study of the British and Irish press coverage of the World Whores Congress (1986), the composite picture which emerged was of a woman forced into prostitution; a discourse of the prostitute as a 'dope' which was resisted by the practitioners' discourse in which they defined themselves as active agents (Ryan, 1987). This tendency is also present in the sample used for this current study, although this issue is not of direct concern.

12 While I go on to consider this aspect of prostitution in Chapter Eight, one example of this attitude is found in a *Guardian* story. Overhearing a woman (who was a prostitute) telling about being raped, 'the taxi-driver ... said that it wasn't really rape – she just didn't get paid' (CHEAP TRICKS LEAVE CITY GIRLS NO TIME FOR LEGAL NICETIES, 6.5.95).

13 I focused upon this because of a tendency abroad, although not novel, to expand the definition of prostitution to refer to exchange of drugs (goods) for sexual 'services' (cf. Gossop et al., 1994). The only instance of such a definition being used is in a story outside the data set (WOMAN TELLS RAPE TRIAL OF DRUGS NEED, *Irish Times*, 15.2.95).

94

The relevance of this definition, particularly in this story, is that rape is deemed not to have occurred because the woman 'exchanged' sex for drugs.

14   Comments made throughout this section relate only to the media in Western industrialised societies.

15   The figures for television viewing are as follows: 1986 (26.32 hours per week); 1991 (26.4 hours); 1993 (25.41 hours). Television viewing time varies across gender and age. Hours spent reading broadsheet and tabloid press are not available.

16   As Jalbert points out, 'while we do not know how many possible understandings could be derived from a particular text or communication, we can nonetheless make arguments of the kinds of understandings that can be achieved' (1995: 7, emphasis in original). This is the approach I adopt (discussed in Chapter Four).

17   A contemporary example of this would be O.J. Simpson's remarks on the media presentation of his 16-month trial. He argued that there was an enormous discrepancy between what went on in the courtroom and the media reports of the trial (*Irish Times*, 3 October 1995).

18   In addition, as Curran (1990: 136) noted, the mass communication readers tended to promote the view that the two models were fundamentally different, which he claims, at least in respect of his co-authored work (*Mass Communication and Society*), was as much a pedagogic device as an attempt to reject 'sterile' US consensus theorising in order to assert the centrality of Marxism in British sociology.

19   Analysis of ideology in the news by those working within a discourse analytic framework draws upon a long and varied sociological tradition, generally starting off with a rejection of Marx's understanding of ideology as a distorted view of reality and moving to Althusser's formulation of ideology (and the interpolation of S/subjects) in his seminal paper 'Ideology and ideological state apparatuses' (1971).

20   This formulation echoes Gramsci's (in Bocock, 1986) formulation of ideology as common-sense in his discussion of hegemony.

21   In relation to sexual assault crimes against women, feminists have argued that the media have constructed a false 'reality' of street violence; Stanko (1993) discusses this in relation to the concomitant effect of ignoring the 'reality' of women's vulnerability to violence in the home.

95

22 See Richardson and Corner (1986) and Morley (1993) for excellent synopses of the trends within media reception studies. Freund (1987) documents a similar tendency within literary theory.

4 Methodology and methods of analysis

4.1 Introduction

The present inquiry into broadsheet press coverage of prostitution underwent a transformation over the course of the study, as noted in Chapter One. This chapter outlines the research process, specifically the methodological choices made over the course of the study and the implications such choices had for the way I handled the data. It follows on from the criticisms noted in Chapter Three regarding the viability of a content analytic procedure for the analysis of media discourse. It is necessarily detailed because I consider that the changes that were introduced are of crucial significance for the analysis of press discourses.

Given that the research process rarely matches the ideal-type of research process as outlined in text-books on method and given also that my experience of carrying out this particular piece of research was punctuated by periods 'at sea', an experience I shared with Halson (1992, p. 83), this chapter aims to point to the step-by step decisions I made in the face of problems encountered.[1] In short, I aim to bring the reader on a retrospective voyage of the research process, the destination being the point where the methodological questions raised by ethnomethodology and Goffman are outlined. Particular issues of concern relate to the reading process. This 'voyage' starts at the originating point of the preliminary analysis of one newspaper report on prostitution, which was approached with the aim of applying methods of formal discourse analysis based on the work of Zellig Harris and informed by Michel Pecheux, as mentioned in the introductory chapter. The theoretical bases of these approaches are not fully explicated as they no longer are central to my analysis. My initial aim vis-à-vis methods of discourse analysis was to eschew a priori

97

interpretations of the data, to attempt to specify the formal features of the texts *before* moving to their interpretation. This latter objective was influenced by linguistic analysis and, as became increasingly clear, could not be sustained in the analysis of textual content as opposed to textual form (structure).

4.2   Starting points: Qualitative research design

A recent text-book (Tesch, 1990) on qualitative research notes that despite the increasing acceptance of qualitative methods in sociology, it is impossible to give a strict codified list of procedures for the qualitative analysis of raw materials. It is generally accepted that qualitative analysis involves 'intellectual craftsmanship' (Mills, 1959); that the procedures should not be prescriptive, given the creative involvement of individual researchers (cf. Billig, 1988, pp. 198-199).

Various writers on the qualitative research process (Silverman, 1985, 1993; Tesch, 1990; Marshall & Rossman, 1995) and on discourse analysis (Potter & Wetherell, 1987) have produced lists of 'rules' of qualitative research, usually totalling ten, which convey the central principles of qualitative research. Tesch's (1990, pp. 95-96) list conveys these principles in abbreviated form and I have selected from this list the central underlying methodological premises on which this research is based. I include them here because they give some coherence to a research process which was marked for considerable periods of time by incoherence, by, as I noted in the introduction, an increasing sense that the three elements of the research (the substantive topic of prostitution, the discourse analytic approach and the literature on media processes) were not converging. A retrospective view of the logic of the research however, enabled me to see how, despite the problems I encountered, the approach as a whole was consistent. Some key items in the 'recipe' for qualitative research are the following:

1   Analysis is not the last phase in the research process; it is concurrent with data collection. This approach was the hallmark of Glaser and Strauss' (1967) work and underlies the dynamic, processual nature of qualitative research. Unlike the quantitative research approach, the lines between reviewing literature, finding a method, collecting the data and analysis of those data are blurred. This approach, in the current study, meant that the data collection phase began as soon as I started the study and I carried out a preliminary analysis of materials

almost immediately as a way of testing the method initially selected. Concurrently, I was reading the literature on the substantive topic and identifying core themes *and* I was addressing the literature relating to the mass media. These different research activities informed each other.

2 The analysis process is systematic and comprehensive, but not rigid: This principle required that I was always ready to engage in revisions of what was emerging from the data in the light of my research questions. The analysis is complete only when new data no longer generate new insights. In my case, data collection was completed in 1991 and further materials I collected were not included in the core data set but were reserved to serve as 'validators' of themes and foci identified as central. These additional data did not generate new insights, but have the status of being 'confirmatory'.

3 Attending to data includes a self-reflexive activity that results in a set of analytical notes that guide the process. My research question, while it emerged some time into the study, was, as I discovered when I went back over notes made on the data, there 'all along'.

4 Data are 'segmented', i.e., divided into relevant and meaningful 'units'. However, Tesch comments (1990: 96) that the analysis always begins with reading all the data to achieve a 'sense of the whole'. This sense fertilises the interpretation of individual data pieces. As the corpus of materials was not complete when I started the analysis, this reading was ongoing: each new addition was added to the existing corpus and the entire corpus was read again. The unit of analysis, initially words (in order to identify different 'voices' or discourses by way of lexical cohesion) in the text was, ultimately, 'descriptions' which were comprised of individual words and sentences.

This process of reading the data, of reading and reading once more, is a central feature of qualitative research. I concur with C. Wright Mills' (1959) argument that reading is a form of research; my reading continually provided pointers for analysis, which in turn led to the refinement of the research questions.

A further feature of the qualitative research process relates to what is termed by Glaser and Strauss (1967) 'analytic induction'. This characteristic was of critical importance in my case for it dictates that rather than imposing my own ideas on the materials to be analysed, I attempted to 'let the data themselves speak'; in short, taking up analytic induction means shunning a priori approaches to one's data.

4.3   Starting points: Preliminary analysis

Kane (1983) notes that research techniques are a bit like fishing flies; the researcher chooses the right one for the fish s/he wants to catch. Hence the research question(s), and relatedly, materials collected, influence the selection of method. The present study was, at the outset, an exploratory study: whilst the initial interests in newspaper discourse and the representations of prostitutes were explicit, I did not know before I started the study what I was going to find. I did not know how extensive coverage would be or nor what the focus of the newspaper stories would be. In this sense the data collection phase (outlined in Chapter Three) was a journey into the unknown. The method I initially adopted was concerned to detail the structure of the news reports; to parse the texts into distinct discourses by ways of Harrisian discourse analysis.

I began my preliminary analysis with a broadsheet story on prostitution. In September 1987 *Lyn: A Story of Prostitution* (Levine & Madden) was published, attracting considerable publicity including radio interviews and public meetings at which the co-author of the book, June Levine spoke. In October, Nuala O'Faolain, a regular columnist in the *Irish Times*, devoted a column to this book, headlined LYN'S GROUP IS THE MOST DEPRIVED OF ALL (5.10.87). The start of this study coincided with the publication of this article and I decided to base my preliminary analysis on it. This article was of interest for a number of reasons: while it is generally recognised that media analysts are dealing with pre-interpreted products, products which bear the marks of the organisational practices of news production, O'Faolain's article is clearly a discourse of interpretation, a book review with a commentary. It was also an extended sequence of discourse and my initial aim was to see if I could identify conflicting discourses in this text. In detailing the initial analysis, I want to draw attention to the issues and problems which arose for me and to indicate how this initial analysis served as a springboard to the process of refining the research problem, from the representations of prostitutes to the questions of how the press stories are read as stories of prostitution; how are the women in these stories categorised as 'prostitutes'?

The initial approach to the analysis of this text aimed to identify the key discourses and to consider the structure of the text. Zellig Harris' (1952a, 1952b) presuppositionless distributional analysis was to serve as a starting point.[2] Harris' method aims to analyse connected speech and writing above the level of a sentence and he suggested that his method could be used with the analyst possessing information only about the morpheme boundaries: 'To establish the method for its own sake ... *no prior knowledge* should be used' (1952a, p. 3, emphasis added). Given my concern to avoid a priori theorising, with the strategy of analytic induction, this approach seemed a valuable starting point. The starting point of this distributional analysis is to consider the more frequently repeated words of the text, the aim being the construction of an 'outline' of the structure of a text according to equivalence classes and in this way, according to Harris,

> sometimes show how one section of one sentence is equivalent to a different section of another sentence and therefore contains the same classes. The extent to which we can do this depends on the amount of repetition in the text (1952a, p. 19).

The task of the analyst is to search for repetitions of strings of words within sentences, labelling each string A, B, C, and so on in the order in which they occur. The analyst then considers the environments of each of the strings and groups them into equivalence classes, so if A occurs in sentences AP, AQ, AR then P=Q=R equivalence class X (Torode, 1985, p. 7). This approach works from the bottom up in an attempt to specify the organising principles of a discourse.

I therefore looked for repetition of words and identified the occurrence of these words in terms of discourses. However, the first problem the presuppositionless discourse analyst runs into is the problem of valency: the same word may have a different meaning according to its use (a point the ordinary language philosophers, Austin, Searle and Wittgenstein, and the structuralist, Sausseure emphasise). The following extract illustrates this problem.

S1   I've just read a *book* called 'Lyn', which is the real life story of Lyn Madden, who was a Dublin *prostitute*.

S2   She was with a *man* called John Cullen one night, in 1983, when he finally succeeded in murdering Dolores Lynch a former prostitute, who had crossed him.

S3   He set fire to Dolores's *house*: her mother and her aunt died in the flames, and she died of her burns next day.

The four words: book, prostitute, man, house were the basic words selected and these words are repeated throughout the 75 sentence text. However, 'prostitute' in the first sentence clearly refers to Dublin prostitutes whereas later on in the text 'prostitute' is used in a general way:

S20 For example, prostitutes are very often abused in childhood …

The occurrence of 'prostitute' in S1 and in S20 refers in the former to an individual prostitute (Lyn Madden) and in the latter to all prostitutes. My interpretation of this was that 'prostitute' in S1 was being made equivalent to 'prostitutes' in S20 – Lyn Madden's experiences were to stand for all prostitutes. Similarly, 'home' is a key word in the text (being repeated numerous times).

S21 Of the 389 children sleeping rough in Dublin this week, 50 per cent of the girls have been abused in the home.

S22 Home.

S23 In the word of Lyn Madden is reported from there aren't homes there is housing …

S31 Why did Bernie keep Mick in BMWs with which to commute to his charming home …

How were 'home' and 'house'/'housing' to be analysed? They are clearly not the same, the one is the obverse of the other. Yet, in reading of the article, the 'home' of the 50% of girls who have been abused is linked to the 'house' of the 'world' of Lyn Madden. Similarly, 'man' in S2 was identified as a key word. The 'man' here is a pimp. In S43 'men' are customers. Men also refers to 'men with money' (S50). Distinctions between these 'men' cannot be made with the method of identifying repetitious words.

However, this way of parsing the text can be of use, for example, in identifying the discourse of the book:

S1 I've just read a book …

S6 The book is about Lyn …

S7 She wrote it …

S8 Her friend June Levine brought the book to publication …

S 9 No other book exists like it in Ireland.

S10 We are in her debt for it …

S11 It is a nearly intolerable book …

S17 The book is full of ruined children …

S29 Not that simple social action would be enough for all the questions this book raises …

S47 In her narrative as printed in this book …

S66 the people in the book …

S73   the people in Lyn Madden's appalling book ...

S75   ... after reading this book.

Other discourses identified by way of repetition of words were of the home, of children, of prostitutes and of the world of Lyn Madden. The discourse of the book is the dominant discourse; other discourses, for example of children and of childhood, are not present to the same extent:

S12   Lyn was broken by her childhood ...

S14   She had three children

S15   Cullen had three children by his wife, three by a mentally defective prostitute ...

S17   The book is full of ruined children, just as it begins with a ruined childhood.

The book discourse includes a biography of Lyn, moving to discuss her childhood and the childhood of other children.

A structure, however simple, was discerned in the text. However, the relevance of this structure to my research question was not clear. The relevance of structural analysis has been subject to criticism. Thompson, reviewing the work of Michel Pecheux who aims to provide a structuralist account of texts with a view to explicating the ideology/ideologies articulated in them,[3] comments that whilst his approach is meticulously descriptive, the results do not speak for themselves, raising the question of interpretation:

> ... the necessity of elaborating the results is a striking demonstration of the thesis that, however elaborate the formal methods of analysis in the social sciences may be, such methods could never be more than a limited and *preliminary* stage of a more comprehensive interpretative theory (1984, p. 251, emphasis added).

Thompson's argument misses the point, as I understand it, of a formal method. Harris stated that while the

> ... formal findings ... can ... reveal peculiarities within the structure ... this ... is still distinct from an interpretation of the findings which must take the meaning of the morphemes into consideration ... [S]uch interpretation is *quite separate* from the formal findings, although it may follow closely in the directions that the formal findings indicate (1952a, p. 29).

I understand formal analysis in terms of analytic induction and my criticism of the method relates to the presumption that a formal method can be applied prior to interpretation: the identification of words depends on the analyst's knowledge of language use, a knowledge which is used in the application of the formal method. One of the key methodological issues which formal discourse analysis raises relates to the moment of interpretation and when that arises, i.e., at what point does the analyst *interpret* the data/datum? I argue that it cannot be excised from the analytic process, *at any stage*.

In my case, an additional problem emerged: my interpretation of the text diverged from the 'formal findings' (I had parsed the text into distinct discourses). In my interpretation I relied on theoretical points made by Berger and Luckmann (1966) to make sense of what I thought was 'going on' in this text. I did not base my interpretation on the formal structure identified, a move which anticipated the abandonment of the Harrisian method.

My reading (and countless re-readings) of this text led to the issue of the construction of the world of prostitution as an extra-ordinary world, outside of our ordinary, known-in common world, and the inhabitants of this world are similarly placed. The 'pub', the 'chip-shop', the Canal, the streets are all places in that world. The setting up of an opposition between our world, referenced by 'home' and the prostitutes' world referenced by these public places echoed Berger and Luckmann's comment that

> ... the reality of everyday life always appears as a zone of lucidity behind which there is a background of darkness which is removed from the 'here and now' (1966, p. 59).

A paraphrasing of O'Faolain's article is in the following passage:

> ... the interpretation of realities of marginal situations within the paramount reality of everyday life is of great importance, because these situations constitute the most acute threat to the taken for granted, routinised existence in society. If one perceives the latter as the 'daylight' side of human life, then the marginal situations constitute a 'night side' that keeps lurking ominously on the periphery of everyday consciousness (1966, pp. 115-116).

O'Faolain writes that

S25   We, the Irish, have created this world.

S26   Having created it ... we ignore it.

S27   Maybe there's an occasional glimpse ...

This is a glimpse into this extra-ordinary world, characterised by terror, murder and chaos.

The article works to suggest that this dark side is being brought into the home: 'Why did Bernie keep Mick in BMWs with which to commute to his charming country home?' Mick, is her pimp, and lives in our world – 'there are no homes in the world of Lyn Madden ...'. de Beauvoir (1952) has argued in respect of the public/private sphere divide that women remain immanent, i.e., caught in the private sphere, while men are transcendental, they are able to move between worlds. Here, it is the women caught in the extra-ordinary world of Lyn Madden, with the 'men in the cars', the 'men with money', able to move between this world and our ordinary world.

My interpretation of this article thus departed from the formal structure identified. While Lyn may be identified by the formal analysis as a passive subject, with things done to her, detailed discourse analysis is not required to reach this conclusion. In short, the search for textual structure was, for this study, misplaced and the findings yielded by a formal method of analysis were assessed by me as jejune. However, the analytic experience was to prove valuable in directing my attention to a range of issues vis-à-vis textuality, for example, that of inter-textuality which was raised by the analysis.

Bob Hodge has commented that

> Texts and discursive practices typically make claims about their own transformational histories indicating which texts and statements from the genealogical chains that constitute them. The task of recovering all these missing texts is usually impossible (in Torode, 1989, p. 101).

My initial attempt to match sociological discourses on prostitution to the discourse of prostitution in O'Faolain's text was not concerned to see how her journalistic account drew upon these discourses. I was concerned to attempt to uncover the discursive chains between O'Faolain's article and the book, upon which it was based. This 'matching' of discourses enabled me to trace similarities and differences. I attempted to trace what was in the book and what was in O'Faolain's article by matching the paragraphs in the newspaper article to the contents of the various chapters. The following is an attempt to indicate where the book and the discourse on the book, in O'Faolain's article, converge and diverge.

Paragraph 1:	Chapter 1 [what the book is about]
Paragraph 2:	Chapter 27, 28 [the trial]
Paragraph 3:	Chapter 27 [the trial]
Paragraph 4:	Chapter 3 [her relationship with Craig]

	Chapter 13 meets Cullen, reference to Theresa being 'mentally slow' (1987: 130).
Paragraph 5:	Chapter 16 (about Cullen's knife attack on Lyn)
Paragraph 6:	Chapter 9 (about shoplifting), chapter 5 (Lyn on Valium), 'They (Craig and Lyn) knew nothing about life in the real world' (1987, p. 116).
Paragraph 7: (Having created this world we ignore it)	Chapter 1 'There is a vital need for all women, everywhere, to take a long hard look at the reality of prostitution' (1987: 6).

The article follows the book, not surprisingly perhaps, as it is a commentary on the book. It reproduces Levine's message that prostitution is a 'reality' which is ignored in Ireland (by both officials and ordinary people – readers of the *Irish Times*), a stance reproduced by O'Faolain. This exercise indicates how popular literary discourses are taken up and reproduced by journalists.

While I started with what, in the course of attempting to carry out a formal analysis on the selected text, emerged as a utopian desire to suspend my everyday knowledge of words and their meanings, I soon realised that my identification of key words relied on this everyday knowledge. In addition, I began to question the validity of such a method of analysis and the relevance, to my project, of methods of analysis which uncovered the structure of a text. In conversation analysis, the turn-by-turn sequencing of a conversation is clearly relevant to what gets accomplished over the course of an interaction, and a similar approach to texts holds in terms of a description of the accomplishment of writing (for example, stories begin with a beginning and so on). As newspaper texts are read, a consideration of reading as a course of action, which is accomplished over time, is necessary, as is a recognition that detailed attention to a text in terms of how it is read requires that the analyst posit a reading strategy and an ideal reader who reads the text in orderly fashion.

In the search for a method with which the analyse the data, I also used the socio-linguistic work of Gunther Kress (1985) and Norman Fowler (1985, 1991). Their approach aims to specify the production and maintenance of ideology in spoken and written texts by analysing the functions of different linguistic devices (modality, nominalisation). Fowler argues that the social context of the discourse needs an initially independent description into which the linguistic description is to be reintegrated (1985: 75).

I wish to suggest, on the basis of my attempts to apply this work to my data, that it is a priori – the social context is used in a way which makes analysis redundant; all that is proposed is an unceasing reproduction of power differentials. Finding the source of the ideology articulated in various texts is also problematic. In essence, the socio-linguistic work was not appropriate to my research endeavour.

O'Faolain's article served as a springboard to this study, not only because of the problems I experienced trying to apply formal discourse analysis to this text but also because of the content. Sentence 48 in particular raised questions for me:

> She is telling us about lives in which there is no God … This world derives from prostitution … Tonight, drunk, stoned, sick and despairing women will be climbing into the cars of men with money.

In reading this, particularly the last sentence, I automatically read 'prostitutes' will be climbing into the cars of men with money. In short, the characteristics (drunk, stoned and despairing) and more importantly the activity (climbing into cars) direct my reading. Why should this be so? A formal linguistic analysis would see 'climbing' as active, the structure of the text would parse these sentences into their respective discourses, however, the reading of this passage produced a meaning: 'prostitute'.

It was this question in particular and others relating to reading stories of prostitution which ultimately led me to the work of the ethnomethodologists. The work informed by this perspective enabled me to obviate the problems I identified and indeed to begin systematic analysis. It is to this theoretical and methodological approach that I now turn.

4.4   Ethnomethodological approaches

Ethnomethodology, as Atkinson (1990) points out, is neither a theory nor a method in the conventional sociological sense. This makes it difficult to present in a 'methods' chapter.[4] This difficulty is compounded by my attempt to detail the problems encountered in the analysis of the data and their solution. In addition, it needs to be pointed out here that my use of ethnomethodology was selective; it focused particularly upon the ethnomethodological contribution to sociological understanding of classification procedures.

The central analytical concern of ethnomethodology is oriented to the question of *how* the social order is produced or 'accomplished' by members' activities. By combining the terms 'ethno' (meaning 'folk' or 'members') and 'methodology' (meaning 'methods of reasoning' or 'sense assembly procedures'), Garfinkel, the founder of ethnomethodology aimed to capture the topic of what he argued was a neglected domain of inquiry in sociology (Atkinson, 1990, p. 455; cf. Garfinkel, 1974 on the origins of ethnomethodology and its scope). Ethnomethodology takes what is generally treated as a 'resource' and turns it into a topic for research. For example, taking language as a topic of inquiry means considering how language not merely reflects things which are treated as being of sociological interest, but rather how language is, itself, a social activity. Bailey (1987) regards the 'method' of ethnomethodology as the explication of 'indexicals'. Garfinkel and Sacks defined this as expressions

> ... whose sense cannot be decided by an auditor without his necessarily knowing or assuming something about the biography and the purposes of the user of an expression, the circumstances of the utterance, the previous course of discourse or the particular relationship of actual or potential interaction that exists between the user and the auditor (1970, p. 348).

The relevance of this is that, as will be shown in the analysis, where the utterance is placed in a sequence of expressions (or sentences) determines its sense. Elliptical expressions have sense only by reference to past utterances. The categorisation of the hearer by the writer/speaker can be analysed by reference to the relationship between them (for example, place formulations, discussed in Chapter Six, are selected on this basis).

Indexicality is a central concept of ethnomethodology; it refers to how language is reducible ad infinitum; we can never fully explicate what it is that we mean as each background assumption leads to other background assumptions (cf. Garfinkel's writing experiments, 1967, Chapter Two). As Albert notes, the content of communication could never provide the sense that we come to understand; if we look to lexical definitions for the sense of an expression, we can be assured to be looking in the wrong place (1982, p. 98). This means that it is not a matter of, for example, counting words, rather what is at issue is how the sense of expressions are produced – what the procedures are which are used in the production and hearing of expressions. This, of course, draws upon the work of ordinary language philosophers (Austin, Searle, and particularly Wittgenstein, 1953) regarding the performative character of words. As Turner puts it, it is about explicating procedures for 'analysing utterances into activities' (1971, p. 171). Very simply put, it means that words do things, they do not reflect social reality, they construct it.[5]

It is not my concern to provide a comprehensive review of ethnomethodological work. Various excellent reviews (Schegloff, in Jefferson, 1992; Rustin, 1993), collections (Turner, 1974; Psathas, 1979, Coulter, 1990), studies (Garfinkel, 1967; Atkinson, 1978) and critiques (Bauman, 1973; Giddens, 1976) exist which fulfil this function. My focus is quite narrow, honing in upon the elements which informed my analysis of the data. A central claim which is implicit in my comments is that the ethnomethodological work I selected, while primarily being concerned with activities in conversation, can be shown to have relevance in the analysis of written texts (cf. McHoul, 1982).

4.5   Ethnomethodological approaches to reading

My introduction to ethnomethodology was via a consideration of media 'bias'. In the late 1970s, a debate in the journal of the British Sociological Association (*Sociology*) was sparked off by the publication of a paper by two ethnomethodologists, Digby Anderson and Wes Sharrock (1979). The target of their paper was Graham Murdock, who rejoindered their claims (1980). McKeganey and Smith (1980) entered the fray in its closing stages. The debate was lengthy and I am not going to recapitulate it in detail. The key claims of Anderson and Sharrock were that media scholars themselves produce 'bias' through their 'contrived surprise'.

They argued that in Graham Murdock's work ('Youth in contemporary Britain'), his analysis of headlines of stories about 'youth/s' was illegitimate. Taking one headline as an example: YOUTH FINED FOR INDECENT EXPOSURE, Anderson and Sharrock remark that they find nothing in the headline to read 'youth' as implicative of a social group 'youth': 'we find nothing in the text to lead us to invoke the charge of stereotyping' (1979, p. 380). They suggest that what is needed is an analysis of how members actually use and monitor or evaluate the use of concepts such as 'youth' or 'age'. Readers, possessing a 'common stock of knowledge' use such devices ('age', 'youth') as membership categorisations which provide for the correct categorisation of actors by reference to specific acts. Crucially, for current purposes, they suggest that before analysis can be done on a text it must be read, therefore, analysis is properly analysis of reading practices. The ongoing debate is not of direct relevance here, and so I want to stop at this point.

Anderson and Sharrock's comments alerted me to the role of the reader, not in the sense of the 'audience' (as in active audience theory, cf. Chapter Three) but in respect of how texts are actually read. How are the stories of prostitution produced by the reader's interaction with the text over the course of reading? There exists some ethnomethodological work on reading, for example, McHoul (1982), who begins his studies by noting ethnomethodology's 'shyness' of textuality. He aims to explicate members' methods in the performance of reading.

He uses Garfinkel's (1967) infamous 'breach experiments' technique in order to show how reading is characterised by a retrospective-prospective approach, that is, how, when reading, if we come across something that we do not understand, we make sense of this by reference to what has come before, and further, use this to anticipate future occurrences. I consider one important section in McHoul's work to be his ethnography of reading. In this ethnography, he details how he reads a text. He is aiming to explicate the technical resources he uses, and shares with other readers, in making sense of the utterances composing a text (1982: 108). His ethnography alerts him to how, as he reads and is confronted by 'puzzles', he does not immediately stop reading but carries on, searching to find answers. A question-answer sequence is thus to be identified in the course of reading work.[6]

The ethnography I carried out on a randomly selected newspaper story yielded similar findings; namely that the occasion of reading is not unrelated to other social experiences (a particular feature of my reading). The news item is read as part of an ongoing story and refers back or recalls information already (presumed by the journalist) to be held by readers. At the same time reading is constructed in terms of what is to come, hence the occasion of reading is constituted in a mutual and reflexive way by texts and their readers. The author is a textual effect produced over the course of a reading (cf. Lury, 1982, p. 8). Texts are thus dialogical, text and reader together produce the occasion of reading as a task of understanding work (McHoul, 1982, p. 138).

This, then, was my starting point for considering how readers read newspaper reports.[7] It situates the activity of readers firmly at the centre of the analysis and crucially directed my attention to how I was reading the texts as 'stories of prostitution'. How was such a reading produced? In addition, Celia Lury's 'Ethnography of an Ethnography: Reading Sociology', a discussion of the ways in which sociological texts accomplish the traits of objectivity, facticity and validity (1982, p. 21), alerted me to how the question of facticity was critical in newspaper discourse and I began to focus upon how I as a reader accepted the descriptions of women as *unequivocally* 'prostitutes'. What was going on in these (86) texts? Ethnomethodology requires that the researcher become 'anthropologically strange' (cf. Garfinkel, 1967) – to view the ordinary, mundane and common-place as unfamiliar (this is, effectively, what is proposed in the deconstructionist strategy of placing words 'sous ratour', that is placing an invisible cross over them, problematising their meaning, in an attempt to understand how they are used). While this 'anthropological estrangement' is an important step, it alone cannot be the basis of analysis. I found this basis in Harvey Sacks' work on descriptions.

4.6 Machineries of description

Harvey Sacks and Michael Moerman point out in a lecture in 1971 that sociology, like anthropology, is fundamentally concerned with 'culture'. Defining culture as a 'system of shared understandings' (cited in Silverman, 1986, p. 118), Sacks also understood culture 'as an apparatus for generating *recognisable actions*' (1992, p. 308). In his 'Notes on Methodology' Sacks argues that overwhelming order, 'detailed order', is evident 'at all points' and further that:

> That sort of order would be an important resource of a culture, such that, for example, any members of a culture, encountering from their infancy a very small portion of it, and a random portion in a way (... the experiences they happen to have, the vocabulary that happens to be thrown at them in whatever utterances they happen to encounter) would come out in many ways much like everybody else and be able to deal with just about anybody else (1963, p. 22).

One fundamental aspect of 'culture' is the way members describe the events and individuals or groups. These descriptions constitute the character of activities or persons. Sacks argues that description in sociology is a technical problem arguing that

> Sociologists frequently treat some categorisation that Members have done as providing the sociologist with materials that are descriptive in the sense that such materials may then be used – as they stand – for further sociological investigation (1992, p. 33).

He suggests that no category of sociological description (for example, 'suicide') should be adopted as part of the sociological attempt to explain behaviour without first focusing on the common-sense ways in which members themselves use this or other categories: even if it can be said that persons produce descriptions of the social world, the task of sociology is not to clarify these, to say what 'they are really about' or to criticise them, 'but to describe them' (1963, p. 7). In his lectures, he stated that sociologists' business is to 'analyse how it is that something gets done or how something is a something' and not employ it as a resource in analysis, but rather, make it the topic of research (in Jefferson, 1992, i, p. 295). Selecting as an example the category 'suicide' Sacks asks how is it categorised as 'suicide'; what methodic procedures are involved in the classification (and hence production) of 'suicide'? He argues that unless and until we describe the category of suicide and produce a description of the procedure employed for assembling cases of that class of activities, the category is not part of the sociological apparatus (1963, p. 8). Two main published papers provided the basis of Sacks' method for explicating the production of categories. The aim is outlined in the following passage:

> What one ought to seek to build is an apparatus which will provide for how it is that any activities which members do [are done] in such a way as to be recognisable as such to members. [That is how they] are done and done recognisably (1974, p. 218).

This apparatus was first developed in the analysis of calls to a suicide prevention centre in which Sacks outlined how 'I have no-one to turn to' was produced as a recognisable description of a person's situation. Further, if members of society have a phenomenon 'possible descriptions' which are recognisable per se, then one need not know how it is that, for example, 'babies' and 'mommies' behave in order to examine the composition of such possible descriptions as members produce and recognise. A key argument of my approach is that the procedures involved in the production of descriptions (and their reception) operate in a similar manner in both scriptual (McHoul, 1982) and spoken utterances.

Sacks' lectures (Jefferson, 1992) are centrally concerned with this issue of description, their production and recognition. Sacks (1967, 1974) outlines the central features of an analytic approach to descriptions which comprise categories (e.g. 'mother', 'teacher'); membership categorisation device (a collection of categories) and category-bound activities (how identifications of doers of activities are produced). The production of categories is governed by 'rules' or 'maxims', for example, the 'hearer's maxim' (when a person uses two or more categories to describe at least two members of a population and it is possible to hear the categories as belonging to the same collection of categories, then we hear them that way); and the 'economy rule' which holds that a single category from any membership categorisation device can be referentially adequate. These are the central features of the apparatus and each is described in more detail below. The operation of the categorisation production and recognition procedure involves the use of norms. Crucially, the categories that Sacks is dealing with are members', not analysts', categories.

4.6.1 Category bound activities

Sacks refers to category bound activities as activities which are taken by members to be done by particular or several particular categories of members where the categories are categories from membership categorisation devices (MCDs). For example, one can assess the behaviour of another by reference to 'stage of life' categories (baby, adolescent, teenager). So for example, if 'crying' is subjected to a 'test' of stage of life category (baby), then its candidacy as a member of the class 'category bound activities' is warrantable. Crucially, Sacks remarks that

> One way to decide that an activity is category bound is to see whether, the fact of membership being unknown, it can be 'hinted at' by naming the activity as something one does (1974, p. 223).

Given that my initial recognition of the problem of descriptions in one datum (LYN'S GROUP IS THE MOST DEPRIVED OF ALL, *Irish Times*, 5.10.87) was the reference to 'drunk, stoned and despairing women will be *climbing into the cars* of men', an activity which was read as the activities of 'prostitutes', Sacks' terse reference to 'hinting at' here was extremely suggestive. How else might this 'hinting' be at work? Volume One of Sacks' lectures (Jefferson, 1992) devotes considerable attention to this issue of description. He comments that one other way that people go about identifying is by 'hinting':

> ... it involves picking some activity which has some properties, whatever they may be, which provide for the activity to be hintable with ... some membership identification category ... And then one comes to see that doing 'hinting at an identification' does not necessarily ... involve that you intend to do 'hinting', but that there may be, e.g., things which are said and things which are done which are properly seeable as 'hinting at an identification' (vol. i, p. 579-580).

Categories 'hintable at' by naming an activity are 'category bound activities'; Sacks proposes that

> What you have to do is, each time that you want to say that something is a category bound activity, have some ways of *proving* that it is so … what are the ways of proving? [One would be] that the category is hintable at by naming the activity, [this] is one way of coming to see that it is one of those. But even here you have to be able to show that what took place was a 'seen hint' or a 'seeable hint' (i, p. 583).

The viewers' maxim as one of the class of relevance rules (that is assessment of the relevance of a categorisation) holds that for an observer (or, I suggest, reader) of a category bound activity, the category to which the activity is bound has a special relevance for formulating the identification of its doer (1974, 1992).

These points are suggestive. However, in some of Sacks' remarks a shadow is cast over the 'hearing' of descriptions. He gives an example of a data extract which is as follows:

[Therapist] So what interests did you have before?

[Client] I was a hairstylist at one time. I did some fashions now and then, things like that.

[T] Then why aren't you working? …

[C] Well, I'll tell you. I'm afraid – I'm afraid to go out and look for a job. That 's what I'm afraid of. But more, I think I'm afraid of myself because – I don't know, I' m just terribly mixed up …

[T] Have you been having sexual problems?

[C] All my life … Naturally, you probably suspect, as far as the hair stylist and, uh, either one way or the other, they're straight or homosexual, something like that (1992, i, p. 579).

Sacks, on the basis of this extract, comments that when he names that he's been a hairstylist etc., the client seems from later talk to take it that he's hinted that he's a homosexual. It appears then, as one, and 'not at all unusual', way, that there are some categories that identify oneself, which one can hint at by belonging in, by naming some activity that one does.

Allied with this is Sacks' comments about norms, norms being rules of proper behaviour. In ethnomethodological fashion, which rejects that rules govern behaviours, but are rather oriented to by members to find the sense of activities, utterances and so on, Sacks comments that it is not the case that there is simply good behaviour for category members (such as mothers) but that one can use a norm to see who it is that's doing something which it can characterise (vol. i, p. 253). Now, he states

> ... that's a different sense of norms regulating activities where sociology says norms are followed. They provide also ... for how it is that person who knows neither of the people comes to choose what categories s/he *ought* to choose ... to see what is going on. And in that sense they provide rules of relevance for selecting categories (ibid.).

Further, norms provide for the relevant membership categories in terms of which they formulate identifications of the doers of those actions for which the norms are appropriate (vol. i, p. 260). Finally, Sacks comments that

> What is at work is more than a matter of narrative technique of discourse organisation although these may be involved. Rather, common-sense knowledge of the world, of the culture and of normative courses of action enter centrally into discriminating those actions or events (vol. ii, p. 306).

In yet another lecture, Sacks argues that the machinery [of description] can clarify where it might not be proper to say certain things about another person; what one can do is to propose membership in some category where that category stands as the adequate basis for inferring those certain other things. Drawing on the above transcript, Sacks comments that 'while it might not be proper to say that the client is troubled by possible homosexual tendencies, he finds a way to invoke a subset of occupational categories (hairstylist) which constitutes an *adequate* basis for inferring homosexuality' (i, p. 47). Sacks himself here draws on common-sense knowledge, the inferred homosexual tendencies of the client is only inferred via the occupational category 'hairstylist' because of a gendered division of labour in the structural organisation of society. More of the transcript would be required to ascertain if the therapist analysed the category (hairstylist) as a 'sexual' category. The gender of the speaker is thus crucial to determining what is being 'hinted at' in this talk. This has direct relevance for my analysis. Appearance, place and time as membership and activity formulations are so only by virtue of the gender of the subject of the descriptions, that is women.

   Atkinson (1982), reviewing Sacks' work on description, refers to how it overcomes critical issues in the problem of how categorisations are accomplished. He states that interactionists' response to this resided in the result of some

... vaguely defined process of negotiation which was always won by the most powerful person or group involved. The breakthrough of the ethnomethodologists, then, was to take the problem of how member's categorisations are accomplished as a central and fundamental problem in studying social order (1982, p. 195).

This sums up the crux of the matter, the machinery which Sacks aimed to produce focuses on the 'how' of production, a 'how' which is seen to include 'norms' embodying common-sense knowledge. However, Sacks 'redeems' his approach over the course of his lectures, pointing to a movement *out of* the ethnomethodological paradigm of consensus when he briefly considers the issue of the *function* of category identifications.

In the *Spring Lectures* (1970) he discusses the witnessed status of stories (dealing with the telling of stories), remarking that there is an important distinction between what you see and what you infer from that seeing. The inference is, of course, culture bound. He states that (in a discussion of the category of a 'hot-rodder'):

Members of categories are taken as representative of their category, what is known about the category is known about 'groups' and the fate of each is bound up with the fate of the other so that one regularly has *systems of social control* built up around these categories which are internally enforced by the members because if a member does something like rape a white woman ... then that thing will be seen as what a member of some applicable category does, not what some named person did ... [C]ertain categories are owned by a group other than those to whom they apply – these are dominant categories (1992, volume 1, lecture 18, emphasis added; 1979).

Sacks' example of this is 'teenager' which is a category used by adults, as against 'hot-rodders' which is used by teenagers themselves who engage in drag car racing. He states that what the dominant categories basically own is how it is that persons perceive reality (vol. i, p. 9). This is suggestive; for example, findings from a study of British and Irish press coverage of the World Whores Congress in 1986 reported the women's demands to be called 'whores', not 'prostitutes'; the former word articulated their voluntarism, while the latter that the women are 'dopes' forced into prostitution, an approach which denied agency (Ryan, 1987).

In another suggestive comment Sacks argues that the teenagers' category (hot rodder) constitutes an attack on the culture, a culture which is stable because everyone sees the world as it is. He says that on the basis of this analysis the problem of social change can be addressed: this would

... involve laying out such things as the sets of categories, how they're used, what's known about any member and beginning to play with the shifts in the rules for application of a category and with shifts in the properties of any category (vol. i, p. 14).

Sacks' approach to the problem of descriptions is primarily dealing with description in talk. On the basis of my introduction to Sacks' work, I began to consider not only the technical resources employed by me, as a reader, upon each occasion of reading, but I also focused upon how categories are produced: 'who' is the prostitute? How was this identification of 'prostitute' recognised in and through my reading?

4.7 Ethnomethodological indifference

Ethnomethodology contains a number of 'policies' outlined by Garfinkel (1967) and Garfinkel and Sacks (1970). These are underlying methodological directives and of particular relevance for the current project is the ethnomethodological policy of indifference. Broadly speaking this holds that the ethnomethodologist simply approaches her data (any data, as Sacks (1984) pointed out, will do), and analyses it *without regard* for an assessment of its correctness, validity, truthfulness and so on. This is, I consider, especially problematic. As Rustin points out, the critics of ethnomethodology consider that the ethno-methodological in-depth focus on everyday practical reasoning was

> ... an irresponsible diversion from sociology's substantive responsibility to understand the larger social world and the human problems to which it gave rise (1993, p. 178).

While I consider that ethnomethodologically informed studies (such as this current one) *can* inform understanding of the 'larger social world', this point has a relevance, especially given Sacks' (1984) suggestion that the 'big issues' (which as Kathy Davis (1988) points out, include asymmetrical gender relations) be left until 'later'.

Jalbert, who is an 'ethnomethodologist of the media' (for want of a better description) has specifically addressed the problem of ethnomethodological indifference. He suggests that if certain critical formulations become part of the explication in analysis, they need not be seen as a departure from analysis. He expresses puzzlement as to the attribution of 'polemic' to an analysis in which critical factors emerge, noting that the ethnomethodological aim of explication of the analyst's resources does not preclude the analyst from trading on her own critical resources for the production of an analysis of meaning (1995, p. 8). The policy of ethnomethodological indifference (that is the abstention of judgements of adequacy, correctness or otherwise of practical actions) is

> ... sometimes held to preclude the kind of methodological device under which whereby adopting a *critical* standpoint towards some phenomenon can enable us to obtain access to some aspect of its organisation, logic or structure not otherwise readily available [is deemed illegitimate] (1995, p. 10, emphasis in original).

The methodological imperatives of ethnomethodology remain unchanged in Jalbert's scheme; as Sacks (1984) argued observation is to form the basis of theorising and this remains central:

> The only issue is, *using the texts and only the texts, the communicated reports and only the reports as data,* how to provide for whatever viewings of such materials [that] can be claimed to [be] available to viewers (1995, p. 11, emphasis added).

Jalbert (rightly, in my view) suggests that it is not so much that 'bias' exists but rather that recipients could have logical grounds for discerning bias within, for example, a newspaper story. Hence, the background knowledges of readers become central but not in the sense of investigating those different background knowledges, rather, the central position (which is worth quoting in full), is that:

> The analyst, who restricts [herself] to that form of analysis which begins and ends with the *text*, which locates the *text* at the center of [her] analytical attention, is *never* interested in criticising producers or recipients, their background commitments or organisational affiliations, [she] is interested only in portraying as faithfully as possible the intelligibility structures and devices inhering in the text as well as the background commitments which interact with any such structure or devices so as to generate a given possible understanding and assessment. [Hence], [a]ssessments can be critical but they need to be grounded in the possibilities made available by the analysis of the text (1995, p. 12, emphasis in original).

These statements are of crucial relevance to the current project – the aim is to 'interrogate' the text, to find, not (as in the content analysis) the number of times that, for example, a particular category is present, but, as will be demonstrated in the following chapters, to show *how* such a category is used, to ask what is at work in the journalistic selection of categories.

At this point I depart from Jalbert, but taking with me his comments about grounding critical inference in the analysis of empirical materials. The point is that the analyst must refrain from attempting to assess whether one or other category is, by some standards, reasonable to invoke (1995, p. 17) before describing how that category selection works, that is the procedural basis of the selection. Further, as Anderson and Sharrock argue, the analyst is precluded from stipulating a *definitive* content to any given reading or viewing for any given text (cf. 1979, p. 367).

4.8 The Goffman additive

As will become clear in the analysis of the data, Erving Goffman's work provided me with observations which I could use in the consideration of what was 'going on' in the stories of prostitution. Goffman's work can be seen as one step on from the ethnomethodological preoccupation with production of social life; as Sacks remarks in respect of incongruity, Goffman does indeed refer to it but does not detail how it gets done (in Jefferson, 1992). Further, Garfinkel argues that Goffman's work is a-temporal and hence cannot appreciate the ongoing nature of social action:

> ... all of Goffman's analyses either take episodes for illustration, or turn the situations that his scheme analyses into episodic ones (1967, p. 167).

Schegloff (1988) has also criticised Goffman, particularly in respect of his analysis of conversational interaction. This is not of concern here. He complains that Goffman largely ignored the constitution and recognition of courses of action per se. Schegloff also declares that Goffman's work, contrary to popular opinion, is marked by the absence of empirical data, citing Sacks' (1984, p. 25) criticism that although Goffman's 'stuff' seems to work at the time, 'it is not and does not describe, the way people actually conduct themselves' (1988, p. 132).

In contradistinction to these criticisms, Schegloff opens his paper with the following remark:

> How many readers, and hearers, [feel] revealed and exposed, give out embarrassed giggles at the sense of being found out by his accounts? (1988, p. 91).

Schegloff further notes that the ethnomethodological criticism of Goffman's work (particularly that advanced by himself and Sacks, who were Goffman's students) is limited to parts of that work. The ethnomethodologists want to 'build on Goffman's insights in some aspects, although not in others' (ibid.).

I consider that the ethnomethodological work with which I am concerned is eminently compatible with Goffman's approach to the organisation of social life (and vice versa), a view also advanced by Travers (1994). As will be seen, the work on practical reasoning, on the production of a moral order (cf. Sacks, 1972) displays close similarities to Goffman's work. The ethnomethodological work of McHugh (1970) concerning conventionality and theoreticity can also be seen as building upon Goffman's approach (1963). In many ways, a 'genealogy' of ethnomethodological ideas could be traced back to Goffman's observations, subjecting them to more detailed analysis and disassembly.

4.9   Conclusion

The above sections detailing the ethnomethodological approach which formed the basis of my analysis of the data has been, necessarily, an abridged account. As Coulter (1990) notes there are over 14,000 published ethnomethodological works available. I have been concerned to specify the particular features of this research programme which influenced my understanding of both the data themselves and of the analytic procedure which was required. The outline of Sacks' work on description required detail as I consider that synoptic versions (cf. Silverman, 1985; Cuff et al., 1979) do not adequately display how Sacks reached the conclusions that he did, how, precisely, he analysed materials.[8] Goffman's work did not receive detailed consideration as I was not attempting to use his methods (if I could have discerned a precise method in his work, given Goffman's lack of explicit attention to methodological considerations, cf. Drew & Wooton, 1988; Ditton 1980). Rather, I am using Goffman as a 'signposter' (if you like), taking his observations about social life and 'seeing where they will lead' (Sacks, 1984). Before moving to the analysis, I want to conclude with a comment regarding methodology.

Billig argues that when social scientists advocate the use of a methodology, they are presenting rules of procedures about matters such as the collection of data and their analysis is an attempt to standardise the practices of the social sciences. He suggests that scholarship, which is individualistic and hence anti-methodological, is vital to the production of interpretations which, while they may be questioned, lead to new questions and suggest possibilities for answers. Importantly, in respect of the current study, he comments that traditional scholars

> ... do not attempt the impossible task of laying bare all the intellectual experiences which lead up to the ability to make a scholarly judgment (1988, p. 199),

and refers to how, in his work on political culture, the

> ... identification of a common political culture was not achieved by methodological means as much as by the practices of traditional scholarship. Texts had to be sought out and read and half-hinted allusions had to be noticed and then interpreted (1988, p. 203).

Billig's approach resonated with my experience of analysis; the existing approaches to the analysis of discourse were not applied successfully (or indeed satisfactorily applied in the initial stages of this research endeavour, given my undoubted inexperience).

The most crucial juncture in the research process was when I realised the relevance of Berger and Luckmann's (1966) comments. This realisation brought with it the (appreciation of the) necessity of abandoning methods of formal discourse analysis. They were simply not of use for my purposes. The resulting method which was applied to the data was a hybrid which had its origins in the initial work I had carried out but also drew selectively upon ethnomethodological approaches in order to 'ground' the analysis. In this sense, my work falls into the 'scholarship' category to which Billig (1988) refers. Given that some of the core arguments levelled by ethnomethodology against mainstream sociology have been adopted and currently are a 'common-sense' of qualitative sociology, the work cannot be described as purely ethnomethodological.[9] It is recognisable as ethnomethodological in its (my) aim to avoid reading context into the data until the features of that data have been fully explored, hence, the delay until Chapter Eight in referring to the contextual web.

Notes

1   Recounting the 'messiness' of the research process, the cul de sacs and so on encountered is a contemporary feature of qualitative research reports (cf. Davis, 1988; Marshall & Rossman, 1995). Such accounts fall into the confessional mode of ethnography as described by van Maanen (1988).

2 Harris stated that the aim of his method was to obtain a structural picture of the text (1952b, p. 475), however Coulthard (1977), noting Harris' comment that analysis should be judged according to how interesting the results are, comments that we can take it that, as Harris' method has not been used since the 1950s, they do not yield findings of interest. While I would now agree with this, Harris' approach seemed relevant at the time of the initial analysis.

3 Pecheux's work is similar to Harris, he aims to discover the traces of the underlying structures of the texts, without using any knowledge of the meaning of its morphemes, free of any subjective addition.

4 Another difficulty presented to any reviewer is the presentation of ethnomethodological work in a succinct way. This arises because, given the empirical thrust of the approach, specifically the way explications tend to relate so closely to the data used, it is difficult to summarise work without also reproducing relevant transcribed extracts (cf. Atkinson, 1990).

5 Rustin notes the convergence between Foucault and the ethnomethodologists; the position that discourse is the constituting element of social life parallels ethnomethodology's focus upon linguistic routines and accounting procedures as the elements of social action. Both are concerned with how forms of social classification construct the social being rather than merely reflect or represent it (cf. 1993, p. 191). This comment accounts for what may be perceived as the 'Foucauldian tint' to this study.

6 McHoul (1982) draws upon ethnomethodological conversation analysis in his work. I also attempted to apply conversation analytic techniques to the data (with modifications) and the results relate to the function of headlines, leads and the like. Space constraints do not permit a discussion of this work.

7 See Schenkein (1979) for an ethnomethodological analysis of newspaper reports.

8 The publication of Sacks' lectures (Jefferson, 1992) has been crucial in this regard. These lectures display fully the brilliance of Sacks' thinking and I reiterate Silverman's (1993) curiosity in wondering how Sacks might have proceeded had he not died in 1975.

9 My instrumental use of ethnomethodology would be, as noted, criticised by ethnomethodological 'purists'. ten Have (1986) attacked Torode for this. Garfinkel, discussing the origins of ethno-methodology, noted that ethnomethodology constituted a

'shibboleth' of a range of different studies (in Turner, 1974, p. 18). I follow Rustin (1993) in arguing that ethnomethodology offers valuable insights, insights which are 'lost' by some ethnomethodologists' refusal to consider the wider application of their work.

5 Identifying 'the prostitute': Information signs

5.1 Introduction

The various discourses in which prostitution has been or is currently conceptualised have been discussed in Chapter Two. Assumptions about prostitution and those who engage in it reflect notions about female and male sexuality, different notions about the desirability and function of prostitution and different understandings as to the causes of the persistence of prostitution. A commonality shared by the different discourses is the problems encountered in attempting to define prostitution (see Appendix I), and, as a concomitant, and more relevant to current purposes, defining who is 'a prostitute'.

My initial approach to the data used in this study was to attempt to establish what were the main topics in the British and Irish press stories. The 'anatomy' of the corpus is descriptively outlined, by way of content analysis, in Chapter Three. This procedure enabled me to ascertain the core news topic categories; violence, form of prostitution (e.g., street, brothel, etc.), disease/public health; illicit drug use, police activities and legal issues. Also coded were categories relating to the definition of prostitution given, the reasons for entry into prostitution and the terms used in referring to women in prostitution. The (quantitative) content analytic procedure provides a superficial picture of the corpus of data, indicating key topics across the stories. However, the superficiality of findings (including the issues raised by coding procedures) means that as an approach it is incomplete. That said, content analysis is recognised as a viable component within a wider qualitative research design, as providing an initial starting point for more detailed qualitative analysis.

While I found the results of the content analysis procedure useful in terms of providing an overall snap-shot of the data, I was still left, following this exercise, with an intuitive feeling that something else was 'going on' in the 86 stories whose topics were diverse, ranging from coverage of the Jeffrey Archer trial in 1987 to reports dealing with politicians' calls for amendments to the prostitution legislation. Kathy Davis' (1988) account of her initial encounters with her data (taped general practice consultations) resonated with me as I read and reread the press stories. She comments that when she listened to the tapes several times her (unexpected) feeling was that the GPs

> ... seemed unabashedly and unswervingly *nice*! ... My response was mixed. At first I was inclined to reject these tapes as exceptional ... Upon returning to the larger collection of tapes [from which she selected a sample] and listening to them, I discovered that, by and large, they all shared this same quality of niceness (1988, p. 48).

Davis comments that her surprise was due to her reading of the feminist literature regarding women's treatment by medical professionals. Returning to the tapes she eventually found what had been there all along, namely, countless examples of, for instance, GPs making moral judgements about women's roles as wives and mothers, not taking their complaints seriously and so on. She remarks that she was not surprised that these instances were in her transcripts, what *was* surprising was that they were not immediately available in her material. She nearly missed them:

> Ultimately, it was this experience of sensing that *something* was wrong without being able to put my finger on the source of that feeling which caused me to stop dead in my tracks. A kind of conversational déjà vu. I was reminded of the countless, everyday experiences of ... not being taken seriously ... (1988, p.50).

As noted in Chapter One, I approached my materials with the same optimism, an optimism which quickly evaporated, for the stories were *unremarkable*. They were not full of the sensationalist vocabulary of the tabloids.[1] That the data are representative was proved by my checking procedures, described in Chapter Three. I continued to read and re-read the stories and, like Davis, came to a point where I 'stopped dead in my tracks'. This 'event' was brought about not only by my reading of these stories and the examination of the different discourses in which prostitution is variously constructed (which included magazine articles about prostitution) but also by my reading of the feminist literature (that is, feminist discourses) on rape and violence against women generally, and the concept of provocation which is so central in both legal and feminist discourses of sexual violence.

What started to emerge as critical in *my* readings of the 86 stories were the descriptions of the prostitutes, the descriptions of the places identified as places of prostitution and the time at which prostitution occurs.[2] Sacks (1970) has suggested that tellers of stories in conversation must tell the story in the way *anyone* would tell it. While Sacks argues that his points regarding story telling are specifically to do with story telling in conversation, his observation led me to question how the stories were being told, that is, how I was reading these stories as recognisably, adequately and, most crucially, *unequivocally* stories of prostitutes. My self-reflexivity is thus critical to my analysis. To this, a further consideration must be added, that relating to the concept of visualising (that is making something visible to the mind even if it is not visible to the eye). Ericson et al. argue that this is the essence of journalism as a method, noting that it has as its corollary, that rule violation must be visible, a matter of public knowledge (1987, pp. 4, 5). While not arguing that prostitution is deviant behaviour (a claim that would have to be warranted by reference to the press discourses), the issue of visibility started to emerge as critical. Morgan and Scott have noted that the identity of the fop or dandy is 'impossible to imagine without seeing it in physical, bodily terms' (1993, p. 17). How then is the identity of 'the prostitute' produced?

As noted in Chapter Four, I turned to ethnomethodology in my attempt to overcome the difficulties I was having, and Harvey Sacks' work on the production and hearing of descriptions of events and persons provided an analytic approach. In addition, an introduction to Erving Goffman's (1959, 1963) work on impression management, on the ways in which social interaction is organised by reference to the information participants have about each other, provided me with another interpretative frame with which to focus in on the descriptions of prostitutes in the data.

The steps taken in the analysis of the materials can be summarised in terms of the following: I firstly 'transcribed' all stories, taking the sentence as my unit of analysis. Some stories were comprised of two sentences, others of over 100 sentences. The aim in doing this was to identify where in the news story the descriptions of 'prostitutes', their activities and place and time of those activities (of display of prostitution) were located. This 'transcription' also enabled me to identify devices such as back-referencing. Secondly, I searched the 'transcripts' for descriptions and attempted to employ what Barthes (in Coward & Ellis, 1977) has called 'slow motion reading' in an attempt to explicate what

Garfinkel termed the 'ineffable' parts of a text – 'prostitute' as a category identification was sometimes missing from the descriptions so the question of common-sense knowledge I brought to the text was raised. Thirdly, I extracted the descriptions and ordered them according to the following criteria:

1 physical descriptions and descriptors (e.g., hair colour, height, make-up, demeanour);

2 clothing descriptions and descriptors (e.g., dress, 'skimpy');

3 place descriptions and descriptors (e.g., Canal, 'seedy');

4 time descriptions (e.g., day, night).

These three steps were initial ways of organising the data. The analysis of the 'machinery of description' involves interpretation. Interpretation is not a distinct stage following the analysis, despite Thompson's (1990) argument to this effect, as my preliminary analysis demonstrated: the focus of analytic concern emerged from my reading and making sense of the stories as stories of prostitution. In addition, I was concerned to explicate what was meant by Peter Sutcliffe's statement à propos of a woman he murdered, that he 'knew she was a prostitute'. How could he know?

5.2 Formulating categories: Physical appearance

In this section I consider the physical appearances of 'prostitutes'. An *Irish Times* story about the background research for a book on prostitution tells of the initial problems the researcher encountered:

S26 … Ms Taylor had a problem.

S27 How was she to start researching the book?

S28 She didn't know any prostitutes.

S29 Should she go to a red-light district?

S30 *How do you know whether a woman is a prostitute or just someone waiting for a friend?* (PROSTITUTES AND THE LIVES THEY LEAD, *Irish Times*, 11.3.91, emphasis added).

Mary Cummins, reviewing a book about prostitution in Dublin, comments that 'I was desperately curious to see what they looked like' (*Irish Times*, 30.3.95). What 'they' 'look like' has been a concern articulated not only in

128

journalistic accounts.[3] It has been a feature of medical discourse and occurs in the popular feminist discourses of prostitution.

The identification of 'the prostitute' by reference to physical appearance in the medical discourses was seen in Acton's remarks (cf. Chapter Two). Robert's cites a physician's assessment (Lipert, 1848):

> By the daily practice of their profession for many years, [prostitutes'] eyes acquire a piercing, rolling expression; they are somewhat unduly prominent in consequence of the continued tension of the ocular muscles, since the eyes are principally employed to spy out and attract clients. In many, the organs of mastication are strongly developed; the mouth, in continuous activity, either in eating or in kissing, is conspicuous ... The forehead is often flat; the occipital region is at times extremely prominent ... The rough voice is the physiological characteristic of the women who has lost her proper functions – those of the mother (cited in Roberts, 1993, p. 228).

June Levine, discussing Lyn Madden (a prostitute), is concerned to show that she is still 'womanly' and does not look different. She writes that

> Lyn never matched the stereotype of the whore. By day, Lyn always fulfilled those aspects of a woman's role which are most acceptable; shopping ... looking nice ... Her hair was black, her eyes blue with long lashes and well shaped brows. Her high cheekbones were accentuated by the palest skin. Her mouth was full and she never wore lipstick ... (1987, pp. 7-8).

These passages raise the question, what is the stereotype of the 'whore'? Lynn's un-whore-like-ness is constructed on the basis of physical features, suggesting that from (women's) physical appearance, category membership can be formulated.

Lynda Nead (1988) has suggested that in the 19th century the construction of the stereotype of the prostitute was centred on the physical appearance of women. This was related to a notion articulated across medical, legal and popular discourses that an individual's physical appearance reflected inner moral turpitude. Walkowitz (1980, p.37) has commented that British writers in the 19th century focused particularly upon the remarks of Parent-Duchatelet who conducted a survey of Parisian prostitutes in the 1930s, emphasising the prostitute's physical deterioration. This theme of physical deterioration as a 'sign' of moral downfall was a critical element in the dominant narrative of prostitution. The notion that moral deviance was visible and available to onlookers' perception via physical appearance was also articulated in the work of the early criminologists, such as Lombrosso and Fererro and was applied not only to prostitutes but also to homosexuals (cf. Smart, 1986, Marshall, 1990). What these discourses also, as a concomitant, articulated was an assumption that the prostitute was *immediately available* for categorisation. Twentieth century deviance theorists also drew upon the notion that 'prostitutes' display physical features. Lemert (cited in Lauer, 1986, p.83) argued that 'prostitutes age more quickly than other people' and Lauer considers it 'unlikely that the physical and psychological strains they are subjected to would fail to leave their marks' (ibid.). Hence, correlation between physical and moral states, a feature of the discourses on prostitution in the 19th century has persisted into this century. The concern with physical attributes and appearance is also evident in the newspaper stories on prostitution although its reliability may not hold.

S9   My friend and I dragged ourselves into our clothes and went to see what was happening.

S10   A *dark complexioned girl and a blonde* opened the door.

S11   One look told me all I needed to know: working girls. My friend disliked my instinctive assessment – which turned out to be correct – that they were hookers (THE GIRLS NEXT DOOR ARE BONKERS, *Independent*, 10.9.91).

Her assessment procedure 'one look' (S11) is partially based in the physical attributes of the two women, but it was also an 'instinctive' categorisation, suggesting that 'something' alerted her to their 'hooker' status. Use of descriptions of skin colour are not adequate descriptions which can warrant the category 'prostitute'.

S1   Dave Foster, aged 34, wearing a dark suit, white shirt and red tie, gave £80 to a clip girl in cash.

S2   She did not come back ...

S14   He was walking around asking other girls if they had seen a tall black girl ... (HOTEL BOOKING SCAM LEAVES FRUSTRATED PUNTER STRANDED, *Guardian*, 9.7.90).

The futility of his search is evident.

The narrative of physical deterioration and of accelerated ageing referred to above is not a strong feature of the stories, although references to age are common.

'You become old very quickly. Physically and in every way' (THE RENT BOY DAVID, *Guardian*, 5.11.88).

The prostitute was a dark haired mother of three called Debra Murphree or Debra Hedge. She is tattooed and looks worn, much older than her 28 years. (GREAT BALLS OF FIRE, *Observer*, 28.2.88).

One of the stories (a 'biographical' story) about a prostitute reverses the 'accelerated ageing' evident in 'prostitutes':

S1   Dolores French will be 38 this October but she doesn't tell that to her clients on the phone because she knows she doesn't look it and it would not be fair to give them the wrong impression. (WHEN PROSTITUTION IS JUST ANOTHER JOB, *Irish Times*, 17.4.89).

However, this reversal occurs as part of a wider reversal:

S17   She is at pains to say that she wasn't forced onto the streets ...

S108 Everyone wanted to see the woman who decided that Hooking Is Real Employment and founded HIRE, the first union for prostitutes; the prostitute who instead of getting murdered, diseased or despairing, got a respectable husband, a great deal of money and the thing she set out to get (ibid.).

S108 sets up the reversal of the 'usual' career of prostitutes: murder, disease or despair – and looking older than their 'real' age.

And a police officer's observations also articulates this:

S35   Brian said of his patrol area, 'This is the bottom end, the sordid end of the market ...'

S36   Trade is brisk.

S38   And at £10 a time minimum, the 'Toms' easily earn £100 a night.

S40   But it's a lifestyle that takes its toll.

S41   'I've seen them go from girls to middle-aged women in a matter of five years,' says Brian (WAR ON VICE GIRLS, *South London Press*, 6.3.87).

Here, age is linked to place via the hierarchy of prostitution (bottom-end being the area of the police patrol). This linkage between age and place is noteworthy:

S55   If you are young and attractive you will charge as high as you can get, but working below the rate is not tolerated.

S56   A woman in her teens or early twenties can earn up to £250 a night.

S68   If someone says I'm too dear, I say, 'Get over the quays – there's a sale on there,' says Sharon who's been working the canal for the past ten years.

S69   The women who work the quays are older, more haggard looking.

S70   Some have drink problems, others are homeless …

S74   They use the dark, derelict and run down lanes in the area (TWILIGHT WORLD OF PROSTITUTION, *Irish Times*, 30.1.89).

'Older', 'haggard', 'derelict' and 'run down', age and place formulations here are read as 'fitting together'. Person formulations and place formulations work in two directions: to provide for the adequate description of 'type of person' with 'type of place' and vice versa. Goffman, discussing presentational strategies in interaction, commented that 'ageing prostitutes' in 19th century London restricted their place of work to dark parks in order that 'their faces would not weaken their audience appeal' (1959, p.216).[4] In another story[5] about HIV infected prostitutes, the journalist comments that

S18   The prostitute with whom I spoke …

S19   But the blonde, 29 year old, later admitted that AIDS was rampant among Dublin's ladies of the night.

S24   She is also very beautiful *even* if she looks about eight years older than she is (*Sunday World*, 22.2.87).

Here, we see Sack's anti-modifier device ('even if') operating to distinguish between 'beautiful' and 'looking eight years older'. While this description of the prostitute articulates the 'physical deterioration' discourse, it can also be read as part of a wider AIDS commentary (Watney, 1987). One of the 'signs' of AIDS is that the individual with AIDS 'looks older', the diseases associated with the syndrome include wasting and physical deterioration. In this story the prostitute's 'arms are pock-marked with years of mainlining the lethal drug' (heroin). The notion that women who are HIV antibody positive are also prostitutes is a common-sense one (at least in the late 1980s, cf. Henderson, 1990).

Physical appearance then may be reliable in pointing to HIV status of the individual and from that a membership categorisation of 'prostitute' may be made; this is 'co-categorisation' in Farraday's (in Plummer, 1981) terms.[6] In an article about prostitution in central London, AIDS is not a distinct topic but a reference to AIDS facilitates interpretation of the subsequent text:

S55   Since AIDS a lot of them like French (oral sex) or hand relief ...

S69   Less understandable, he [a police officer] says is why anyone would pay for sex with Dolores, another woman cautioned later that evening for soliciting outside a 'crack house' in Inverness Terrace, Paddington.

S70   She has cut her wrist by accident and is wearing a bandage round it which is dripping with blood.

S71   Skeletal with illness, she spews out a torrent of abuse as the van draws up ...

S78   The latter area [Paddington] is the worst.

S79   The girls are often on drugs and poor.

S80   They are not professionals (Curbing crawlers on the red-light night shift, *Guardian*, 9.7.90).

The link between AIDS, blood, and 'skeletal with illness' is one possible reading a reader may make. In addition, S78, S79, S80 link back to the earlier 'AIDS', 'blood' and 'skeletal with illness' references. Other news stories have identified the 'source' of HIV as 'unprofessional' or 'amateur' prostitutes who are drug dependent (*Sunday World*, 22.2.87; *Irish Times*, 30.1.89).

Physical differences, rather than physical deterioration, as 'marks' signifying occupational category or status category, are not a feature of the press discourses. In only one story (ARCHER PAID – PROSTITUTE, *Irish Times*, 11.7.87) is a physical feature of the body of the prostitute included. Monica Coghlan, testifying at Jeffrey Archer's libel case, describes their sexual encounter:

S10   Then he got undressed.

S11   He commented on how lovely I was.

S12   He was quite taken aback by my nipples.

Coghlan's body elicits surprise from her client, her body is 'extraordinary'.

In her analysis of 19th century paintings of 'wayward women', Nead (1984, 1988) considers how a particular creature, the rat, was used to symbolise the moral corruption of the prostitute and was one of the key signs of the prostitute's degraded state and further to symbolise the spread of prostitution (rats can 'pop up' out of drains anywhere). This 'rat' symbolism was not explicitly present in the 86 stories. In a magazine story, the 'rat' imagery reverberates in the following passage:

Against a brick wall a mini-skirted girl lolls in the gloom. Chief Inspector Fisher pulls in and opens the passenger window ... 'If you're here again in two minutes, you'll get lifted,' he tells her. She looks relieved. 'Awright,' she mutters and *scuttles smartly away into the night*, her high-heels tap-tapping (JUST WORKING GIRLS, *Plus*, June 1991).

The sounds of her heels reminds the reader (me at least) of the sound of rats scratching, frenetically. In a local newspaper (*South London Press*), a police officer's identification of women as 'Slug, Rat Face and Minnie the Mouse' is explained:

'So I just take one look at them and call them the first thing that comes into my head.'

Slug and Lentil Burger? Now there's a thought!.

'Slug is a slow, fat and disgusting woman from Liverpool,' says Brian.

And Lentil Burger?

'Well, she looks and talks like hippy Neil from the Young Ones,' he said (WAR ON VICE GIRLS, 6.3.87).

A slug is defined as 'anything slow moving' (Chambers). The term activates in the same way as 'rat' images of dirt (slugs are slimy creatures) and represents a tenuous (given that there are only two instances) link with 19th century discourses.

Physical appearances and attributes include hair colour, weight and height. However, while the descriptions of women operate as referential devices (Maynard, 1984) they cannot be said to categorise a woman as a prostitute. Their relevance is evident in respect of 'ageing', a common-sense notion that women in prostitution are 'marked' by their activities is evident in the stories. The descriptions of physical appearance in these stories need to be contextualised within the wider context of the routine reportage of women's physical appearance as news in the media (Bardsley, 1987; Wolf, 1991).

5.3   Body gestures

Physical appearance provides information which is 'given off' (Goffman, 1959). The individual cannot control its transmission. Physical appearance is one element of personal front (Goffman, 1959, p.34), a front that includes physical attributes (size and looks, racial characteristics) and clothing. Information which is 'given' is controlled by the individual.

One way of 'giving' information is via the use of 'expressive equipment', equipment which includes clothing (discussed below).[7] Hence personal front needs to distinguish between physical appearance/attributes and clothing.

One aspect of personal front is 'bodily gestures'. Henley (1977) in her discussion of body politics notes that women's sexual invitation is commonly assumed to be evident on the basis of external appearance, citing the instance of a court case in Copenhagen in 1975 in which a woman was convicted for soliciting because a policeman testified that he determined her intention from her walk. Bodily gestures are considered important in determining membership of a category: Rock in his study of deviant behaviour comments that the prostitute 'must visibly emphasise the differences between herself and conventional women, citing a London prostitute who speaks of slowing

> down to walking pace ... Then the slacks must be worn with a different air, bold and flaunting. The walk must become a swing, a flirt of the hips, an invitation ... (1973, p. 113).

In 'Where the Action Is' (1967), Goffman reiterates his point that when the individual is in a social situation [s]he is exposed to judgement by the others present and that this involves their assessing him/her in regard to primary capacities and to qualities of character. Goffman is specifically concerned with behaviours which can be employed as a serious invitation to a run-in (p. 252). One such ('truncated') behaviour is the use of style of standing or walking as an open invitation to action to all others present, for example, the 'delinquency strut', a form of walking which communicates an 'authority challenge' to adults present. These remarks are suggestive in the light of the above comments: are there particular body gestures which are described in relation to women formulated as prostitutes in the press stories? Various references to 'standing on the corner' (*Guardian*, 13.7.90), 'standing in the shadow of the city's Anglican cathedral' (*Observer*, 28.2.88), 'waiting in an alleyway' (*Observer*, 14.6.87) are made but there is nothing distinctive about the behaviour, other than mere presence, as I argue in Chapter Six. Andrieu-Sanz & Vasquez-Anton's statement that

> Whenever prostitution is discussed in everyday situations the stereotype of sleazy night-life is evoked, as if prostitutes spent all their time slinking along walls wearing mini-skirts and cloying perfume (1989, p.70),

is born out in a magazine story:

Against a brick wall a mini skirted girl *lolls* in the gloom (*Plus*, June, 1991).

The gestures of prostitutes are then not a feature of descriptions in the British or Irish press. However, the clothing worn is focused upon to a greater extent.

5.4   Sartorial style

The aspect of Sacks' work on membership categorisation I find most suggestive relates to the 'hinting' work that, in particular, category-bound activities perform for the formulation of membership. In this section, I consider the descriptions of clothing in the press stories and I want to focus on the descriptions of clothing to see if they are doing the work of 'hinting' at membership category. One convincing starting point comes from a story about a woman who was denying allegations that she was a prostitute:

S1   When does a sex therapist become a prostitute?

S16   'But I am categorically not a prostitute.'

S18   However, circumstantial evidence concerning Miss Dale's occupation includes the many published photographs of her variously attired in black stockings, leather basque, rubber mac, studded leather choker, sometimes arms akimbo with whip imperiously in hand.

S26   No evidence has been offered that Miss Dale offers sex for money.

S27   Yet this week she has endured the epithets of 'Miss Whiplash', 'the tart in Mr. Lamont's house' and 'busty vice girl' (LAMONT LODGER MAKES HER EXCUSES – AND STAYS, *Sunday Telegraph*, 21.4.91).

S16, Ms Dale's claim, is denied by 'evidence' presented in S18. Importantly, the evidence of being a prostitute is not so much that the photographs exist but that the clothes she is wearing in the photographs are read as those that a prostitute would wear. S26 is not effective in denying the allegations and S27 brings in the other terms common-sensically used to refer to prostitutes and indeed women who are sexually 'available'.

The reading process involved is particularly evident in the following excerpt:

S1   The dark haired girl urges 'Don't call me a prostitute'.

136

S2   She is clad in black fishnets, lime green mini-skirt and leather bomber jacket.

S3   'We like to be called working girls.'

S4   'Prostitute sounds really common doesn't it?' (JUST WORKING GIRLS, *Plus*, June 1991).

In addition to the question raised by the headline; who and what are 'just working girls', S1 raises the question – why should this 'dark haired girl' be called a prostitute? S2 raises a further puzzle, the clothes described are, in common-sense knowledge, the clothes of 'a prostitute'. What would be an adequate reason for not 'calling' her 'a prostitute'? S3 resolves the puzzle and contradiction posed by S1 and S2, by making 'prostitute' substitutable by 'working girls'. Working girl is equivalent to prostitute, and we (the readers) would find that she was a prostitute 'all along'. The 'type of clothes' go with the category 'prostitute' properly, that is, are read as adequate and warranted descriptions. A description of the dark haired girl as a prostitute is warranted by the descriptions of clothes, hence the description works both in a retrospective and prospective way in our making sense of the description (cf. Garfinkel, 1967; McHoul, 1982).

Joan Nestle has commented that:

> Throughout the history of prostitution runs the primacy of dress codes. Prostitutes historically have been identified by their dress and to make sure that the prostitute did not pass into the population of true women, different states have set up regulations throughout the centuries controlling her self-presentation (1988, p.234).

Nickie Robert's history of prostitution contains ample evidence of this statement, for example, in the middle ages:

> Authorities throughout Europe turned their attention to the whore's sartorial niceties. In Leipzig it was decided that she should wear a yellow coat, trimmed with blue; whereas in Vienna the whore should tie a yellow kerchief across her shoulder; in Augsberg she would wear a green sash. Bern and Zurich, meanwhile, decreed red caps; Bergamo, yellow cloaks; Parma, white cloaks; and Milan black cloaks. In Bristol, as in London, striped hoods were to be worn, while officials in Avignon banned furred cloaks, especially of squirrel or lined with fine cloth. Also outlawed were silk and cloth-of-gold bonnets, gold and silver rings, and chaplets of coral, amber, silver of precious stones … Finally the whores of Avignon were ordered to distinguish themselves by wearing a red shoulder-bow as were those of Paris (1993, p. 79).[8]

The desire that 'the prostitute' be readily available for recognition and identification and that the method of ensuring this was via clothing, has a long history. Cyprian (3 AD) decreed that:

A virgin should not only be a virgin but she ought to be known and considered as such ... No-one on seeing a virgin should doubt whether she is one (cited in Corrigan, 1988, pp. 4-5).

He further called for

... chaste and modest virgins [to] shun the attire of the unchaste, the clothing of the immodest, the insignia of brothels, the adornments of harlots ... if a woman looks like a harlot, it is to be taken that she is one (ibid.).

The sentiments expressed by Cyprian are echoed in Goffman's argument that:

Society is organised on the principle that any individual who possesses certain social characteristics has a moral right to expect that others will value and treat him in an appropriate way ... The individual who explicitly signifies that he has certain social characteristics ought in fact to be what he claims he is [exerting] a moral demand on others to treat him as he appears and he also implicitly foregoes all claims to be the things he does not appear to be and hence forgoes treatment that would be appropriate for such individuals (1959, p. 24).

In other words, as Corrigan (1988) has pointed out, Cyprian assumed a correspondence between appearance and reality, while Goffman assumes that uniform methods of interpretation exist. Goffman's work alerts us to the types of interpretation without considering, as the ethno-methodologists do, the ways in which writers (journalists) and readers perform a job of analysis on descriptions.

Taking a story from outside the data set (although within the data collection period) about the conflict situation in Beirut, the following sentences occur mid way through a full page news analysis/commentary story:

Women who knew the good old days wait in *fishnet* and fag ends in dimly, red-lit bars. Side streets smell of raw meat ... (A FAREWELL TO ARMS, *Guardian*, 18.11.89, emphasis added).

While the 'red-lit bars' may serve to concretise the identification of these women as 'prostitutes', I suggest that it is the reference to fishnet (read as fishnet stockings) which activates the identification. The reference to 'raw meat' raises an association (in my mind) with references to 'meat racks' in respect of male prostitution. 'Good old days' raises the association of 'good time girls'. These associations are culturally available to readers, however, as noted, readers do not necessarily make such associations.

Goffman has suggested that incumbency in a role 'tends to be symbolised through status cues of dress permitting those who engage in a situation to know with whom they are dealing' (1961, p. 77). People coming into a social occasion assume a correspondence between dress and social categories. The fitting of a category member to the category can occur over a course of reading. The following excerpt illustrates this:

LYN'S GAME PLAN FOR SAFER SEX

S1   The two sailors were offering the *teenage prostitutes* only £10 each – in Italian lire – when Lyn Matthew stepped in.

S2   'It's twice as much as that, mates, and you have to use these,' she said, waving a box of condoms before their astonished faces.

S3   Protected only by her leather jacket and Liver bird feistiness, Lyn, 34, has taken on one of the most challenging tasks of the anti-AIDS drive: persuading *prostitutes* in Liverpool's red light district to insist on safe sex.

S4   Standing in the shadow of the city's Anglican cathedral at midnight, in an area known to *working girls* as 'The Bock', she is dismissive of kerb crawlers.

S5   'The mushes can wait,' she said, using *working girl* jargon for clients.

S7   Her priority is to get through to the women who are in the front line of danger from AIDS through their many partners and, too often, their addiction to heroin.

S8   One *girl*, almost freezing in a *mini-skirt and strappy shoes*, said: 'Some smack heads will do anything for gear' (*Observer*, 28.2.88, emphasis added).

In S1 the category 'prostitute' is given, S3 reiterates this but in S4 and S5, 'prostitute' is substituted for 'working girl'. In S8 the category 'girl' (which could in Sacks' (1974; in Jefferson, 1992) model be heard/read as 'stage of life') is read as prostitute/working girl, a formulation which is read as 'correct' because of the descriptions of dress which accompany this formulation. S8 can be seen as a person description which involves, as Maynard (1984) points out, a two part construction:

Person description = Reference Form + descriptive item
one girl + miniskirt and strappy shoes.

The sequential placement of a person description is important: 'Placement of an utterance within an ongoing sequence of talk is critical to its recognition as a person description' (Maynard, 1984, p. 121). The reading of 'girl' as a prostitute is realised through its sequential placement, 'girl' back-referencing to 'working girl' and thus to 'prostitute'.

Of course, an alternative reading is that the reader would automatically assume that 'girl' is 'working girl' / 'prostitute' because of the topic of the story – safe sex practices by prostitutes. Goffman's (1959, p. 213) argument that 'dress carries much of the burden of expressing orientation within a situation' begs the question, how much of the burden? That is, how much of the burden of formulating categorisations rests on dress? And is there a collection of items which are unambiguous cues to identity? In a *Sunday Correspondent* feature article (Survival stories, 14.1.90), Alison refers to how she

> ... never had any trouble getting business – I had long hair dyed luminous green and wore my jeans and a Snoopy sweatshirt. I suppose they [clients] like me because I didn't *look like a real prostitute* (emphasis added).

On the other hand, a story in the *Irish Times*, about male prostitution in the AIDS era, contained the following:

S11   Since AIDS, male prostitutes have found it much harder to find business ...

S13   Then Michael had just started 'on the game' and the women around the canal didn't mind the men working the same area as them.

S14   Some of them became good friends.

S15   'It was normal then for the fellas to stand around that same place as the rest of us, many of them would be in drag. They'd *look just like us*,' laughs Colette, a *prostitute* in her mid-thirties. 'They'd wear mini's, high heels and make-up and the client's wouldn't know which was which' (I'm really careful with clients, *Irish Times*, 30.1.89, emphasis added).

Alison's assumption about 'real prostitutes' being recognised via dress (or the physical and clothing aspects of personal front) is of interest: mini-skirts, and high heels (and make-up) are the items which are used in the formulation of category membership, a point made by Colette in the second excerpt.[9] The idea that the prostitute is readily available (at all times) for recognition as a prostitute is raised in a story about Cynthia Payne (an ex-brothel madam):

Cynthia Payne's dress sense has never courted much interest ... Payne's taste in clothes is simple, demure even. 'People always expect me to look like a tart or a madam. They're always disappointed when they see how normal I am' (ALL IN THE BEST POSSIBLE TASTE, *Guardian*, 20.11.89).

The 'uniform' of the prostitute is described in detail in the following excerpts:

Under her sheepskin coat she is wearing the hookers' uniform: tiny mini-skirt, black lace stockings and hurt-me heels (*Plus*, June 1991).

Nightly she would tour the champagne bars in her silver-fox-type fur coat, mini-skirt and stiletto heels (*The Sun*, 6.11.86).

There are times when she makes the world of dressing men up in diapers seem normal, and you have a lot of sympathy for her in Amsterdam, where she went to try out the sitting-in-windows side of prostitution, because she says the cobble stones were very hard on the high heels (WHEN PROSTITUTION IS JUST ANOTHER JOB, *Irish Times*, 17.4.89).

Key cues of 'a prostitute' would seem to turn on 'mini-skirts and high heels, although McLeod has argued in regard to women working in prostitution that

There is nothing distinctive ... about the clothes women working as prostitutes wear, except that they tend to dress smartly and neatly (1982, p. 11).

While the stress on the ordinariness of women in prostitution is a feature of both feminist and practitioner discourses (Roberts, 1993; Silver, 1993), the common-sense assumption of distinctive appearance is central to popular understandings that the prostitute will be visually noticeable[10] and indeed goes against the prostitutes' own accounts of how they manage their sartorial style to 'give' the impression of membership of the category 'prostitute'. Working clothes are to be distinguished from 'non-working clothes':

And when her working day is over and the leather, lycra and lurex are neatly folded away ... (PROSTITUTES AND THE LIVES THEY LIVE, *Irish Times*, 11.3.91).

141

Wilkinson noted in her study of prostitutes in London that the women

> ... change their clothes for work, putting on platformed shoes, which because they have become almost de rigeur for prostitutes, many dislike wearing (1954, p. 81).

Doreen (a woman in her study) commented that 'the great high heeled shoes with ankle straps [are] very common. I hate being seen in them ... [but] you've got to dress for the part or it's not worth doing it' (ibid.). This 'uniform' has, Wilkinson suggests, the effect of 'sanctioning' approach. Nearly forty years later, Bella, refers to her preparations for street prostitution:

> I was young and dressed like a real tart: I have to look like a tart when I'm going on the street [I wore] a bright-red jacket with a little mini-skirt (1993, p.13).

In Jaget's' *Prostitutes: Our Life*, 'C' comments that the wearing of high heels is 'most important' (1980, p. 106). In these accounts, from prostitutes' discourse, an assumption that 'dressing up' for the purposes of street prostitution is evident. That prostitutes are *intentionally* dressing in particular ways in order to signal their 'availability for hire' is a central tenet of these accounts and they stand in contradistinction with McLeod's assessment. The implications of this are further discussed in the next chapter and in Chapter Eight.

However, while dress is described and made relevant by reference to category ('prostitute', 'working girl', 'tart') in the press reports, sociological discourses about the nature of dress have pointed out that dress or appearance may not be the most reliable indicator of a person's category membership. Bauman, discussing segregatory strategies, argues that

> ... with segregation by appearance losing much of its practical value, more importance is acquired by segregation by space (1990, p. 64).

This is echoed in the press, specifically in feature stories about fashion. An *Observer* story (FLESH IS FUN, 14.8.88) referred to how

> ... it seems that there is now a new definition of 'proper dress' ... Short skirts and body conscious clothes ... are not about sexual availability, rather they are about narcissism. The owner is enjoying her own body not offering it. The onlooker too has a different response (or is being forced to shed his old response) and does not see revealing clothes as an invitation. This acceptance has made the short skirt a norm rather than an outrageous garment *worn by only certain types* (emphasis added).

However, the article comments that while 'poseurs wear as little as the prostitutes ... the difference between their dress code is *dangerously fine*' (ibid., emphasis added). Attempts to account for the changing cues of dress form another discourse in which the recognisability of 'the prostitute' is problematised, although residue from the traditional notion that a prostitute can be easily and unproblematically recognised by her dress remains present.

5.5 Conclusion

In this chapter, I have focused upon personal front (Goffman, 1959) which includes physical appearance and attributes and sartorial appearance. The ways in which personal front is employed in category descriptions rely not simply upon a listing of attributes or clothing items. The attributes and clothing items are read within the context of an ongoing story and can derive their relevance and recognition as adequate descriptions on the basis of their sequential location in the story. However, appearances may be deceptive: there is a popular discourse which, like the sociological discourse, problematises appearances: one is not what one may appear to be. This means that other means of identificatory practices must be employed.

Bauman's (1990) argument in effect privileges Goffman's contention that individuals can assume from past experience that only individuals of particular kinds are likely to be found in a given social setting, over his more central argument that

> ... if unacquainted with the individual observers can glean clues from his conduct and appearance which allow them to apply their previous experience with individuals roughly similar to the one before them, or more importantly to apply untested stereotypes to him (1959, p. 13).

In relation to the *reading* of press stories on prostitution in which person and clothes descriptions are present, this means that appearance alone may not be accepted by the reader as adequate descriptions of 'the prostitute'. Something other will be necessary in order that the category 'prostitute' is warranted. That something other is locational analysis on which activities and category membership can be identified as belonging to the category 'prostitute'. Personal front is interpreted via time and place, its elements are indexed in their context of display. In addition, as I will suggest, location or place may be of relevance only if temporal qualifiers are added.[11] It is to the question of location and temporal formulations that the focus of the next chapter is directed.

Notes

1   A *Sun* article (TRAIL OF RAPE AND HORROR) illustrates this point:

S1   Muscleman John 'Rambo' Steed was unmasked yesterday as the M4 monster who blasted to death a vice girl and raped a string of innocent women.

S2   The handsome blue-eyed beast ... (*The Sun*, 6.11.86)

The discourse of femininity in which women are constructed as 'innocent' or 'guilty' [vice girl] is immediately evident. Also evident is a particular discourse of criminality: 'monster', 'beast' which serve to make his crimes 'unmanly', abnormal (see Hollway, 1981).

2   Once 'discovered' these features of the newspaper texts became glaringly 'obvious'. Apposite in this context are Wittgenstein's words:

> The aspects of things that are most important for us are hidden because of their simplicity and familiarity (one is unable to notice something because it is always before one's eyes) ... [We] fail to be struck by what, once seen, is the most striking and most powerful (cited in Pollner, 1987, p. ix).

3   I would suggest that the cultural anxiety about the sameness of prostitutes to non-prostitutes is a central mechanism in the descriptions of appearances. One magazine article (THE WORLD (AND UNDERWORLD) OF THE PROFESSIONAL CALL GIRL, *New Woman*, January, 1988) has as a pre-headline the following: 'They look just like you and me, but their minds and good looks belie a shocking truth: they are call girls. And they could be living next door to perfectly respectable you'. As this chapter will suggest, this acceptance that the 'prostitute' does not look *noticeably* different from others is not a general feature of stories of prostitution.

4   'Prostitutes' are supposed to be 'beautiful' (as in the functionalist scheme outlined by Kingsley Davis, 1937), and physical attributes of 'attractiveness' are frequent: to take an example from a magazine feature story on prostitutes:

> It is a freezing morning at Birmingham New Street station ... The majority are male commuters, with a few wealthy housewives and mothers with kids in tow. *One woman is less easy to categorise. She is tall, and attractive, in her mid-twenties perhaps, with short red hair* ... (THE NINE-TO-FIVE PROSTITUTE, *Marie Claire*, June, 1990, emphasis added).

5 Three stories from the tabloid press were included in the data set, their inclusion does not invalidate my arguments about stories of prostitution in the broadsheet press.

6 In a second tabloid story (THE AIDS TIMEBOMB, *Sunday Mirror*, 13.8.89) the lead paragraph is followed by a description of the 'AIDS timebomb':

> S2   The 24-year old scarecrow blonde says she has slept with 300 men in two months.

> S8   Drawing nervously on yet another cigarette, the under-nourished, unmarried mum says, 'I've known for two years that I've got the AIDS virus ...'

7 This sign equipment can include make-up. deBeauvoir refers to young women who 'imitate prostitutes': 'they use heavy make-up, associate with boys, act coquettishly and provocatively' (1959, p.291). Make-up (or its excessive use) was not mentioned in the stories (apart from a reference to Monica Coghlan, a prostitute (*Irish Times*, 11.7.87) who was involved in a court case).

8 Roberts (1993) argues that sumptuary legislation was expressly targeted at prostitutes, as in the passage cited, however de Marley (1986) has suggested that this was not the case, prostitutes were affected by the legislation only in their capacity as working-class women.

9 In a story about children's views of their nannies (NANNIES: HERE'S WHAT THE CHILDREN THINK, *Independent*, 22.1.95), a girl referred to one of her nannies as being 'kind of a bit of a tart really ... this really young woman with knee-high boots and really heavy make up.' The 'tartiness' of the nanny was warranted as a correct categorisation by virtue of the subsequent description of her personal front.

10 In one unidentified news story (which was therefore excluded from the data set), Pamela Bordes, a House of Commons researcher who was 'exposed' as a call girl, was depicted in a cartoon (in the *News of the World*) as a 'scantily clad prostitute walking the streets' (RIVALS CLASH OVER PAMELA STORY, *Guardian*, 1989/1990). As a reader I can 'imagine' this cartoon – not reproduced in the story – as showing a woman with a short/mini-skirt and high-heels, that is, I read 'scantily' as meaning 'mini-skirt'.

11 Rosie Summers commented that en route to a client, she stopped in a diner: 'in that small town my walk, my short dress ... and my being out of doors so long after dark marked me off as a hooker'

(1988, p. 115). Here the complex interaction between demeanour, dress, place and time in the formulation of 'the prostitute' is especially evident.

6 Zones of prostitution and localised times: Formulating identity by place and time

6.1 Introduction

While Bell (1991) has suggested that time and place constitute the setting of a news event, this holds true for all social life (cf. McHugh, 1968, p. 3).[1] Considering the impact of the televisual and electronic media, Meyrowitz argues that they 'have greatly changed the significance of physical presence in the experience of social events' (1985, p. vii). While his work is concerned with the impact of communications upon interpersonal behaviour, his points are of relevance to the current project in respect of the ways the media have expanded the audiences of performances previously 'contained' with audiences limited to those present. Discussing information accessibility he refers to how, in contemporary society, 'where one is has less and less to do with what one knows' (p. viii). Via the electronic and televisual media

> ... things that were once kept in the 'backstage' area of life, such as sex and drugs were [in the 1960s] being thrust into the public arena (1985, pp. 2-3).

Whilst Meyrowitz is referring to specific media, notably not including the press, I contend that his remarks have relevance to the medium of the press which, it can be suggested, performs a similar function. Mark Connelly's analysis of public discourses on prostitution in the progressive era (including vice commission reports and medical literature on venereal disease) argues that these narratives functioned as 'vicarious "tour guides" to the red-light districts for individuals who would not go there in person' (cited in Walkowitz, 1980, p. 132). The press reports which are concerned with the located (visible) presence of 'prostitutes' also can be seen as 'tour-guides'.[2] They serve to map out places of prostitution, providing an ecology of the city, and identify persons (especially women, but also men) in these locations.

Person categorisation on the basis of personal front is, as suggested in the preceding chapter, problematic, particularly so given the changing 'signs' of dress in contemporary society. Even with these 'shifting signs', dressed bodies are apprehended in context – Goffman's (1959, 1963, 1971) comments about occasions and social situations draws attention to the ways in which performances are bounded in 'regions', that is, in places. He (1963, p. 12) further notes that 'social setting establishes the categories of person likely to be encountered there' (a notion also advanced by Bauman, 1990). Hence, another way of formulating identity is through the formulation of places and times. In this chapter, I want to consider how place and time descriptions are used in categorising women as prostitutes, drawing upon Schegloff's elaboration of Sacks' model of categorisation in this analysis. I have included place and time within one chapter because of their interconnectedness – the identity of a place can change over time, from day to night (cf. Giddens, 1989, p. 110).

I conclude this chapter with a discussion, based upon the ethnomethodological work of Peter Blum and Peter McHugh, of the functions of the descriptions in the press stories. I suggest that their significance lies in the evidential work they perform; that the formulation 'prostitute' is inextricably bound to questions of intent and motive. I also suggest that the descriptions of personal front, location of presence and time of that presence are used in the telling (by journalists) and reception (by readers) of stories of prostitution to warrant the identity of the women categorised as prostitutes as unequivocally 'prostitutes'.

6.2   Spaces of prostitution

In the content analysis in Chapter Three, Tables 3.8 and 3.9 detail the focus of British and Irish press on form of prostitution and 'type' (that is gender/age) of prostitution. As was evident, prostitution is understood as a sex specific offence with 100% of the articles referring to women as compared with only 7% of stories referring to male prostitutes. This is possibly due to the legal understanding at the time of this study of prostitution as a gender-specific offence. The main focus was on street (36/86, 42%) and brothel (28/86, 33%) prostitution. The remaining stories were concerned with clippers, phone sex, and so on. A further content analysis of 'place' (as opposed to form of prostitution) yielded the following:

Table 6.1
Places of prostitution

Place	British	Irish	Total
General area	14	1	15
Brothels/bars/hotels	4	9	13
Street	14	12	26
Not specified	15	12	27

This table is more detailed than Table 3.8 in that the distinction in that table was between form of prostitution rather than actual coverage of where it occurs. As the table indicates, street prostitution is a dominant topic of the British and Irish stories on prostitution. In addition, I considered the location of event in terms of city/country (as stories about prostitution occurred throughout the newspaper, both in the home news and international news sections). The findings from this indicated that newspaper coverage (at least over the five year period that this study was concerned with) was explicitly concerned with prostitution in the capital cities, London and Dublin. Newsworthiness as a criteria for inclusion of reports about prostitution outside these 'epicentres' would appear to be based on murder, child prostitution or other 'unusual events'.[3] Prostitution, it could be inferred on the basis of these findings, is represented as an urban problem. Indeed, Waters (1989) refers to Western notions of prostitution as a town planning problem (cf. Wilson's comments on the city, 1991).

6.2.1 Place formulations

Loosely following Atkinson (1982) who considered headlines of newspaper stories to see whether (medical and sociological) theories of suicide were evident in the headlines, I firstly focused upon the headlines of the data (86 stories) to see if location was a 'macro-topic' (van Dijk, 1988) heralded by the headlines. 16 explicitly mentioned place, reproduced here is a selection for illustrative purposes:

1   VICE: DUTCH EURO MOVE;
2   ONE WOMAN'S ESCAPE FROM THE SAVAGERY OF DUBLIN'S STREETS;
3   EXPOSED: THE REAL WORLD OF DUBLIN'S BRUTAL PIMPS;
4   SOHO GIRLS PONDER NEW OFFENSIVE;
5   WENDY: VICTIM OF LOW LIFE IN A SORDID SQUARE MILE;
6   THE GIRLS NEXT DOOR ARE BONKERS.

These six headlines indicate the variation from Europe, to city (Dublin) to specified area in a city (Soho, in London), to unspecified areas, to home. However, as noted above the lack of reference to place in the headlines belies the concentration on places of prostitution in the stories proper.

Schegloff's work on location formulation is concerned with how places are correctly identified in conversation and, like Sacks' work on membership categorisation procedures, the model upon which the analysis is built involves (verbal) recognition on the part of hearers of a place identification. This is obviously not a feature in reading a news story. However, the model is explicit about the work a hearer does in analysing the use of particular formulations: the reader also has a job of analysis to perform in her reading of newspaper stories in which place descriptions are given.

Schegloff argues that the 'problem' of location formulation is that for any formulation to which reference is made, there is a set of terms, each of which by a correspondence test is a correct way to refer to it. On any occasion of its use, not any member of the set is 'right'. The problem is then how is it that some terms are selected on particular occasions? (1972, p. 81). Place terms can be used to perform non-place formulations, so they can be used to formulate, for example, stage of life (school-age).

Of relevance to the descriptions of places that occur in newspapers are Schegloff's comments about the 'analysis' speakers perform. He proposes that location analysis focuses on the ways in which the selection of a location formulation requires of a speaker (and will exhibit for a hearer) an analysis of his own location and the location of his [or her] co-conversationalist(s).[4] Using an excerpt of data from telephone calls to a US city police department, he notes that for conversational topics, a formulation under which the co-conversationalists are co-present will be rejected. Calls to a police department are assumed to be from within the city where the police department is located. The question 'where are you?' does not then arise. Further, the analysis performed in the course of the selection and hearing of a place name is to determine the competence (of the hearer) on which the speaker must rely if he is to use some locational formulation adequately (p. 94). This means that the speaker must categorise the hearer in her/his selection of place formulations.

One of the features of the newspaper stories is that they will identify general areas, without giving street names as it will be assumed that the bulk of the readers will not be in a position to use information about specific street names, that is London street names will mean nothing to a reader in Lancashire, and Dublin street names will not mean anything

150

to a reader in Kerry. Hence, Schegloff's argument that 'relation to member terms' (e.g., Jane's place) are used in preference to geographical place identification, 'G' formulations (e.g., street address), does not hold in the case of press stories. If the street name *is* given, then location formulation of the place/city will be required: in a story about Monica Coghlan, the place of prostitution is a key issue:

S2   On Thursdays she travelled to the Mayfair area of London seeking clients.

S3   In a good weekend off Curzon Street, she could earn up to £1,500 before returning to Lancashire.

S6   She began her career on the streets of Manchester's Moss Side when she was 18.

S8   After more than 20 vice convictions in Manchester, she joined the hundreds of women commuting to London's lucrative red light districts.

S9   In her heyday, she rented a £600-a-week flat in Mayfair (COGHLAN COMMUTED FROM ROCHDALE TO LONDON, *Irish Times*, 25.7.87).

In S2, the general area of 'Mayfair' is identified as the destination of 'prostitute' Coghlan. S3 provides a more detailed place description: Curzon Street. Readers who do not know Mayfair would be able to guess that Curzon Street 'belongs' in the Mayfair area. The mention of 'Manchester's Moss Side' may constitute a puzzle for readers unfamiliar with its 'poverty' status, but the 'beginning of a career' here along with the vice convictions in S10 might produce a reading of 'street prostitute'. The 'exodus' of women from northern towns to London is a feature of women's magazine stories on prostitution and the reader may here make an association of 'Away Day girls'. The explicit references to street names are unusual, given that the *Irish Times* is an Irish national paper; in a sense, the references to specific streets are redundant for an Irish reader but are explained by the fact that the news report is filed by the Press Association, probably from its London office. Schegloff notes the ways in which the organisational constraint(s) on media discourse is (/are) related to the need of the mass media to formulate the location of the events in terms recognisable to strangers (1972, p. 90). However, despite his argument regarding the preferential use of more general terms if speaking (or writing) to strangers (which is related to the relationship between membership categorisations and the selection and hearing of locational formulations), the data present a somewhat different picture. In the stories specifically concerned with prostitution in a particular area, detailed place formulations are selected.

In a story about police activity in central London, street names are given, perhaps as a strategy to inject 'realism' or indeed, to serve a function of mapping out the area in terms of key prostitution areas. The story also uses place formulations to establish membership categories.

S1   Midnight in Mayfair.

S2   A grey BMW stops in Park Street and an attractive man in his late 30s gets out.

S3   He crosses the road, and rolling up the sleeves of his pink and white stripped shirt, starts to follow a girl in a long jacket and jeans walking past.

S4   He is looking for sex (CURBING CRAWLERS ON RED LIGHT NIGHT-SHIFT, *Guardian*, 9.7.90).

This lead paragraph identifies general area, Mayfair, and a specific place within that area (Park Street). S2 begins an identification of the man as a kerb-crawler, confirmed by S4.

S7   Eventually Charles Barber has had enough.

S8   An inspector with the street offences squad, whose job it is to keep kerb crawlers and prostitutes off the streets of central London, he confronts the man and flicks out his ID.

S9   'Good evening, sir, can I ask you what you're doing in the middle of a red-light district?'

S10   Peter Punter, as he is known in the trade – all names in these reports have been changed, except those of the police – is aghast.

S17   'I didn't know this was a red light area.

S18   It isn't is it?'

S19   'Yes sir, it is, and you are right in the middle of it ...'

S27   'I own a building near here, in Enford Street, and I was worried about my property.'

S32   Like a lot of men stopped on Park Street, he was lying (ibid.).

The exchange between police officer and the man, identified as a 'punter' by virtue of his presence on the street, culminates in the S32. His claim of S27 is not followed up. S32 formulates a type of member 'liar' by reference to place, 'Park Street'.

Later in the story (S82-S88) about the 'worst' area of prostitution in the 'patch' of the street offences squad, another 'punter' is cautioned and leaves the area (S88: Thoroughly humiliated he trembles back to Kent). We are not told where in Kent, it is a general place formulation. As Schegloff suggests

> ... for some names, recognition can be expected of the members of some membership categories. And not only recognition but adequate recognition, i.e., not only can it be expected that they can perform some operations or analyses, but the ones that yield adequate-for-the occasion outcome (1972, p. 91).

The selection of 'Kent' is thus adequate for the current occasion of telling a story about prostitution in Central London.

Of relevance in the above story is the identification of a man as a 'punter' in a particular part of Mayfair and his activity, following a woman. The woman is not immediately identified as a prostitute, rather this 'fact' is made known by the police officer's designation of the area as a red light area in S9. Nowhere is 'prostitute' mentioned, but the woman 'Peter Punter' was following is taken to be a 'prostitute'. Again, it is apposite to point out here the speed of the reading process; membership categorisations are almost instantly made, even if the reader is then going to stop and revise this categorisation (for example, S3 could be read as harassment of a woman).

Schegloff suggests that one type of location formulation is 'course of action' places, i.e., places that are identifiable by what goes on there and are so formulated and gives the example of 'where battle X was fought'. In relation to places in which prostitution occurs, 'red-light area' performs adequate reference work. This type of formulation converges with 'topic or activity analysis'. Different forms of prostitution are identified by reference to different places, for example 'Clipping is the latest form of private enterprise exclusive to Soho' (*Guardian*, 9.7.90). A magazine story about prostitution in London detailed the places of prostitution across London (Soho, South London (Streatham), Mayfair, North London) and identified the 'type' of prostitute to be found in each area; for example in Soho, 'predominantly black, young(ish) tarts', in Mayfair, 'upmarket girls are usually to be found ... [m]any of the girls here are well dressed and educated' (SEX FOR SALE: PROS AND CONS, *Midweek*, 12.4.90). The ecology of cities constructed by reference to 'type of prostitution' and 'type of prostitute' is especially evident in the following excerpt from a story about prostitution in Dublin.

This story indicates a feature of Irish press stories, in contrast with those in the UK broadsheets, namely that when they discuss male and female prostitution explicit references to place and 'type of prostitute' in the capital city are made.

S28   There are well known beats: *for women* around the Pepper
       Cannister Church, the Grand Canal, Fitzwilliam Square,
       Waterloo Road, Burlington Road and the area along the quays,
       around Benburb Street; *for men* around Burgh Quay, Parkgate
       Street and the Wellington Monument in the Phoenix Park.

S32   Prostitution is nothing new to the streets of Dublin.

S39   By the early Thirties much of 'Monto' had disappeared due to
       slum clearances and prostitutes were dispersed to different
       parts of the city.

S40   By 1960 women prostitutes were beginning to use the area along
       the Grand Canal.

S51   One prostitute spoke of what she called the 'happy amateurs'.

S52   These are women who, because they cannot find the money to
       feed their children or buy them shoes, go on the areas to make
       the extra cash they need (*Irish Times*, 30.1.89, emphasis added).

S52 refers back to S28: the areas they 'go on' are predetermined by a pre-
existing ecology of prostitution throughout the city (so they will not be
found at Wellington Monument).

S70   The women who work the quays are older, more haggard
       looking.

S73   Prostitution is less organised here; the women are willing to
       bargain and don't keep their own flats.

S74   They use the dark, derelict and run down lanes in the area.

S81   Some prostitutes work in hotels, particularly when there is an
       All-Ireland or a rugby match on, or even a big business conference.

S84   Rates are much higher here, with up to £100 being charged for
       a night (ibid.).

Different place names are used to identify male and female prostitution,
'rates' of prostitution,[5] and 'sub-classes' of prostitutes (the 'haggard
women' in the quays).[6] Hence, reference to prostitutes on the 'quays' is
heard as the 'bottom end' of the prostitution hierarchy. Schegloff's model
suggests that telling stories of prostitution may involve three orders of
analysis: a location analysis, a membership analysis and a topic analysis,
involving the selection of place, category of member (predominantly
gender-based) and activity. And, of course, as suggested in the previous

chapter, category of member and activity can be 'hinted at' (Sacks, in Jefferson, 1992) by appearance.[7]

Further, the detailed descriptions of prostitution in specific, fixed places suggest Goffman's (1959) argument that the 'setting' tends to stay fixed geographically; that 'those who use a particular setting as part of their performance cannot begin their act until they have brought themselves to the appropriate place and must terminate their performance when they leave it' (p. 33), this is discussed further below.

6.2.2 Inmates of the underworld[8]

As noted in Chapter Four, the preliminary analysis of one datum (LYN'S GROUP IS THE MOST DEPRIVED OF ALL, *Irish Times*, 5.10.87) served as a spring board from a detailed linguistic analysis to a more superficial interpretative approach. In addition, the analysis raised themes which were to become central to subsequent analyses of the data, namely O'Faolain's reference to the 'world' of Lyn Madden. In this analysis, I suggested that prostitution was presented as an activity occurring in an extra-ordinary world. This was established through the setting up of 'our' (the journalists' and readers') world in opposition to the world glimpsed through Levine and Madden's (1987) book:

S22   Home

S23   In the *world of Lyn Madden* is reported (sic) from there aren't any homes, there is housing.

S24   This is *the world* of Valium and take-away curries and clothes bought from shoplifters and phones that are always broken and cries for help that are not answered.

S25   We, the Irish, have created *this world*.

S26   And having created it, by a series of political and social choices, we ignore it.

S27   Maybe there's an occasional glimpse – a cleaning woman who can't come in because both her arms are broken, a knife in a chip-shop, blood in the hallway of a pub.

S28   But on the whole we leave dealing *with that world* to the Gardaí and taxi-drivers and the Legion of Mary, and we leave the alleviation of the suffering in that world to a few, frail organisations and individuals.

S36   But even more important – the prostitutes inhabit a *world of parody*.

S48   She is telling us about *lives in which there is no God*, and not even a trace of goodness or grace.

S49   This *world derives from prostitution*, which, as I write, is flourishing as never before in modern Ireland (emphasis added).

S22 to S28 constitute a distinct discourse within the text, which is resumed as the story proceeds. This is a discourse about the 'extraordinary' reality of prostitution in Ireland. Apposite here is Berger and Luckmann's comment regarding the interpretations of realities of marginal situations as a threat to the taken-for-granted everyday reality and the perception of the latter as a 'daylight' side of human life, with the marginal situations constituting a 'night side' that keeps lurking ominously on the periphery of everyday consciousness (1966, pp. 115-116). The 'worlds' discourse echoes Levine's comments in the preface to the book (*Lyn: A Story of Prostitution*) that 'we have externalised the problem of the existence of women in prostitution in our own lives (1987, p. 13). Other reviews of the book stressed the chaotic, nightmarish nature of this 'world of prostitution': in a summary statement we are told that 'Mary Maher has been reading Lyn Madden's story, published today, about her *nightmare* struggle to break free of the brutal *realities of the game* (ONE WOMAN'S ESCAPE FROM THE SAVAGERY OF DUBLIN'S STREETS, *Irish Times*, 7.10.87).

A further review of the book (EXPOSED: THE REAL WORLD OF DUBLIN'S BRUTAL PIMPS, *Evening Press*, 7.10.87) referred to the 'shocking *nightmare lives of women* who live in fear', to the book as 'redolent with blue movie fantasies changed to nightmare reality'. What emerged as significant is the use of the words 'twilight zone':

S11   Despite months and months of listening to Lyn Madden, the days she spent at Cullen's trial, the personal encounters with the *women who work the twilight zones of Dublin*, the book is for Ms. Levine a political statement (emphasis added).

This conceptualisation of prostitution as an activity carried out in a 'twilight zone' emerged as a central element in the data. A story headlined TWILIGHT WORLD OF PROSTITUTION detailed how

S17   Three times a week, since that night 20 years ago, Joan has worked the Grand Canal.

S18   It's her haunt.

S19   She knows the other women there and the regular clients.

S20   She knows how to survive.

S21   'When we go up there to the canal we change completely.

156

S22   We're playing with danger.

S23   We're entering a twilight zone' (*Irish Times*, 30.1.89).

In stories collected from outside the core data period (1987-1991) there were other instances of this 'transformation' discourse:

> Josephine said she resorted to pain-killers to prepare her for a night's work. 'Then I'm out there. I change completely. I'm a different person' (HOOKER'S RIGHT TO TREATMENT, *Star*, 14.6.94).

> The Star met with two prostitutes ... to get a behind-the-scenes insight into their lives ... 'When I'm out working at night, I'm a totally different person than when I'm at home around me kids' (IT REMAINS A DANGEROUS PROFESSION, *Star*, 17.8.94).

Prostitutes inhabit a twilight zone; in another story from outside of the data set, this 'twilight zone' in which prostitution occurs is present. The story is about the murder of three women, identified by police spokespersons as 'prostitutes' (again with no legal evidence of this status):

> A 30-year-old prostitute ... was last seen on 3 March in the shadows of the service station. Witnesses recall a figure lurking in the twilight area between the bright lights of the petrol station and the green-and-yellow fluorescence of the restaurant block (FEAR OF A 'RIPPER' HAUNTS DETECTIVE, *Independent on Sunday*, 7.8.94).

These additional data suggest that the understanding of prostitution in terms of a 'twilight zone' is not unique to the data collected for this study.

The 'twilight world' as a world characterised by chaos, is in the Irish reports presented as lurking at the margins of (especially)Dublin society. In the UK press reports, this concept was not used, although in the story LYN'S GAME PLAN FOR SAFER SEX, *Observer*, 28.2.88) which is 'about' the work of a safe sex educator who works with prostitutes, Lyn Matthews' work is described as '[travelling] along the *underbelly* of one of Britain's major cities'. This would seem to be another version of the 'twilight zone', along with 'underworld': in an *Irish Times* opinion story about a politician caught by the police with a rent boy (the Emmet Stagg affair) Fintan O'Toole refers to how

> Already, in the drama of the last two days, it is forgotten that the whole matter entered the public domain under the cloak of concern for the misery of young boys selling their bodies on the streets. A real and disturbing insight into the *underbelly* of official Ireland ... (A SAD EPISODE TURNED INTO A VENDETTA, 9.3.94, emphasis added).

Connected with this notion of a 'twilight world' and the 'underbelly' of cities and societies is a conceptualisation of women in prostitution being 'in a life'. Together these present a view of prostitution as outside of the ordinary, everyday, mundane world which 'we', the readers of these stories, inhabit.

A story about THE RENT BOY DAVID quotes David:

> When you're whoring you make the whoring unreal. And your whole life becomes unreal ... The rent boy scene is very much its own society with its own laws, its own rules (*Guardian*, 5.11.88).

The early sociological conceptualisation of 'the prostitutes' world' as a 'counter-society' (Rolph, 1954, p. ix) is articulated in such discourses.

Being 'in the life' is presented as all encompassing. However, when prostitution (or rather the activities associated with prostitution) start to move, amoebic like, into ordinary society this is the cause of concern on the part of ordinary members. In WENDY, VICTIM OF LOW LIFE IN A SORDID SQUARE MILE, these concerns are explicit:

S1 News of a young girl's death in an illegal drinking den spread through Southampton's 'red-light' district within minutes, driving the prostitutes off the streets and sending shudders through the underworld of pimps, drug dealers and shebeen operators ...

S3 It lasted for 24 hours and then the girls began to reappear, operating on street corners in the afternoon between noon and three, when they stopped to pick their children up from school, and back again in the evenings for the businessmen on their way home.

S10 It was a sordid tale, exposing the seedy side of Southampton life, where in one square mile, residents are forced to live alongside shebeens, walk children past prostitutes and turn a blind eye to drug dealers.

S13 It was bad publicity, too, for Southampton City Council and the Nicholstown and District Action Group which, with the help of the police has been cleaning up the area's image.

S16 However, last year there was a resurgence and the council realised that it had to keep up the pressure if Nicholstown was to be kept clean.

S19 The two are inextricably linked, with working girls and active or retired pimps often managing the make-shift bars. where drink prices are often marked up by 50 or 100%.

S21   There are drugs, usually cannabis, and always the potential for violence, found in any place with the volatile mixture of drink, narcotics and people used to living outside the law (*Sunday Telegraph*, 9.12.90).

The 'sordid square mile' is an area where ordinary and extra-ordinary worlds meet – the world of the residents and that of the 'extra-legal' groups of pimps, prostitutes, drug dealers and shebeen operators. (An *Observer* story (10.2.91) also referred to groups 'living precariously outside the law'.) In this scenario, the 'cleaning up' operations have failed and hence the containment of prostitutes, which is one method of the social control of prostitution, has been unsuccessful.

Schur (1980) suggests that geographical and visual containment are particular strategies for the regulation of prostitution. These strategies aim to ensure that public 'display and disturbance are to be kept to a minimum so that avoidance possibility can be maintained' (1980, p. 111). In the 'sordid square mile' the world of the prostitutes is threatening to take over the ordinary world.

This is a common theme in the press stories (e.g., *Irish Independent*, 9.8.90). A fundamental concern relates to visibility in the social and legal regulation of prostitution. The cleaning up of Nicholstown (S13, S16) is a concern about 'image', that is, about what is visible. Cohen, reviewing the literature on crime control planning, notes that (in the US) the city, in the 1950s, became identified with crime ... it was a mnemonic not for order, but for the separate parts of a collective cultural nightmare'. This nightmare included visions of decay of whole blocks of cities, taken over by freaks, derelicts of all sorts, with a vision of a physical landscape devastated by vandalism and the like (1985, p. 213). He notes that this vision of urban decay and chaos has become 'banal' over the past decades. The sordid square mile, where residents and prostitutes live side by side, represents such chaos. Cohen makes reference to two strategies employed in the social control of social space, a clearly critical concern à propos of street prostitution, that of 'vomiting out' and 'swallowing up' (1985, p. 218). The former mode is exclusionary: temporarily or permanently deviants are driven beyond social boundaries or separated into their own designated spaces. The latter relates to integration or inclusion. However, his inclusion of this latter is somewhat specious: as he notes, 'reforms motivated by the inclusionary impulse often end up by being exclusionary. This might happen when the decision about *whom* to include calls for an act of formal classification' (1985, p. 219). This latter mode (of inclusion) was not evident in the data.[9]

The exclusionary mode is far more usual: as 'C' (a prostitute) stated, 'People want us to exist but they don't want us in their line of vision' (in Jaget, 1980). A story in the *Irish Independent* story articulates the exclusionary mode:

S3   There was an undoubted and noticeable increase in the level of prostitution. 'We should not turn a blind eye to the problem.'

S5   Mr O'Dea's remarks came after residents of Pery Square, Limerick set up round-the-clock vigils in an effort to clear the locality of prostitutes, who move in about 6pm and stay until around 1.30am.

S8   'We want the prostitutes to go back to their old pick-up spots on the Dock Road,' said one house-wife. 'We are determined they are not going to stay in this area' (REFORM PROSTITUTION LAW: TD, 9.8.90).

The operation of a 'vomiting out' discourse in which the containment of prostitution activities in one area is the goal is evident in S8. This mode of social control is activated by noticeable presence.

6.2.3 Conclusion

This section has focused upon descriptions of place in the press stories of prostitution. Schegloff's model of place formulations indicated how membership, activity and place work to produce and sustain the topic, namely prostitution. It is difficult to do justice to the variations across the different stories. Allied with place formulations in producing and 'fitting with' a topic are time formulations, and it is to these that I now turn.

6.3   Timed displays of prostitution

Like space, time has been recognised a neglected feature in sociological theory and time-space relations have become an increasingly important topic for sociological analysis (cf. Martins, 1974). Time figures both in the narrative sequence of press discourse (for example, most recent news comes first, so that temporal order is reversed, cf. Golding and Elliot, 1979; van Dijk, 1988; Bell, 1991) and in the reading of stories (cf. Garfinkel, 1967; McHoul, 1982). Time also figures in our experiencing of social life (Bourdieu, 1990; Hassard, 1990). There have been different ways of conceptualising time.[10] Most importantly for my purposes, a distinction between quantitative and qualitative time, astronomical/clock and social times respectively has been proposed by Sorokin and Merton (1937).

The centrality of time as one factor in press understandings of prostitutional activities was one which emerged from my focus on place. The headlines to the stories do not explicitly mention time, there was only one headline in the corpus: CURBING CRAWLERS ON THE RED LIGHT NIGHT-SHIFT, (*Guardian*, 9.7.90). Other headlines did use time reference but in relation to HIV, not time periods:

THE AIDS TIME BOMB, *Sunday Mirror*, 13.8.89.

PROSTITUTE WITH AIDS A 'WALKING TIME BOMB', *Evening Press*, 12.12.87.

The discourse of AIDS draws upon a metaphor of anticipated explosion and these articles were concerned with how many men the women had had sexual contact with. These 'time bomb' headlines are specific to HIV but both include details about place and time of the prostitutes' activities.

Other time-related headlines included BODY OF PROSTITUTE, 15 'KILLED BY PIMP', FOUND EIGHT YEARS LATER, (*Guardian*, 22.1.91). This headline reports events with a temporal gap – that between the killing and the finding of the body. On the basis of an analysis of headlines, time would not appear important. But the stories, varied as their main topics are, are explicitly concerned with time of activities, from the 'scene setting' functions of time references (e.g., S1: Midnight at Mayfair, *Guardian*, 9.7.90) to linkages established in a woman's biography:

S10   Annie took her out that first night.

S17   Three times a week, since that night 20 years ago, Joan has worked the Grand Canal (*Irish Times*, 30.1.89).

A content analysis of time periods (day, night) was carried out to ascertain the main focus of the stories on prostitution, i.e., at what times did the activities of prostitutes occur? Table 6.2 (overleaf) illustrates that night-time activity was the most frequently reported. This concentration of night-time activity reflects common-sense understandings of prostitution, and indeed, legal discourses in which 'prostitute' is equivalent to 'nightwalker'. As this table indicates, press reports on prostitutional activities focus overwhelmingly (when time is mentioned) on night-time activities. The Irish press were nearly twice as likely to refer to night-time than the British press and there is a greater spread of references to other time 'slices' in these (British) stories than in the Irish press. Nearly 50% of the stories made no reference to time. These stories would include, for example, the story of the outcome of a court case:

BROTHEL KEEPER LOSES TAX APPEAL, (*Guardian*, 19.5.90); PROSTITUTES WITH HIV 'SHOULD GET SICK PAY' (*Independent*, 11.6.91); ATTACKS ON BROTHEL POLITICIAN WRONG (*Irish Press*, 25.10.91); WHEN PROSTITUTION IS JUST ANOTHER JOB (*Irish Times*, 17.4.89).

Table 6.2
Time periods of prostitution in the British and Irish press

Time	British	Irish	Total
24 hours	1	0	1
Hourly	0	1	1
Day	2	1	3
Afternoon	3	0	3
Evening	2	0	2
Night	**9**	**17**	**26**
Dawn	1	0	1
Weekend	0	1	0
Not specified	29	15	44

6.3.1 Temporal formulations

Schegloff's (1972) analysis of location analysis was concerned primarily with how place formulations can do non-place formulations (i.e., how a place can be selected and heard as an activity identification). While he does make reference to temporal formulations, this is done only to note that they exhibit similarities to place formulations. These temporal formulations can operate in the same way as 'G' terms and as Rm terms: so, following Schegloff's earlier analysis, in 'T' terms we would be dealing with general times (e.g., 2am, Monday, afternoon, etc.) whereas Rt terms would be dealing with what Sacks (in Jefferson, 1992) termed 'private calendars' (for example, the time our dog died). If, as suggested by Schegloff and illustrated in the preceding section, place formulations can 'produce' membership categories and topic or activity analysis, it can be proposed that temporal formulations do the same work. Hence, in legal discourse (e.g., The Town Police Clauses Act, 1847, s.28 'Every common Prostitute or Nightwalker loitering and importuning Passengers for the Purpose of Prostitution ...'), the category 'nightwalker' uses a time formulation. Similarly, James Joyce in *Ulysses* refers to 'Monto' (Montgomery Street) as Night-town. In the data, time is used to hint at and produce membership categorisation and to formulate activities.

The references to the 'twilight zone' of prostitution relates to a place and to a time; 'twilight' is that 'faint light after sunset and before sunrise' (Chambers). It is a liminal time. Only one of the stories uses this definition literally, and while not referring to 'twilight' refers to 'Dublin's *low-light world*' (*Irish Press*, 16.10.91, emphasis added). As shown above, the press discourses draw upon other discourses, such as the criminological, in their conceptualisation of prostitutes as inhabiting an extra-ordinary world. The extra-ordinary world has no time, it is the one and unchanging 'twilight' zone between sun-down and sun-up.[11]

Giddens, discussing the processes of spatial migration to, and within, cities, states that these have been accompanied by a 'migration' into the time-zones of evening and night (1989: 110). At least four patterns of time-space organisation can be discerned in this migration and these patterns can be identified in respect of places of prostitutional activities.

1. *continuous use* (incessant areas):

S5   The decline of the Reeperbahn has been resoundingly confirmed by the closure of Germany's biggest brothel, the Eros Centre

S6   The entire six-floor building was formerly a hive of activity, from its upstairs bedrooms to the 'contact precinct' on the ground floor, where several hundred prostitutes displayed their wares to wide-eyed potential customers *24 hours a day* (*Guardian*, 3.4.88, emphasis added).

2. *evacuation* (empty at night):

S70 The women who work the quays are older, more haggard looking.

S72 This is the only area in the city where prostitutes *work during the day*.

S74 They *use the dark, derelict and run down lanes* in the area.

S75 *After dark* they stand under the street lights, on the corners along Benburb Street, near Collins Barracks, where the long distance truck drivers park overnight (*Irish Times*, 30.1.89, emphasis added).

(S72 and S74 suggest that it is during the day that they use the 'dark lanes', leaving these after dark.)

3. *invasion* (especially active at night):

S5   Mr O'Dea's remarks came after residents of Pery Square, Limerick, set up round the clock vigils in an effort to clear the locality of *prostitutes, who move in about 6pm and stay until about 1.30am* (*Irish Independent*, 9.8.90, emphasis added).

4. *displacement* (shifting from day to night):

S3   It lasted for 24 hours and then the girls began to reappear, operating on street corners in the *afternoons between noon and three*, when they stopped to pick up their children from school, and back *in the evenings* for the business men on their way home. (*Sunday Telegraph*, 9.12.90, emphasis added).

All four kinds of time-space organisation can be found in the stories of prostitution. However, despite this, night time activity, associated with darkness is the dominant time zone of prostitutional activity. Deviations from night time activities are noticeable:

The other prostitutes who work the same sleazy strip, where rooms are rented more often by the hour than by the night, said he'd picked them up too (GREAT BALLS OF FIRE, *Observer*, 28.2.88).

A *Sunday Tribune* story (MEN LIKELY TO BE CHARGED IN TIPP 'CHILD-SEX' SCANDAL) tells of how

S14   One man in his sixties was up the street every night with a torch to watch them.

S16   He claims the *sex sessions took place after dark* every evening.

S17   Fr Irwin, a part time lecturer at Thurles Seminary, was direct.

S18   He told parishioners that the *nightly sexual activities* in his village should stop (7.2.88, emphasis added).

Sorokin and Merton suggested that 'periods of time acquire specific qualities by virtue of association with the activities peculiar to them' (1991, p. 61). In the press discourses of prostitution, the period of time in which the activity of prostitution occurs is predominantly night-time. Sexual activity, in this case prostitution, is closely bound up with darkness and night-time; as Lynda Nead (1984) has argued, Christian notions of light and darkness are associated with (sexual) purity and (sexual) impurity. Again, Berger and Luckmann's (1966) comment that mundane reality constitutes a daylight side to be contrasted with the extraordinary reality which constitutes a night-side of everyday life is of relevance here. The twilight world is suspended between light-times, it is a faint light and the activities that occur in this world do so under cover of darkness. The time of this world is an unchanging night-time, a 'nightmare' (*Evening Press*, 7.10.87). The night-time status of this world of unending sexual activity is reinforced by an underlying idea that sexual activity is 'properly' a night-time activity. To refer back to the symbolism used in connection with prostitution in Chapter Five, I drew attention to the ways in which, historically, the rat has been used to symbolise prostitution (cf. Nead, 1988). The naming of one of the women (by a police officer) as a 'slug' is connected to the knowledge that slugs, like rats, come out at night. The metaphors associated with prostitution, especially those of darkness, are not confined to press discourses. deBeauvoir refers to how 'marriage is directly correlated with prostitution, which, it has been said, follows humanity from ancient to modern times like a *dark shadow* over the family' (1953, p. 287, emphasis added).

6.3.3 Prostitution time

Goffman refers to fantasy as 'the time away from ordinary life' noting that Georg Simmel's concept of 'adventure time' approximates to this (1967, p. 162). The concept of 'adventure time' has been examined by Mikhail Bakhtin in his essay 'Forms of time and the chronotope of the novel: notes towards a historical poetics' (1981). In this essay Bakhtin asserts the essential connectedness of temporal and spatial relationships that are artistically represented in literature, that is the chronotope. He considers the Greek romance, a genre which had three sub-genres involving methods for fixing time and space in the novels. Suggestively, one of these novels includes 'adventure time'. One of the features of this 'adventure time' is that it lack progression, when the hero and heroine meet at the start of the novel they are at marriageable age, the novel then goes into adventure time in which hero and heroin are separated and faced with different tasks and experiences. The novel concludes with the hero and heroine still at marriageable age (hence the meeting —> marriage plot is not interrupted by the events that occur in between (i.e., the —>): the adventure time is an extratemporal hiatus between two moments of biographical time:

> ... all events in the novel that fill this hiatus are a pure digression from the normal course of life; they are excluded from the kind of real duration in which additions to a normal biography are made ... adventure time lacks any natural everyday cyclicity (1980, pp. 90-91).

Further, the world of the Greek romance is an alien world. However, this world is not made exotic as exoticism presupposes a deliberate opposition of

> ... what is alien to what is one's own, the otherness of what is foreign is emphasised, savoured ... and elaborately depicted against an implied background of one's own ordinary and familiar world (1981, p. 101).

While at this point Bakhtin moves in a direction relevant to the specificities of his own project, I consider that his initial remarks are of relevance to the current study. The world of the prostitute is, like that of adventure time, atemporal, unchanging, its alien nature constitutes its newsworthiness – the fascination with the prostitute and her life has been noted (cf. Leigh in Delacoste and Alexander, 1988). It is a world in which we are audiences, via the newspaper story, the investigative journalists who go to this 'underworld' bring us back 'news' from 'there' (cf. Torode, 1987, for a discussion of the subject positions available in press stories).

6.3.4 Conclusion

The activities of prostitutes are 'episodic' (cf. Goffman, 1971). The press stories, as noted, are not concerned with prostitution per se; but rather with the activities of prostitution, with loitering and soliciting in particular. Only one article, ARCHER PAID – PROSTITUTE (*Irish Times*, 11.7.87) records prostitution (the giving of money for sexual services).[12] Loitering and soliciting are the documentary evidences of prostitution, they are the appearance of the reality of exchange of money for sexual 'services' (cf. Garfinkel, 1967). It is these activities which are the visible performance of prostitution, not the giving of money, nor the activities which ensue or precede this giving). It is loitering and soliciting which are 'read' (by observers) as prostitution. Indeed, this is, as Chapter Two documented, the legal approach to prostitution. Loitering and soliciting are thus activities in a sequence of activities; they are the predictive, and recognisably predictive, **activities of prostitution proper but can be** made to stand for prostitution itself. Loitering and soliciting are thus predictive actions. The temporal sequence involved in prostitution involves loitering —> soliciting —> prostitution. The temporal order of the world of prostitution is one involving repetition: loitering, soliciting and exchange of sexual acts for money. The loitering and soliciting aspects of prostitution are the 'visible' parts of prostitution, they constitute 'evidence' of prostitution (as seen in the press stories) and this 'evidential' dimension is of critical importance in respect of appearance, place and time of performance.

6.4   Evidence of intent: Identifying prostitutes

Appearance (both physical and sartorial), presence in a location, and time of presence are, it has been argued, central features in stories of prostitution. The consistent use of these descriptions by journalists across a range of differing stories suggests that the telling of a story of prostitution (and its hearings or readings) relies upon these devices both in conjunction with the category 'prostitute' and in order to 'hint' at category membership. This indeed has been the ethnomethodological approach to the production of categories and to the selection and hearing of descriptions as 'recognisably correct'.

My initial response to the (analytic) identification of appearance, place and time as what I saw were the constitutive elements of stories of prostitution, was to propose that the stories were articulating rules of appearance, of presence in specific places and of time of that presence; these rules were applicable to all women.   However, stopping the analysis at this point (namely at the preceding section) would have ignored a crucial aspect of the work that such descriptions perform and would have resulted in a superficial analysis. While I was conscious of the fact that the stories are not concerned with prostitution per se (as noted, in only one story is the exchange of money for sexual services documented, *Irish Times*, 11.7.87) but rather with the activities associated with prostitution, i.e., the *pre*-prostitution behaviours, I did not accord much attention to this (after all, I was concerned with the construction of 'the prostitute', not with press reports of sexual behaviours). However, like the initial stages of the research when I had a sense that 'something was going on'(namely the insistent descriptions of appearance, place and time), now, post-analysis, there was 'something *else*' going on in these data. While I picked up on this 'something else', I did not explicitly come to formulate what this was precisely until the later stages of the study.

This 'something else' was that the descriptions of appearance, place and time not only formulate 'prostitute' but, crucially, they are selected to produce, and are heard/read as, evidence of intent to prostitute. These descriptions are critical to the production and hearing of stories (containing the categorisation 'prostitute', and its variants, e.g., working girls) as recognisably and unequivocally 'stories of prostitutes'. This section therefore attempts to move on from the preceding discussion of how categories and activities are produced in stories to the question, why are the devices of appearance, place and time used in stories of prostitution? In so doing, it still remains within the (hybrid) ethnomethodological sphere with its concern with production procedures; asking 'why' relates to the next 'level' of analysis, namely that concerned with the production of motives, of intent and the display of that intent via appearance, place and time.

6.4.1 Pre-prostitution: Visible presence as predictive

The legal approach to prostitution, as outlined in Chapter Two, is explicitly concerned with criminalising the presence of women who intend to engage in prostitution. It is a criminalisation of visibility (Roberts, 1993). It does not concern itself with the act of prostitution (the exchange of money for sexual 'services') but is concerned with loitering or soliciting *for the purposes* of prostitution. This legal discourse on prostitution started to assume prominence: whilst as Chapter Two demonstrates there are a range of issues and topics which are the concern of the different discourses (from the medical to the feminist) and, as demonstrated, these concerns relate to prostitution as institutionalised behaviour, to its centrality in the maintenance and reproduction of asymmetrical gender relations in a system of patriarchy, to its functional effects, to prostitution as behaviour which occurs in all societies throughout history. As is evident, my concern has been to consider how some women get categorised as prostitutes, a focus which has been overlooked in the discussions of prostitutes, whether conceptualised as sexual deviants (the religious/moral discourse), as mentally aberrant (the psychopathological discourse), as enterprising women (a variant of the feminist discourse) or as 'dopes' forced or driven into prostitution (another variant of the feminist discourse).

The legal concern with prostitution is as a problem of visibility, specifically a problem of visibility in public places and as a problem actualised in the presence (loitering) of women in public places. It therefore explicitly divides the 'episode' of prostitution into two clearly defined sub-episodes: loitering and soliciting, which are the public display of prostitution and the act of prostitution (exchanging money for sexual 'services'), which occurs in 'private'.[13] This same separation is present in the newspaper stories indicating that it is the pre-prostitution behaviours which meet the criteria of 'newsworthiness'. I would suggest that this concern with loitering and soliciting rather than with prostitution itself relates to the problems of definition of prostitution; which behaviour is viewed as prostitution has been the subject of much debate (cf.

168

Goldman, 1979; Gossop et al., 1994). I would further suggest that prostitution, the exchange of sexual 'services' for monetary payment, is prostitution by virtue of the activities of loitering and soliciting, activities which are prior to the act of prostitution.

Peter McHugh's (1970) ethnomethodological analysis of deviance gives support to these claims. His analysis focuses upon how people account for social events within their common sense reasoning. Of relevance to the comments above is his suggestion that if a man is found at the bottom of a flight of stairs, the deviance is not being at the bottom of a flight of stairs, rather the deviance resided in some *prior act* of which the man at the bottom of a flight of stairs is an extension (p. 173, emphasis added). He further argues that deviant acts are not identified in terms of their effects (although an act might have effects) but the social processes of deviance, in which members call one another into question, inhabit the identification of acts, whatever their effects.

Acts are identified as deviant by the operation of two assumptions relating to what McHugh terms conventionality and theoreticity, and acts are empty until they are given treatment, namely until conventionality and theoreticity are assessed. Conventionality refers to the judgement taken that alternatives existed or did not exist for the actor; theoreticity relates to judgements in which the actor is deemed to know what s/he was doing or deemed not to know what s/he was doing (in the latter judgement, the actor would be identified as a practical actor). In short, 'conventionality and theoreticity are the processes by which deviance is recognised, responsibility ascribed and labels designated' (1970, p. 170), an idea of deviance which makes it unnecessary to look at the act itself, hence we do not need to look at prostitution but rather at the processes of judgement made vis-à-vis this behaviour. Via the operations of conventionality and theoreticity McHugh aims to describe the production of deviance, an approach which, he suggests, advances on the traditional concern with causes and effects:

> Without its items of production – with only its cause and effects – we will not have identified or described deviance and thus will be left holding a conglomerate of causes and effects of nothing (p. 156).

The causes do not describe the procedures members use in organising themselves as social actors and are extrinsic to the performance of deviant treatment.

An assessment of an act as deviant requires that a charge is made, namely that alternatives existed and further that the actor knew what she was doing; deviance in this scheme is not the simple correspondence between behaviours and labels. Hence, in relation to loitering and soliciting, if assessed as deviant (as they are by the police and courts), assessing whether the woman had alternatives to this behaviour and whether she knew what she was doing are judgements observers would make. Indeed, *Salmond's Jurisprudence* (7th ed.) states that 'in legal understanding an act is an exertion of the will manifested externally. It implies a choice' (cited in Charlston, 1992, p. 11). As regards the availability of alternatives, an important feature of the press stories are the 'reasons for entry' parts of the stories: Monica Coghlan stated that

'This little boy is the main reason why I am a prostitute' (*Irish Times*, 25.7.87);

The women are driven into prostitution by poverty, not always by terrible childhoods (*Irish Times*, 7.10.87);

Lyn Madden, like everyone else streetwalking Fitzwilliam Square or the canal at night, had experienced extreme privation in her early life (*Evening Press*, 7.10.87);

Young girls are being lured onto the streets at night. This is happening because of their dependence on the deadly drug heroin (*Sunday World*, 22.2.87);

Julie ... Last year, her income support was cut off on a technicality. After months of looking for work, she went on the game. Since then, the kerb-crawlers of Streatham have been her one hope of survival in the big city (*Guardian*, 13.7.90).

The stories of prostitution in the British and Irish press are, when the theme arises, all (bar one, WHEN PROSTITUTION IS JUST ANOTHER JOB, *Irish Times*, 17.4.89) dealing with women forced or driven into prostitution.[14] In terms of conventionality, their prostitutional activities could not have been otherwise. However, and of more direct relevance for current purposes, theoreticity (that she knew what she was doing) is assessed. Behaviour which is theoretic is rule guided, that is, observers, in making a judgement, assess whether the actor chooses to do 'badly', i.e., is held to be the agent of her own behaviour:

An actor can be said to have *intended* to do what [she or] he did if [she or] he is held to have behaved in consideration of a rule, and if [her or] his behaviour can also be said to have been conventional ... then so can [she or] he be said to have intended, wanted or meant to do what [she or] he did, i.e., [she or] he can be treated as an agent of [her or] his own behaviour, [her or] his act is a motivated act (McHugh, 1970, pp. 168-169).

In invoking the concept of 'rule' McHugh is, in the ethnomethodological tradition, proposing that we do not see behaviours as rule-governed but rather that rules are invoked in assessing behaviours, that is in assessing their theoreticity and conventionality. Intentions, McHugh suggests, are a central feature in deciding on the character of an act. Acts are not viewed as theoretic or practical in an unchanging world. For example, madness, once viewed as a theoretic choice, is now understood as involuntary.

However, determining the intentions of an actor is somewhat more problematic. My readings of the legal textbooks on mens rea (meaning broadly, guilty mind) led me into a convoluted and confusing maze of differing definitions and case rulings on what constitutes intention; there is no consensus as to what it constitutes, at least in English and Irish law. In legal discourse, intention is theoretic action (that he [or she] meant to do what he [or she] did (Clarkson and Keating, 1992, p. 12)). Smith and Hogan note that numerous offences are defined so as to require proof of 'intention', to cause specified results. Two rulings, that of *Hyam v DPP* (1975) and *A v Maloney* (1985), resulted in the jury being told that it would be left to their good sense to decide whether the accused acted with the necessary intent. While these cases produced two different rulings on what constituted intent I do not have space to detail both outcomes. The *A v Maloney* case produced the current ruling on intent: a court of jury can infer intent when the result is a virtually certain consequence of the act, the actor knows that it is a virtually certain consequence (Smith and Hogan, 1992). Motive is not considered a part of the crime; however it is an element of intent.

Blum and McHugh (1971) consider the social ascription of motive and argue that motives formulate social types of people (like Garfinkel's (1967, p. 106) jurors, attributions of motive require that jurors assess what culturally known types of people drive in what culturally known types of ways), they are a grammar of application. They propose that the provision of a motive is to formulate a situation in such a way as to ascribe a motive to an actor as part of his [or her] common-sense knowledge, a motive to which he[or she] was oriented in producing the action. Thus, to give a motive is not to locate a cause of the action, but is for some observers to assert how a behaviour is socially intelligible by ascribing a socially available actor's orientation (1971, p. 100). Their approach is to say that recognising the act of suicide as an intelligible event of conduct is to assign to that behaviour its identity as social action, in this case, by formulating a motive. Events are formulated as particular types of events by attributions of motive. Atkinson (1982) in his study of the categorisation of sudden deaths as suicide notes that, in order for a coroner to reach a verdict, intent has to be inferred post-mortem, thus coroners must rely on cues which confirm or disconfirm a suicide verdict.

As Atkinson notes, inferring intent is not a simple process. For instance, a note beside a body could disguise murder, and so the note itself must be categorised as 'suicidal':

> Inferential work relating gestures of the situation in which the note is found are required to read 'cannot go on' as 'cannot go on living' (1982, p. 11).

The notes and other items found in proximity to a dead body are made to have a reflexive quality in relation to other cues, so for example, a note beside folded clothes beside a river would point to suicide. His thesis suggests that the mode of death provides investigators with guidance as to what further evidence should be sought, and in many cases provides a preliminary categorisation which is increasingly confirmed. He found that in coroners' work, mode of death on its own is ambiguous and other factors are required to support a verdict (such as the existence of a note). Modes of death vary according to the degree of equivocality they present and of course the task is to make unequivocal that which has been initially presented as equivocal. Of relevance to the remarks made in relation to categorising women as prostitutes is Atkinson's consideration of the location and circumstance of sudden deaths. He comments on how it became difficult to talk exclusively about mode of death without reference to other circumstances surrounding the death, hence assessments of the whole scene (of death) use location in determining mode of death (to formulate an activity). Using location as evidence requires notions about the nature of suicide (a private act). So, if a sudden death occurs in an isolated area to which the person went, then this would be evidence of intent to commit suicide. Atkinson comments that this approach

> ... may imply that it is simply a matter of making inferences about suicidal intent from an analysis of the location and circumstances of death (1982, p. 126).

However, he goes on to suggest that this is not all that is done. Using an example of a woman whose death by drowning was under investigation, he notes that her presence near a canal at all was portrayed as unusual, particularly at the particular time. He comments that the coroner drew on local knowledge that a special as opposed to a routine reason was required to go there on that day; the intention to commit suicide emerged as a 'reasonable' way of accounting for her presence at the canal.

So it's not a matter of inferring suicidal intent on the basis of an analysis of the scene, but that such analyses are also directed towards ruling out other possible ways of making sense of that particular setting (1982, p. 128).

For example, the woman was not sick, so there was no possibility of her falling into the river. Hence by a process used by the coroner (common to the attribution of conventionality and theoreticity, as discussed by McHugh (1970)) in which the categorisations available to her/him render understandable a set of circumstances which would otherwise not be immediately clear. This process thus involves ruling out alternative explanations as incomprehensible.[15]

The works of McHugh (1970), Blum and McHugh (1971) and Atkinson (1982) are all concerned with the imputations of intent. My argument draws upon this work and I want to suggest that physical and sartorial appearance, place of presence and time of presence are all used to produce a recognisably correct 'verdict' of intent to prostitute. As Atkinson notes, local knowledge, that is common-sense knowledge, is invoked about an event. While his analysis is based upon the case of a woman, he does not suggest that one way the local knowledge operated was via an assumption that women do not go to isolated places on their own; the local knowledge invoked relates to the commonly perceived danger to women in such isolated areas.

Atkinson's work is recognised (Rustin, 1993) as an exceptionally brilliant example of the relevance of ethnomethodology to contemporary sociology. As I noted before, I did not come across it until the latter stages of this study. When I did come to it, I became particularly interested in his work in (coroners') courts. Given that one of my starting points for studying how a woman is categorised as a prostitute in the newspaper stories (given the lack of evidence that she has been formally labelled a 'common prostitute' by the courts), a natural extension of this interest would have been to research courtroom procedures. However, this was not possible in the time period remaining. Having reached my conclusion that appearance, place and time are critical background and routine features of the newspaper stories on prostitution, and further that they were used by observers to infer intent (to prostitute) as a way of accounting for the women's appearance and place and time of presence, I wanted to obtain some confirmation of this.

Sacks in 'Notes on Police Assessment of a Moral Character' (1972), which is clearly influenced by Goffman's approach to the analysis of social occasions, aims to describe the methods used by police officers for recognising 'suspicious' persons. Significantly, Sacks is primarily concerned with the police as a specialised occupational groupingwho are charged with inferring from appearances such a probability of criminality warranting the treatment of, for example search and arrest (and, in our case, it would be cautions for loitering). He remarks that the police use an 'incongruity procedure' (in his lectures (in Jefferson, 1992) he illustrates this by reference to an 'unshaven guy driving a flashy car'). The method involves a warrant for questioning appearance, and secondly users of the method cannot give a definitive list of what features will be found to warrant investigation.

A central issue raised by the use of the method is the question of how the proper use of the procedure is to be decided in any particular case? The propriety of inferences constitutes the condition for determining whether the persons are selected as possibly criminal. This warrant is subject to scrutiny in courts of law:

> And whether the inference was proper is decided in the courts by having the policeman state *what it is that aroused his suspicions*; the judge (or jury) then considers whether an *ordinary person* would have been aroused to suspicion on such grounds (1972, p. 284, emphasis added).

The method used is not, as with other procedures in social life, as ethnomethodology has demonstrated, applied indiscriminately; for example, the time of the occurrence is important. What is normal for a place is normal for a place at a time, suspicions are aroused if activities are observed at particular times (and I would add, at particular places in the police officer's 'beat'). In sum, then, the general warrant of the method is not based on the professional status of the police: its general warrant is that *anyone* can see its plausibility, that is, its warrant in particular cases is that the inference made is one which ordinary persons [that is, anybody] would make (p. 288). In my terms, this means that the inference is unequivocal: anyone can see that what happened is what 'really' happened. Sacks reiterates that the warrant of the police officers' observations is decided by a test of reasonableness for an 'ordinary man'. The relevance of these points is that

> ... the policeman is not simply concerned to develop his sensitivity [to occurrences in social scenes]. *He must balance his sensitivity against his ability to verbalise i.e., to present descriptions of how he became aroused* (1972, p. 288, emphasis added).

The police officer then must be able to describe the observable character of a person's activities as the assembly of a crime.

These points are clearly of direct relevance to the current project. Taking Ericson et al.'s (1987) comments regarding the 'watchdog' role of journalists, it can be argued that the journalist, in the same way as the police officer, must be able to describe scenes relevant to stories in such a way as to warrant inferences as to the status of performers; descriptions of appearance, place and time of a woman's presence warrantably infers 'prostitute'. Further, given the course of action sequence of prostitution, in which loitering acts as a documentary evidence device (cf. Garfinkel, 1967), it is the appearance of the reality of prostitution, loitering can stand for prostitution and hence indicates, as in the legal discourse, intent – 'loitering for the purposes of prostitution'. The 'assembly' of the prostitution act involves loitering as the warrant for inferring the occurrence of prostitution.

The references to 'reasonable men', to the 'reasonableness' of inferences is not the preserve of police officers; it occurs throughout social life, in the descriptions of events as 'reasonable' and as 'adequate'. However, police officers' procedures for inferring intent to prostitute are of relevance. In the UK press, there were two stories of journalists' 'safari' journeys into the 'underworld of prostitution'. In WAR ON VICE GIRLS, Robert Galvin accompanies a police patrol in Streatham, London. This patrol took place at night, in the darkness and

> We saw 13 prostitutes and one possible newcomer (*South London Press*, 6.3.87).

Descriptions of physical appearance are used frequently in this story. In another story, Joanna Coles joined the street offences squad in Central London, again at night, and with descriptions of physical and sartorial appearance (CURBING CRAWLERS ON RED LIGHT NIGHT-SHIFT, *Guardian*, 9.7.90). In a magazine story, (*Plus*, June 1991), the identity of a woman as a prostitute is established by a mere reference: a 'mini-skirted girl lolls against a brick wall', this reference establishes the warrant for police directives to move on. Again, this scene takes place at night, and again, appearance is drawn upon.

As noted above, had this aspect of the findings been 'uncovered' by me earlier in the project, I would have focused upon court-room procedures of sentencing women brought before the courts on a charge of loitering with intent to prostitute.[16] Trying to at least attempt to investigate this aspect, I interviewed a prominent Dublin solicitor who is one of the main defenders of women who are identified as prostitutes and summoned to court. She recounted that the Gardaí have to have 'reasonable belief': this 'reasonable belief' is assessed by judges in their sentencing procedures.

Her examples of the 'verbalising abilities' of Gardaí (police) are particularly apposite to the current study. The three main lines of arguments advanced by Gardaí are:

1. that the woman was dressed in black tights, black high heels and mini-skirt;[17]
2. that she was standing in a known place for prostitution; and
3. that this occurred at a particular time of night.

The assembly of the crime of loitering for the purposes of prostitution is made up of these three elements (appearance, place and time). More importantly, it is not just that this is the basis of evidence which is given by Gardaí, but it is, quite crucially, that this 'evidence' is taken as admissible evidence by judges.

Returning to McHugh's (1970) arguments regarding theoreticity, that the actor knew what s/he was doing, the arguments about appearance, in particular, but also place and time of the display of prostitution, presuppose that 'reasonable men (and women)' would recognise the inference as 'recognisably correct'. Further, that if it is recognised as 'reasonable' to assume that particular types of dress, of time and place of appearance can warrantably be used to infer category membership, then it is expected that unless the actor can be shown to be a practical actor (for example, mentally ill) then as an 'ordinary member of society', with ordinary competencies, she or he will know what precisely she or he is doing. As Goffman, in an article which anticipates McHugh's (1970) arguments, points out, the question asked is, 'does the actor have the capacity and training to appreciate the meaning of his offence and if so, does he in fact appreciate its meaning?' (1963, p. 217) He details different scenarios, e.g., the individual whose repertoire of clothing provides dress that is either too formal or informal for the occasion he must attend, thus forcing him 'out of place'. Referring to the individual who does not appreciate the significance of his act for others he speaks of

> … the individual who accidentally and uncharacteristically intrudes upon a situation in which he cannot fit, thereby committing an offence he wishes he had not committed and *would have been fully capable of avoiding had he known in advance what was going to happen* (1963, pp. 218-219, emphasis added).

I consider that this is an important element in the background, tacit knowledge invoked with the notion of 'reasonable (wo)men'. The assuredness of police evidence, of the newspaper descriptions of 'prostitutes' (which, in the court's stead, label a woman a prostitute) rests on the notion that 'everyone knows' who 'the prostitute' is. In this way

176

we have a link back to Peter Sutcliffe's statement that 'I knew she was a prostitute'. We also have a link to other discourse sites, a link that is further developed in Chapter Eight.

6.5   Conclusion

In this chapter I have followed on from Chapter Five looking at the appearance descriptions of women identified as prostitutes in the stories of prostitution to place and time formulations. I have broken the analytic 'flow' in order to insert more detailed interpretative comments regarding the function of such descriptions in terms of the evidence (of a prostitute) work that is performed in and through such descriptions. I have argued that it is in virtue of the common-sense, that is 'what everyone one knows', nature of these descriptions which is of critical importance in respect of the inferences that the descriptions make, inferences as to 'type of member', that is 'prostitute', an occupational category in which gender is omni-relevant. I have further suggested that methods used by occupational specialists for inferring character, are those which are widely available and are used by journalists in the telling of stories of prostitutes, and further, although not mentioned but in the vein of the arguments advanced regarding formulating membership, are read/ heard by readers as 'recognisably correct'. This 'break' is necessary because I now go on to consider the visual discourses of prostitution which accompany written descriptions in the text proper. The 'photographic' dimension further concretises my arguments regarding the centrality of appearance, place and time as evidences of 'intent to prostitute' and the reading process involved produces not only, as Ericson et al. (1987) note, a mental visualisation, but also a 'visual' visualisation of 'the prostitute' and of times and places of prostitution.

Notes

1   Time and place are also of relevance in the analysis of the positions offered by the news text over the course of a reading as Torode (1987) has suggested. The subject positions of 'here' and 'there' (for reader and event/journalist respectively) can be, Torode suggests, analysed in a formal procedure prior to interpretation. While his analysis is suggestive, I would argue that all newspaper stories locate the reader 'here' in the everyday world and the journalist

'there', on safari to the world of prostitution, which is also 'there'. My analysis in this chapter builds on this notion.

2 de Certeau proposed that 'every story is a travel story' (cited in Keith & Pile, 1993, p. 16), a comment which provides the 'gist' of Connelly's remarks.

3 The *Irish Times* carried a story about men in Adana, Turkey, who were seeking tax rebates for their brothel expenses (SEX EXPENSES, 28.1.88). And a further report about a 'prostitution ring' in Tuam, Co. Galway referred to Garda attention following theft from clients (GARDAÍ INVESTIGATE PROSTITUTION REPORT, *Irish Times*, 3.3.88).

4 This approach follows Sacks' arguments that if A categorises B as old then we can look at B to see how we would categorise A, for example, a 13 year-old calling a 25 year-old 'old'.

5 LYN'S GAME PLAN FOR SAFER SEX (*Observer*, 28.2.88) detailed the rates: £15 for sex outdoors and £30 for sex indoors.

6 In a story about prostitution in Birmingham, a police officer stated à propos of the women, 'Not many are on drugs, like other big cities … you don't even have to be that good looking' (*Plus Magazine*, June 1991).

7 See Perkins and Bennett (1985) for a detailed discussion of place (denoting type of prostitution) and clothes worn for the occasion.

8 This heading is taken from Roberts (1993, p. 266).

9 An example of this type of control is evident in a press story about impending legislative reform relating to homosexuality: 'Mr Tunney said he was aware of the fact that homosexuals existed within our society "but I cannot accept, as some of their spokespeople seem to be indicating, that there should be some kind of an alternative society for these people"' (TUNNEY TO FIGHT GAY REFORM MOVE BY GOVT., *Irish Independent*, 14.10.91).

10 Barbara Adam's (1990) work details the different understandings of time across disciplines.

11 This discussion of prostitutes as living in a 'twilight zone' is not unique to stories of prostitution. Simon Watney, in his discussion of AIDS commentary in the media argues that in this commentary, people with AIDS enter a twilight world (1987, p. 93). While he does not elaborate on this, it is suggested by the entire argument of his work that PLWAs are excluded, they are constructed half-dead. Horton (1989) discussing a concept of social death upon receipt of

an HIV diagnosis refers to entering a vampiric state of the undead. These remarks suggest that a twilight zone is removed from ordinary, everyday life.

12 S2 The 36 year old prostitute told a packed courtroom that Mr Archer paid her for sex on the night of September 8th-9th last year.

    S8 They had gone into Room 6A in the hotel where she asked for her 'present', her fee, previously arranged at £50.

    S9 She told the hushed courtroom: 'I told him if he took some time and made it a bit longer it would be another £20.

    S10 He agreed and gave me another £20 note.' (*Irish Times*, 11.7.87).

13 Of course, 'private' is relative but even if sexual activities as part of the prostitution 'contract' (cf. Pateman, 1988) occur on the public streets, in view, laws other than those dealing with prostitution would be invoked, for example, the laws relating to obscenity.

14 An interesting feature of the press stories, and indeed, in popular accounts generally is that a dominant 'reason for entry' into prostitution is for women to feed children. Their deviance is 'lessened': they know that it is wrong but they are more concerned with fulfilling their roles as mothers.

15 Atkinson also discusses the ways in which biography is invoked to 'explain' a sudden death, not any biography but particular sorts of biographical evidence: in the current study, such biographical evidence relevant to the designation 'prostitute' would be poverty and sexual abuse.

16 This would have involved both UK and Irish courts, as since 1981 in Ireland, the use of term 'I knew her to be a common prostitute' was deemed unconstitutional.

17 The solicitor I interviewed recounted her line of questioning in cases in which this was given as 'evidence': 'Are you saying that the women in the Law Courts are prostitutes?' The occupational 'uniform' for female lawyers is 'black skirt, black tights and high heels.'

7 The photographic dimension: Visual images in the press

7.1 Introduction

A common-place about social life is that much of it is carried on in face-to-face interaction. However, as has been noted, the *technologies* of the various media have fundamentally altered modes of communication. All media enable us, to greater or lesser degrees, to experience vicariously action scenes from places far removed from our everyday life and with people not in our social environment. The technologies of print and particularly televisual media enable recipients to 'see' other worlds and peoples (cf. Meyrowitz, 1985). While studies of television and advertising are particularly concerned with visual imagery, those concerned with the discourses of the press are curiously silent on this aspect of the medium. Both the ethnomethodologists and Goffman have considered the role of the visual in everyday life and their approach is drawn upon in this chapter.

The preceding chapters have outlined the ways in which descriptions of behaviours, imputations of intent and evidences thereof are in many crucial ways tied up with the visual – with seeing what is 'really' there. The thesis is that the construction of the prostitute as unequivocally a prostitute relies upon evidence of intent (to prostitute), specifically intent which is evidenced via the descriptions of appearance, place and time. Throughout, the descriptions have been premised upon a 'correct' reading, a mental 'visualisation', (Ericson et al., 1987), of the construction effected, and the invocation of rules to assess the adequacy of such categorisation. Holland, discussing public imagery of childhood suggests that the pictures of childhood found in a range of media are part of a set of interweaving narratives of childhood and argues that

181

We ourselves become joint authors of these stories … *and look to them for guidance on our behaviour and relationships* (1992, p. 11, emphasis added).

This point has been reiterated by Holland, Spence and Watney (1986) in their considerations of photography and sexual politics who argue that photographs position us, providing us with pictures and descriptions of sexuality, definitions and prescriptions. Similarly, my underlying premise is that photographs, like the written stories and media generally, provide *information* about a scene or a subject, information which is structured by the caption and the surrounding text.[1] In addition, as with the reading process, the meaning of the visual text is 'co-authored' by the viewer.

In this chapter I consider the news photographs which accompany stories of prostitution.[2] I specifically focus upon the photographs of scenes of prostitution, the *quotive glimpses* (the terms are Goffman's, 1979, p. 25) of the sequence of actions which are prostitution. These are central to the process of establishing evidence of prostitution as an activity and to the identification of prostitutes; John Tagg (1988) and Hartley (1992) both refer to 'forensics' in relation to photography. It also strengthens my arguments regarding the importance of the legal discourse of prostitution (as outlined in Chapter Two) and its intrusion into or traversing and structuring of popular cultural constructions of prostitution and of the recognition of the prostitute. That discourse is explicitly concerned with the visual presence of a prostitute.

In contradistinction to the attention accorded to visual images on television, in cinema, in advertising, in magazines, newspaper photographs/images are rarely studied as a phenomenon worthy of detailed attention. The justifications, if advanced, are usually variations on a theme. The rationale advanced by one contemporary theorist of press discourse provides an exemplar. Roger Fowler, who, while noting that his work is the result of over a decade of thinking about newspapers and their importance in performing a functional role in the maintenance of inequalities in society, is

> … well aware that … composition and the deployment of photographs, drawings … tables, maps, captions, etc., are of immense significance in newspaper representation, and that these factors interact dynamically with language proper, the words considered as linguistic structure. Newspaper discourse is so complex that concentration on one aspect inevitably leads to neglect of others, if one wants a book of this kind to remain readable – not inordinately long or methodologically over-complex (1991, p. 8).

Fowler's justification, it seems to me, is rather weak. While journalism espouses 'objectivity' as a working practice, it can be argued that photojournalism contributes immensely to this notion. While press news may be seen as more manufactured, involving more production work (though layout, cropping, processing, captioning and the like) than that of television, the photograph captures 'what really happened', 'who was really there'.[3] As Evans comments, the picture editor selects photographs and juxtapositions photographs with written texts, some unrelated, 'the newspaper reader is unaware of the judgements that open and shut his [and her] eyes' (1978, no pagination).

One discourse analyst, Norman Fairclough, has focused, briefly, upon news pictures, suggesting that the visual is increasingly significant in everyday life and noting how

> It is well known ... that a photograph is often *as important* in getting across the 'message' of a report in a newspaper ... [V]ery often visuals and 'verbals' operate in a naturally reinforcing way which makes them difficult to 'disentangle' (1989, p. 28, emphasis added).

In his work however, little space is devoted to a discussion of the role of the visual, other than a brief discussion of a newspaper report and a discussion of Margaret Thatcher (ex-Prime Minister of Britain). I want to briefly consider what he suggests in both instances as I consider that his approach lacks analytic 'bite'.

Taking as an example a press report (HE'LL DO HIS JOB WELL, SAYS MAJOR'S WIFE, Caption: Major Keeble ... will lead the paras into battle, *Daily Mail*, 1.6.82), the photograph is of a man – identified by the caption as Major Keeble. The visual layout, the typography, assists the reader in 'seeing' Keeble as 'the paras' new leader' and the headline 'He'll do his job well, says major's wife' refers to the subject of the photograph and lets the reader know that he is the paras' new leader. Fairclough comments that the choice of photograph is important because 'different images convey different meanings' (1989, pp. 52-3). The news picture is of a man looking out. Fairclough's analysis is as follows:

> I find my attention drawn particularly by the Major's eyes; he is looking straight ahead, looking the reader in the face ... rather appraisingly, with a serious expression mitigated by a hint of a smile at the corners of his mouth (possibly a cynical one). [T]he photograph in its verbal matrix shows me that Major Keeble is all I would expect a leader of an elite military unit to be (ibid.).

Fairclough tells his readers to 'analyse' the photograph in the following way: to consider the caption and ask whether it registers for us what the picture 'says', does it lead us to 'read' the picture in that way? Further, readers (as analysts) are to 'spot' particular techniques for giving particular impressions of people, to single out further examples of the ways in which images and words interact in the press.

He considers the written text in relation to the 'picture' of the wife realised, introducing a notion of the 'good wife', a term not in the text. I consider that an alternative reading is that the 'wife' 'hopes her husband would not have to go into battle again'. The caption to the photograph however tells us that the major 'will lead the paras into battle'. In this way, the newspaper is signalling that other agents will determine future courses of action, not his wife. My point here is to suggest that how the photograph is read needs to be considered in relation to the reading of the other parts of the news story. And, further, that the reader of the press story would be concerned to judge the adequacy of the story with the photograph, whose meaning is realised by the caption, both in terms of identification of the photographed subject and its relevance for the written story.[4]

I have detailed Fairclough's approach because I consider that it highlights the prevailing lack of attention to the visual in the analysis of press discourses. His inclusion of photographs is somewhat perfunctory and is not related to any particular conceptual scheme. In fact, what it demonstrates is a reluctance to think through issues relating to the interaction of written and visual textuality. Fowler's (1991) point (above) about his approach to the analysis of news discourse as linguistic structure raises the pertinent question of integrating analysis of written discourse (of both the article proper and of the caption) and visual discourse (of the photograph) and has, as a concomitant, implications for a consideration of reading strategies.

The inclusion of photographs as elements of a story poses an analytical question regarding the status of a newspaper article plus photograph plus caption. Can this multi-'text' be analysed as a *story* in the same way as I have approached the newspaper texts up until this point? I suggest that it can, that the presentation of a visual image with its tag, the written text of the caption, coheres with (or perhaps contradicts), and interacts with the written story (which can be accorded the status of a 'macro' story). The everyday adage 'every picture tells a story' is problematical in respect of newspaper photographs, often referred to as 'pictures' (as in 'her picture was in the paper', and the journalistic term for photographs is news pictures, cf. picture library, picture editor, etc.): the story read from the photograph is one which is constructed with a simultaneous reading of the headline and perhaps caption as well. It is near impossible to focus immediately upon the photograph to the exclusion of other, surrounding texts. Moreover, I follow Goffman's assertion that our reading of photographs is much like our reading of scenes from everyday life.

7.2 Images: Written and visual

Writing in 1985, Heidensohn argues that the public presentation of deviant women is a crucial aspect in the construction of deviance, expressing surprise that no major work had, by that time, been done on the images of deviant women.[5] Noting that the image of deviant women is as crucial to the process of deviance definition as the societal reaction, she refers to the legal approach to prostitution in which public nuisance 'caused by women plying their trade' is central, but unfortunately stops short at this point, moving in the next sentence to refer to the abundance of work carried out on images of women in advertising. The discussion of the legal discourse within which prostitution is conceptualised, as discussed in Chapter Two, points to the ways in which the prostitute's presence, her visible presence, is criminalised. Heidensohn argues that the 'considerable' (p. 86) stereotyping of women is drawn from a small repertoire, noting previous feminist work à propos of the madonna/whore dichotomy. However while arguing that the witch and the whore image of women, of the image of deviant women as 'especially evil, depraved and monstrous' (p. 93) her commentary refers to *written* not visual images. She argues that while prostitutes are depicted as sexual deviants in the mainstream media (an assertion not demonstrated nor sources referenced), they are producing their own images through their self-publication of newspapers and handouts. However this statement is not backed up and the drawings/logos of the International Committee for Prostitutes Rights draw upon the same public, conventional 'signs' of prostitutes, specifically the high-heeled shoe with all its connotations of sexual fetishism (cf. Fisher, 1987, pp. 322-3). Heidensohn's work does not provide us with any empirical evidence of the visual images of so called deviant women, despite arguments that 'the contaminating sexuality' associated with prostitution tends to 'leak' into the portrayal of other forms of female deviance. Indeed, as noted earlier, comments such as this provided the impetus to my interest in *empirically* investigating how 'the prostitute' is portrayed.

7.3 Description of the data

To reiterate, the systematic data collection for this image study occurred in the period 1987-1991. I continued to collect broadsheet stories beyond that period. Where these reports include accompanying photographs, I use them to emphasise particular points I want to make or, indeed, if necessary, highlight anomalies in the photographs from the 'core' data set.

The core data set for this study comprises 86 stories of prostitution and of prostitutes. In addition a further 64 stories from the Irish broadsheet and tabloid press were collected covering the period 1993-1995. These included 24 photographs and relevant photographs from this corpus are used, particularly in advancing my arguments about the photographs as 'quotations' (Goffman, 1979) of prostitution. Other photographs which were drawn upon came from British and Irish newspaper coverage of the World Whores Congress, October 1986, of which 3 of the nine newspaper reports included a photograph; from the *Sunday Correspondent* (17.12.89) in which a photojournalistic feature story (which included 10 colour photographs of women) of prostitutes in New York was featured. Finally, the magazine (e.g., *Cosmopolitan, New Statesman and Society*) coverage of prostitution also included photographs and these are presented as appropriate. *Hot Press* in March 1986 carried a series of articles on prostitution and the visually arresting image of the prostitute (Appendix III: no. 3) was taken from this magazine.[6] 31 (36%) of the 86 stories in the core data set included photographs. Some stories carried up to three photographs (e.g., GREAT BALLS OF FIRE, *Observer*, 28.2.88). A total of 41 photographs (including two sketches) were present in the data set. The totals per year are presented in Table 7.1 and the distribution of photographs by subject is presented in Table 7.2.

Table 7.1
Distribution of photographs by year and newspaper

	Irish	British	Total
1987	5	3	8
1988	0	6	6
1989	5	9	14
1990	0	5	5
1991	2	6	8
Total	13	28	41

Table 7.2
Subject of photographs by newspaper

	Irish	British	Total
Prostitute (inc. suspected and dead prostitutes)	7	17	24
Client (inc. suspected client)	1	2	3
Pimp	1	0	1
Places	0	3	3
Sketches (drawings)	2	0	2
Other (inc. single cases: photofit, actress, dead woman, researcher, judge, father of call girl, child, other)	2	6	8
Total	13	28	41

As these tables indicate the UK press stories include a great many more photographs than the Irish press and the distribution across the five year period peaked in 1989 (accounting for 34% of the total) but was roughly similar over the other four years. The main subject of the photographs was 'the prostitute' (59%, although as will be seen this subject is both of prostitution and of the prostitute). Other photographs included subjects of the newspaper story, so for example, a story about a rape case included a photograph of a judge.

7.4 Attributions of news photographs

Various feminist scholars who have analysed the imagery of women in public texts have argued that the reason that the images depict women in a devalued way, in a sexually objectified manner, is that the images of women have been made by men (cf. Heidensohn, 1985, p. 94, although cf. van Zoonen for an alternative view). The photographs in the data collection fell into two groups: those with a 'signature', namely the photographer's name or those without credits. Of the 41 photographs (and excluding the two sketches), nine (9) were photographs taken by male photographers, one was an Associated Press wirepicture and the remaining 20 (51%) were not credited, they were 'authorless'. This feature of the photographs does not concern me, other than to note that the absence of female photographers indicates the extent to which photojournalism is a male preserve.

7.5 Approaching the visual data and finding a method of analysis

The argument that media products need to be considered in relation to their socio-historical context, in which organisational practices and technological developments are addressed and in relation to modes of reception has been advanced by Thompson (1990) and discussed in Chapter Three. This same argument has been advanced by those working with visual images (Myers, 1989).

The data were considered firstly for the answers they might provide, via the use of, metaphorically speaking, analytical spectacles made up from the 'lenses' of Barthes, Goffman and Garfinkel, to the question: what is the public image of 'the prostitute'? In particular Goffman's arguments are drawn upon, and I agree with Richard Hoggart's assessment of Goffman's analytical arguments regarding photographs that 'when you look at the photographs to which they are applied, [they] are exactly right' (in Goffman, 1979, p. vii).

Firstly, considering the status of a photograph: various authors (Hartley 1992) have noted the 'objective' status conferred on photographs. Tagg (1988) provides a history of the development of photography and the increasing use that was made of it by the State through the legal and law enforcement agencies. Marshall (1990) has considered the use of photography in the medical profession, particularly its off-shoot of psychiatry, and later, by criminologists. The reading of a photograph has been addressed by Barthes (1977, pp. 28ff). Garfinkel (1967) has used the example of a photograph to discuss the work of coroners faced with defining sudden deaths as homicides or suicides and Goffman (1979) has focused on how photographs operate and the different types of photographs in circulation in public.

Analysis of the visual image has been particularly influenced by semiotics as developed by Barthes (1977). Semiology of the photograph focuses upon two basic levels of meaning: denotation (that is the literal meaning) and connotation (that is the meaning realised by the image), for example a picture of a red rose denotes a red rose but also connotes love.[7] This work is of relevance to me only in so far as it addresses the issue of the interplay between image and written text. (Only one of the 39 photographs did not have a caption, presumably because the headline performed a dual function of caption and headline). Barthes also talks about 'obtuse' or third meaning, by which he means a meaning that cannot be located by a method but which is nonetheless there in the image. In the example Barthes provides to explain what is meant by obtuse, he presents a photograph of a crowd, a rally in which people are

188

saluting, showing a smiling man in the background. Barthes (1977, p. 60) comments that this smiling man is 'visibly' an 'arse-licker', in other words the obtuse meaning is not situated structurally. Barthes here seems to be developing earlier remarks about anthropological knowledge and how variations in readings which depends on a range of knowledge: practical, cultural, aesthetic, national. The cultural specificity of our viewing of an image is thus acknowledged. Garfinkel's ethno-methodological approach takes a different approach, focusing upon how evidence is 'read' as unequivocally one or other course of action.

Referring to the perceptual processes associated with reading the photograph, Barthes refers to how little is known about this process. Importantly, he draws upon Piaget's argument that there is no perception without immediate categorisation, noting that the photograph is verbalised in the very moment it is perceived. In a suggestive manner Barthes adds parenthetically that 'if there is a delay in verbalisation, there is disorder in perception, questioning, *anguish* for the subject, traumatism ...' (1977, p. 28, emphasis added). I say 'suggestive', because I want to suggest that this is the analyst's condition. Like Barthes' strategy of 'slow motion reading' (referred to in Coward & Ellis, 1977) the analyst reads against the grain; in analysing the photographs the researcher has to explicate common-sense viewings. Indeed, Barthes explicitly refers to common-sense knowledge, referring to a townscape:

> I *know* that this is a North African country because I can see a sign in Arabic script, in the centre a man wearing a gandoura. Here the reading closely depends on my culture, on my knowledge of the world, and it is probable that a good press photograph (and they are all good being selected) makes ready play with the supposed knowledge of its readers (1977, p. 29).

Barthes' comments raise the issue of the researcher as the research instrument; as with the analysis of the written stories, I am claiming to offer a reading which is plausible, and its plausibility should be underpinned and evidenced by the presentation of the data discussed and the analytic framework used.

7.6 Classifying the photographs

The photographs can be categorised according to a number of features. For the purposes of analysis, I made three distinctions between the different photographs:

- those of the journalist and of the subject of the news story;
- between those 'of' prostitution and 'of' the prostitute (cf. Goffman, 1979); and
- between prostitutes looking out at the readers/the camera and those which are, in Goffman's words, 'caught pictures.'

This is a broad classification of the visual materials and was initially helpful in the handling of the different photographs. In the following sections, I want to focus on each of these distinctions before returning to consider the specific features of the materials.

7.7 Classification 1: Journalists as subjects

The photographs in the newspaper stories of prostitution fall into two categories: those of the journalist and those of the prostitute/client/pimp/related actors. This distinction is important and is one which has been overlooked, as indeed (as I contend), has the role of photographic texts in nearly all published analyses of newspaper discourse (for instance, Thompson, 1990; Fowler, 1991). I want, firstly, to briefly consider the photographs of journalists. The inclusion of a journalist's picture occurs mainly in the features genre of news stories (and I include here the newspaper's designation of 'news commentary/analysis').

These photographs are of the 'head and shoulders' variety, often close up shots of a person smiling, friendly, looking directly out at the reader, inviting our gaze. The photographs of journalists, accompanying news stories illustrate these remarks. The question which needs to be posed in relation to these photographs relates to their function in the process of reading. It most explicitly raises the question of authorship.

Caughie has suggested that the outcome of the conceptual displacement of the author as source and centre of the text has 'left the author ... without an adequate place in theory; if the author is not at the centre, he [or she] is nowhere' (1981, p. 2). The ethnomethodological approach, directly concerned to explicate the technical resources readers employ in their interaction with texts, has posed the figure of the author as an effect of textual practice (Lury, 1982, p. 8; McHoul, 1982, p. 5). Lury states that the 'author' and her/his intentions are, like the topic of a text, produced as a textual object over the course of the reading. The interaction is not between reader and author but between reader and text. Similarly, Schenkein (1979, p. 192) dismisses the question of 'authorship'. These works demonstrate how, Caughie observes, if the author is not at the

190

centre, he [or she] is nowhere (ibid.). Yet, it seems to me vital that recognition be accorded, on theoretical and analytic levels, to how the author 'functions as a figure within the rhetoric of the text and of how we use this figure ... in our reading' (Caughie 1981, p. 15).

The inclusion of the photographs within specific genres of news stories explicitly focuses attention onto what Caughie refers to as a fascination with the author. Questions of authorship, of intentionality of the writer of the text, are fraught with difficulties. They demand resolution of who speaks and in whose name. Analyses of newspaper stories do not discuss the discourse in terms of the individual journalist, rather they refer to 'press discourse' not, for example, 'O'Faolain's discourse'. O'Faolain is an institutional subject, speaking the voice of the *Irish Times*. However, I, as a reader of the *Irish Times* and as a recipient of other media products, know that Nuala O'Faolain is a political activist. I recognise her photograph from other photographs I have seen, in different sources, of her.

The effect of these photographs is to name the news story as this or that journalist's views. The photographs of the journalists, placed beside the by-line of the journalist's name, personalise and visualise the journalist. Being attached to feature stories, these photographs work as part of a realist strategy: they work to cover over the manufactured nature of news stories. The inclusion of photographs of the stories' authors articulates the ideology of the reporter as news-hound, out there collecting facts. They suggest that the journalist merits this additional attention; rather, as is usual, than just having his or/her name in print, his or/her visual presence is signalled by the photograph. It may be that this confers a certain prestige on the writer, and that this prestige makes for more engaged reading. Another suggestion is that the inclusion of the journalist's photograph indicates that the content of the article is 'personal'. Editorials in the British and Irish press, as the 'voice' of the newspaper, do not carry photographs of their authors (the editors).

Goffman in his discussion of personal publicity pictures 'one's designed to bring before the public a flattering portrait of some luminary' including literary figures, adds a footnote in which he states that

> For male novelists pictured on the back of their dust covers this means ... rough, open shirts. tousled hair, youthful, virile appearance, and often a brooding look, this last bespeaking the deep thoughts that are proper to the innards of the species ... [Q]ualities of the book are to be seen in the qualities of the appearance of the writer, thus promoting a folk theory of expression along with their books and themselves (1979, p. 11).

Such pictures also have application to the presentation of news events, 'presented through the words and presence of political leaders and the write up of the first is accompanied by a picture of the second' (ibid.). This last remark falls more properly into the second category of photographs I consider below, those of the subjects of the news. In line with Goffman's comments about the male novelists we can say that the appearance of the female journalists (only one of these portrait photographs is of a man) is one of friendliness, not brooding, presumably to project the nature of the writer as someone who is not too serious, as someone who is just like the rest of us. Henley (1977) has argued that smiling is a display of submission, an argument which alerts us to how all of the women are smiling out at us. A quick search through two Irish papers, *The Irish Times* (11.8.95) and *The Sunday Independent* (6.8.95) reproduces the 'smiling' women and 'serious' men portraits which were indicated in the data set.

The above is a tentative approach to the issue of journalists' photographs in the newspapers. It is necessarily incomplete but is included because it points to a further aspect of the presentation of the news stories, an aspect which has been ignored by media theorists but which may be of importance in terms of the reader's production of the intention of the (here, embodied) author/journalist.

7.8   Classifications 2 and 3: The different 'ofs' of photographs and the different types of photographs

The second distinction I imposed on the materials was between the photographs of the prostitute and those of prostitution. This distinction follows Goffman's insightful arguments regarding the need to consider the different 'ofs' of photographs. This distinction is further developed in the arguments I present below regarding the photographs as 'quotations' from an action sequence. Goffman (1979, p. 12) suggests that the significant question is not what a photograph is, but rather what a particular photograph is of, an question which allows us to treat a photograph and its printing press reproduction as the same. Noting the idea that the photograph is an actual picture of things 'out there', Goffman observes that 'just as a photograph can be said to be of its subject' so it can also be said to 'be *of* its model' (p. 13). I consider this to be highly suggestive and its relevance was clarified when I turned to consider how to broadly classify the photographs according to whether the subjects were looking out, pass-port, head and shoulder's variety, and those in which the faces of the people were obscured or unclear.

In initial attempts to analyse these photographs, I followed Goffman's (1959) comments regarding third parties to performances and argued that we, the readers, are cast as voyeurs, looking into a scene to which we should not properly have access. This approach raises questions regarding the vicarious nature of most, if not all, news pictures: they give us a visual glimpse into what has been constructed as an 'underworld' (see Chapter Six). I also continued to designate the news pictures as photographs of prostitutes. However, this designation only accounts for some of the photographs, namely those in which the subject of the photograph is 'explicitly' a prostitute, one who is identified as a prostitute in the accompanying written story. Goffman's 'of' distinction enabled me to account for those photographs which illustrated prostitution (or rather loitering and soliciting) *and* those images of the prostitute; two different subjects of the photographs. Those photographs of close ups/head and shoulders are the images of prostitutes and those where the reader is looking into a photographed scene are of activities of prostitution.[8]

This broad classification of the data served as a useful spring board from which to consider, in more detailed fashion, the specific features of the news pictures. Issues raised relate to reading the images, the captioned photograph and the photographs of the different subjects – prostitutes, pimps, clients and the scenes of loitering.

7.9   An uncaptioned image

Photographs rarely appear in newspapers without an attached caption. Only one of the 39 photographs was not captioned (ALL IN THE BEST POSSIBLE TASTE, *Guardian*, 20.11.89).[9] This story contains a double headline: one introducing the story, acting as a pre-preface, 'In the first of a new series, Cynthia Payne throws open the doors of her wardrobe', positioned above the headline proper (i.e., in bold type and bigger print) 'All in the best possible taste'. The reader of the photograph sees a woman standing holding a dress, smiling out at us and an immediate identification procedure undertaken would be to suppose that the woman in the picture is the Cynthia Payne of the pre-headline (see Appendix III: no. 1). Specific features of the photograph, why was it taken, where was it taken (it looks like a home living room), and, for the readers who do not 'see' Cynthia Payne in the photograph, who it is, are answered by the written text. This text opens with

> When Cynthia Payne suddenly looks away mid conversation, affects a rigid pose and shrieks, 'Sex! Money!' it is an indication that there is a photographer in the room.

This sentence interacts with the photograph, the reader can see Cynthia Payne's pose and contrived smile. The dress in the photograph is not clearly described in the written story – it could be the one referred to in the following passage:

> Payne removes another dress from its feather-light dry cleaning bag … 'I was raided in this,' says Payne with a flourish, presenting a mother-of-the-bride-style green and white patterned dress bought from a shop called French Dressing in Streatham. 'I haven't any photos of me wearing it,' she explains, 'because when the police came they … emptied the camera hoping to find pornography' (*Guardian*, 20.11.89).

Close inspection of this photograph does, however, legitimate a reader's guess that this is the dress that is being held up to our view, because in the right hand corner of the photograph the reader can see the bottom of what most readers would know is a 'feather-light dry cleaning bag'. Goffman comments in a footnote that

> … in a great number of contexts an uncaptioned photograph is understood to present a claim regarding the character and properties of the model (1979, p. 14).

However, the properties of the model, here Cynthia Payne, are not 'read' from the photograph, rather they rely either on pre-existing knowledge that she was a madam of a brothel or they gain this knowledge from their reading of the surrounding written text. Indeed, the properties of Ms Payne are not discoverable from the photograph and as she herself says:

> People always expect me to look like a tart or a madam. They're always disappointed when they see how normal I am (ibid.).

The photograph testifies to the 'normality', referred to in the written story, to her un-tart-likeness or un-madam-likeness.

7.10 Captioned images

The remaining 38 photographs from the core data set were captioned. Barthes argues that the caption 'probably has a less obvious effect of connotation, the headline and article are palpably separate from the image, the former by its emphasis the later by its distance. He suggests that the caption appears to 'duplicate that image', that is to merely comment on what is there (1977, p. 26). Prior to these comments, Barthes had noted that the effectiveness of connotation probably differs according to the way in which the text is presented – the closer the text to the image, the less it seems to connote it.

Examples of unproblematic descriptions of the photograph, contained in the captions are readily available: the photographs, as noted, can be divided into two categories, those of head and shoulders/mugshot type photographs and those of the subject in a scene. The naming of a person (for example, Ms Monica Coghlan, from ARCHER PAID – PROSTITUTE, *Irish Times*, 11.07.87) is unproblematic in the sense that the name of an individual hardly tells the reader anything other than who is in the photograph. However, this example is itself problematic because the 'prostitute' referred to in the headline is almost immediately made dependent on the image and vice versa – the 'prostitute' is Ms Monica Coghlan and Ms Monica Coghlan (pictured) is the prostitute. The 'surprise' in the written text would be if Ms Monica Coghlan was not the prostitute referred to in the headline. (Of course, this reading draws upon legal (particularly UK) and common-sense, popular understandings that the prostitute is a woman.) Barthes further refers to how the text can contradict images giving the example of Gerber's work on women's magazine covers with their 'radiant' cover girl photographs and the gloomy headlines (all of which relate to problems – an example from *New Woman* magazine (January 1993) is the glamorous cover girl with, as one of the headlines: JUST MARRIED? (SO HOW COME YOU'RE SO DEPRESSED?)) Only one example of this 'contradiction' was found in the data and even this is not the contradiction that Barthes speaks of, but rather points to how a reading of the photographs plus captions alone could produce an incorrect reading.

A *Sunday Times* story, ATTACK ON CALL GIRL REVEALS AWFUL TRUTH TO HER FAMILY, with a sub-headline: Anguish of parents who thought she was a cook' (*Sunday Times*, 18.8.91, p. 4). Three photographs (see over) form part of this story: two juxtapositioned with a shared caption: Face of violence: photofit of the wanted man and Sharon Hoare. A third photograph located to the left of the headline is captioned: Kenneth Christopher – unaware of daughter's work as a call girl. Considering these photographs prior to reading the written text, a reader would be able to guess that Christopher is the parent, a member of the family, to whom the awful truth has been revealed. The sub-headline and the caption to the photograph of Kenneth Christopher together answer the question which the headline poses 'what awful truth'? They thought she was a cook but have found out that she was a call girl. The two other photographs (or rather one photofit and one photograph) are of a 'wanted man' whose photofit is the 'face of violence' and Sharon Hoare.

Attack on call girl reveals awful truth to her family

Anguish of parents who thought she was a cook

Sunday Times reporters

Photo

Photo

Photo

Kenneth Christopher: unaware of daughter's work as a call girl

Face of violence: photofit of the wanted man and Sharon Hoare

The puzzle set up by these photographs relates to their connection to the story about revelations of 'awful truths' and to the 'parents' or family. The reader could guess that the 'attack' on the call girl was perpetuated by the 'wanted man', but that leaves the reader to account for Sharon Hoare. If the reader first reads the headline and then the photograph/caption relating to the juxtaposed images then she would, perhaps, read 'call girl' as Sharon Hoare. However, how is the reader to account for Kenneth Christopher, the father? Here, the reader would have to draw upon general cultural knowledge that women commonly relinquish their family surname when they marry, adopting that of their husbands. So, Sharon Hoare could be Kenneth Christopher's daughter. However the opening sentences of the written text are as follows:

One of the leading families of the Scilly Isles faced a double tragedy last night after a violent assault on a London Call girl. The attack, in which Lucy Christopher was battered and left for dead, has revealed to her family and their tiny community that she was working as a prostitute (*Sunday Times*, 18.8.91).

This opening or lead paragraph provides an answer to the headline. The 'call girl' is Lucy Christopher, the daughter of Kenneth Christopher and the 'violent assault' was carried out by the wanted man (whose photofit shows the reader a face of violence). In case there should be any doubt about what a call girl is, the lead clearly identifies call girls as prostitutes. (The lexical ellipsis between written article and captions in this story is evident.) However, the question remains: who is Sharon Hoare? The reader has to continue onto paragraph four to find out why her photograph is present in the story – what is its relevance. The answer is that the suspect, the wanted man, is possibly Sharon Hoare's killer. Sharon Hoare was also a call girl. The story continues with an account of Hoare's killing and the suspected man who is compared to, indeed made equivalent to, the Yorkshire Ripper. He is a 'prostitute hating killer, similar to … Peter Sutcliffe, who killed 13 women'.

Again the position of the photographs within the story is relevant: the photograph of Kenneth Christopher is above the most detailed accounts of the family, while those of the suspected attacker and of Sharon Hoare are located close to the written text in which they are discussed.

Barthes has suggested that the caption functions as a kind of 'vice', directing the meaning of the photograph (1977, p. 39). This may be too strong a term but it does convey the 'grip' the caption has on the photograph. Holland likewise has noted that the text directs us how to read the picture and the picture can act to externalise meanings and make them more concrete (1992, p. 10). Photographs can be considered as a 'puzzle' which can be 'solved' by the caption and further resolved by the written text of the story.

7.11 Reading photographs: Inter and intra-textuality

As with the written texts, the newspaper stories, the visual texts, the photographs, are read intertextually. Writing about the HIV pandemic, Tom Kalin has commented à propos of the cultural imagery of AIDS, that a 'tissue' of texts and images have constituted this epidemic (1990, p. 3, emphasis added). This notion of 'tissue' echoes Fisher's (1986) notion of a 'contextual web' and while Fisher uses this notion to point to the wider context of discourses from the local to the wider social context, these terms are helpful in orienting us to the existence of other texts and other images which pre-exist or exist alongside those which, at a specific point in time, the reader of a newspaper has read. Intertextuality is further discussed in Chapter Eight.

The interaction, or intra-textuality, activated by the photograph and the written text is particularly evident in an Observer story about Jimmy Swaggart and the scandal surrounding his photographed liaison with a prostitute. This story (GREAT BALLS OF FIRE, *Observer* 28.2.88) included three photographs: a central one of Swaggart, a smaller one of Debra Murphree and a still smaller one of Swaggart's cousin, Jerry Lee Lewis and his 'child bride' (see over). Inter-textuality is achieved by reference to the photographs of Swaggart and the identified prostitute (Debra Murphree), photographs not reproduced in other press reports about this event but which are central to the story. Intra-textuality relates to how the captions relate to the written text.

In this story, I want to suggest that the *positioning* of the photographs plays an important role in the reading activity (see opposite). The reader is confronted with two main photographs just below the headline. Further down the text, a picture of Jerry Lee Lewis and the child bride is inserted. The main image, of Swaggart, is the most visually commanding when the story is first approached and its prominence pervades the story as a whole. However, those photographs of the woman (the prostitute) and the cousin and bride, are positioned in what I consider to be 'locally relevant spots'. By locally relevant I mean relevant to the written text which surrounds them. The story opens with a paragraph on Gorman, a man who wanted to get revenge on Swaggart. Paragraph 2 recounts a detective's call to Gorman to alert him that Swaggart was in a motel room

SIMON HOGGART reports on how sex scandals are rocking the pious world of American evangelism

GREAT BALLS OF FIRE

Debra Murphree: Told by Swaggart to pose in porno positions

Most bigoted

Photo

Crying in the chapel: Swaggart was the most righteous of all TV evangelists

Crazy remarks

Swaggart's cousin Jerry Lee Lewis and his child bride

with a prostitute. Gorman rushed to the scene to confront Swaggart (paragraph 3). Paragraphs four and five deal with the subsequent events, Swaggart's promise to confess, his failure to do so and the production of the photographs of Swaggart with the prostitute, taken by the private investigator. Swaggart was summoned by church authorities to 'tell all'. Paragraph 6 starts with

> Or not quite everything. The prostitute was a dark-haired mother of three called Debra Murphree or Debra Hedge. She is tattooed and looks worn, much older than her 28 years. She confirmed Swaggart's claim that they did not have intercourse; she had been told to lie on the bed and pose in pornographic acts and positions.

The location of the photograph and its caption, which is a capsule statement of the expanded contents of paragraph six, is positioned beside the text of paragraph six and as this paragraph is read, the photograph is made sense of and evaluated: does she look older than 28 years, for example? The reader cannot avoid, by starting reading at paragraph 1 to 'see' the picture of the woman looking out at the viewer. The prostitute referred to in paragraph 2 *is* the woman in the photograph, a supposition confirmed by paragraph 6.

Similarly, the photograph of Jerry Lee and child bride is positioned in the middle of a paragraph (20) in which Swaggart is deemed to

> come on, … rather like a rock n' role singer, and that's an important
> [PHOTOGRAPH INSERTED]
> clue. Swaggart … grew up with his cousin Jerry Lee Lewis.

The reader cannot avoid reading the caption or seeing the photograph of Jerry Lee and child bride, before he (Lewis) is mentioned in the written text. In the adjacent column right beside the photograph of Lewis is a biographical description of his life. The positioning of the photographs is not 'natural', rather, picture editors have the job of selecting the photographs to be used as part of a story and the production processes of newspaper production involve decisions about where to place photographs. Such decisions relate to journalistic routines involving tacit, taken for granted knowledge about what constitutes a 'good story'.

What I am proposing then is that the reader can read the story in which photographs are included in a 'zig-zag' fashion (for want of a better term), oscillating between the written text and the photograph, the latter as an illustration of what the written story is about. Barthes, specifically discussing newspaper photographs, argues that the text constitutes a parasitic message designed to connote the image, to 'quicken' it (1977, pp. 25, 26). He suggests that this is a reversal of a historical trend; before, the image illustrated the text (made it clearer), today, the text loads the image, burdening it with an imagination (ibid.). Hence his argument that we are not, contrary to popular imagination, a visual civilisation but a written civilisation.

I would suggest that photographs rarely appear without an attached text, at least in the newspapers, or to qualify this, at least in any of the British or Irish newspapers I have read.[10] However, Barthes goes on to say that while formerly there was a reduction from text to image, today there is *amplification* from one to the other. The words reduce the ambiguous meaning of a pictured scene, they do amplify, but they amplify a particular meaning of the scene or subject photographed.

7.12 Profiling the cast of players: Photographs 'of' pimps, clients and prostitutes

Introduction: The photographs, as detailed in Table 7.2, were of pimps, prostitutes, clients and miscellaneous scenes. The initial approach I took in considering the photographs was influenced by my readings of the literature, the different arguments and conceptualisation of prostitutes and prostitution as articulated by the different frameworks (Chapter Two). In this section I focus on each type of photographic subject, drawing attention to some of the arguments advanced in the various frameworks.

Clients Eileen McLeod (1982, p. 9) argues that the 'stock identity of the client remains that of social misfit and is wheeled into the limelight throughout the media'. Further, Ros Miles, discussing the Hugh Grant story comments that

> The case of Hugh Grant is especially interesting because he is far from the stereotypical client – old, ugly and inadequate (A NEW LOOK AT THE OLDEST PROFESSION, *Independent*, 29.6.95).

Hugh Grant is a media-proclaimed UK sex symbol. While there was no comparable 'event' in the stories I had collected, these comments are relevant in relation to the visual images of clients in the press.

Of the 39 photographs, only 3 were of clients. These included Jeffrey Archer, although the story in the newspaper was about his libel case, not about whether or not he had paid a prostitute for sexual services. Jimmy Swaggart was another client who received press attention. Included in this gallery of clients is Jimmy Bakker. Bakker was a TV evangelist in the

201

US, who was under investigation for conspiracy charges (BLESSED ARE THE MEEK FOR THEY MAY GET A MISTRIAL, *Observer*, 3.9.89). I have categorised his photograph as belonging to the client group because of the following passage

> ... 1987, when it was revealed that Bakker had had sex back in 1980 with a young woman named Jessica Hahn [who blackmailed Bakker] ... Since then Hahn has been accused by newspapers of having a great deal of sexual experience before meeting Bakker and of even having taken money to sleep with men.

This may be illegitimate, but even if this story is removed from this category, the number of stories indicates how little media attention is given to clients. That said, however, it is important to note the preponderance of photographs of women leaning into cars[11] (see Appendix III: no. 2).

Pimps The issue of pimping has been discussed, particularly in the sociological approaches to prostitution. The conception of the prostitute as a helpless passive individual (Goldstein, 1979, p. 149) is reinforced by the 'hoary' view that the prostitute is her pimp's unwilling slave and that he holds her mainly through fear (Benjamin & Masters, 1964, p. 189). Benjamin and Masters (1964) argue that this view has been long discarded and Jennifer James likewise dismisses the myth of the brutal pimp (1978, p. 188). The issue of pimps in the sociological framework has been reviewed by Cohen (1980, pp. 167-170) and is not reproduced here. The concern here is to consider the extent to which pimps are featured (via photographs) in the press.

Out of the 31 stories which contained photographs, only two photographs were 'of' pimps (that is, their subject was of a person not of pimping as an activity). Both of these photographs are in stories which are reviews of the book *Lyn: A story of prostitution* (1987) by June Levine and Lyn Madden. In this sense the photographs are located in, in Fisk's (1987) terms, a relation of 'vertical intertextuality'; they refer to the book, although the book itself does not contain any photographs of Cullen. The first story, EXPOSED: THE REAL WORLD OF DUBLIN'S BRUTAL PIMPS (*Evening Press*, 7.10.87) has a side profile of John Cullen and the caption is 'Cullen ... life plus 15 years'. The reader could ask who is John Cullen and what relation has he to 'Dublin's brutal pimps'? This question is answered in the lead paragraph with the fourth paragraph reporting that June Levine is not afraid of John Cullen 'whose excruciating psychotic behaviour marked the lives of everyone with whom he came in close contact'. The side profile of Cullen's face provides us with a glimpse of a 'face of brutality'. The 'life plus 15 years' referred to in the caption is the prison sentence Cullen received for the murder of an ex-prostitute and her mother and aunt.

The *Irish Times* story (ONE WOMAN'S ESCAPE FROM THE SAVAGERY OF DUBLIN'S STREETS, 7.10.87) includes a large full frontal photograph of Cullen, behind whom stand two Gardaí (police). The preface, which is separate from the story proper, provides the upshot of the story:

> Beatings, gang-rape, mutilation, murder: these are among the means that have been used by Dublin's pimps to enforce their lucrative tyranny over any women attempting to support themselves through prostitution. Mary Maher has been reading Lyn Madden's story, published today, about her nightmare struggle to break free of the brutal realities of the game.

The caption to the photograph is not unproblematical: it goes beyond the identification of the person to provide information about that person's biography:

> John Cullen, Lyn Madden's former pimp, after being sentenced to life imprisonment in November 1983 for the murder of Dolores Lynch. Dolores, her mother and her aunt died when Cullen set their house on fire the previous January. Lyn Madden was a State witness at his trial.

The stream of action from which this image is plucked is probably Cullen entering the courtroom or jail – a handcuff is visible around his right wrist. Unlike the photographs of prostitutes looking out at us, these are 'caught' photographs. The written story provides an account of Lyn's life with Cullen and his violent behaviour.

Prostitutes Much, as noted, has been said of the image of the prostitute. The photographs of the prostitutes were predominantly of head and shoulders variety with the model looking out. The identification of the photographed woman as a prostitute was generally given in the headline (as in the ARCHER PAID – PROSTITUTE, *Irish Times*). The *Sunday Mirror* story, THE AIDS TIME BOMB (12.8.89) carries two photographs, both of which identify the photographed subject as a 'prostitute'/'hooker' (the caption is: AIDS timebomb – but Angie is still a hooker). An exception to this is the photograph of Sharon Hoare (in ATTACK ON CALL GIRL REVEALS AWFUL TRUTH TO HER FAMILY, *Sunday Times*, 18.8.91). The one story on male prostitution in the data set (THE RENT BOY DAVID, *Guardian*, 5.11.88) carries a photograph of the back of a man and the caption identifies the subjects as 'Male prostitute, Piccadilly ...'

One of the photographs included in the story WENDY, VICTIM OF LOW LIFE IN A SORDID SQUARE MILE (*Sunday Telegraph*, 9.12.90) shows a woman looking out from behind a window. The caption identifies the woman as a prostitute by its reference to 'red-light' area: 'Watching and waiting: a woman answers her mobile telephone in the red-light area of Nicholstown, Southampton'. The caption contains a membership categorisation via location. These photographs contain no specific detail or signs which identify the woman/women photographed as prostitutes – there are no identifying marks and hence the caption does the work of identification and categorisation.

As noted, additional newspaper stories on prostitution were collected to be drawn upon as necessary. Additional photographs of women included the *Independent on Sunday*'s story FEAR OF A 'RIPPER' HAUNTS DETECTIVE (7.8.94). The photograph of a deserted service station and the juxtaposition of the 'mug-shots' of the murdered women works to suggest a link between the service station and the women in the photographs. The reference to 'Ripper' draws on historical knowledge that could be expectably held by the reader/viewer – i.e., the Ripper murdered prostitutes. In the same ways as the *Sunday Telegraph* story above, the identification of the women as prostitutes may work by the application of cultural knowledge that the women who are in red-light areas or service stations at night can be 'reasonably' expected to be prostitutes.

7.13 Unequivocal views: Evidencing the presence of a prostitute

Evidence of intent, evidence that the 'prostitute' was correctly a prostitute is, I have suggested, effected through the use of membership categorisations, through place and time formulations (Chapters Five and Six). The question which needs to be addressed here is whether the photographs, with their accompanying captions draw upon these same things in order to make their pictured scenes and subjects legible as a scene of prostitution and of the prostitute. That the photograph operates as a proof of the occurrence of an event is not a novel suggestion: John Tagg (1988), examining the development of photography from a Foucauldian perspective, recounts the history of photography and the concomitant notion that the photograph was a direct reflection of the material reality it captured. He provides a fascinating account of the early uses of photography, particularly its service in police work, in town planners' arguments for building development and the development of a 'regime of photographic truth'. Of relevance to my concerns is his argument that the use of photography in police work was primarily related to its *'value as evidence'*. Tagg cites excerpts from a manual of police photography and the words of a legal specialist regarding legal photography. I reproduce both excerpts here:

> ... A photograph should include everything appertaining to its subject and relevant to its purpose. If this cannot be done with one picture, then others must be taken in order that the whole subject is covered ...

and

> Legal photographs are made for the purpose of ultimate use in a courtroom, or at least to be exhibited to people who are to be informed or persuaded by them. In making photographs for use in litigation, lawyers and photographers should strive for 'legal quality', a term used here for having certain characteristics and accuracy ... any drama in the picture should emanate from the subject matter alone ... Any ... attempt to dramatise photographs may result in their exclusion and a consequent suspicion on the part of the jurors that such photographers cannot be trusted (1988, pp. 95-97).

A certain kind of realism in photographs then was a guiding principle in the directives targeted at legal and law enforcement agents. However, Tagg's analysis, insightful as it is, does not consider how a photograph is read, other than repeatedly commenting that a photograph is seen as an 'objective' translation of the object it captures. The affinity between Garfinkel (1967) and Goffman's (1979) approach to the study of social life is raised in the following passages, particularly as Goffman was so concerned to detail the stream of activity from which the photograph plucks but one instant. Garfinkel, discussing how coroners assess the mode of a death, focuses on the gathering of evidence:

> These *whatsoever* bits and pieces that a story or a rule or a proverb might make intelligible are used to formulate a *recognisably* coherent, standard, typical ... a professionally defensible, and thereby, for members, a *recognisably* rational account of how the society worked to produce those remains (1967, p. 17).

Used in this process are photographs and verbal stories.

Taking as an example a photograph of a slashed throat, where hesitation cuts might indicate a suicide, Garfinkel remarks that

Other *courses of action* are imaginable too, and so cuts that look like hesitation cuts can be produced by other mechanisms. One needs to start with the actual display and imagine how different courses of action would have been organised such that *that* picture would be compatible with it. One might think of the photographed display as a *phase-of-the-action*. In any actual display is there a course of action with which that phase is uniquely compatible? *That* is the coroner's question (1967, pp. 17-18, emphasis added).

Garfinkel's identification of the procedures by which *coroners* identify, and identify unequivocally, cause of death, is remarkably suggestive for me and provided the organising focus for considering my visual data, specifically those photographs of prostitutes, shot, as it were, 'on location'. The presence or identification of 'adequate evidence' is particularly suggestive: what evidence is legible in these photographs? Atkinson has suggested that coroners do not necessarily see clues such as notes as pointing to suicide irrespective of other evidence (1982, p. 116). Rather they have a reflexive quality in relation to other cues. Again, I approached the data with this question in mind – what cues are present to lead us to formulate a reading of the photographs as unproblematically and unequivocally photographs of prostitutes.

As a starting point I want to consider one of the stories which deals with the TV evangelist, Jimmy Swaggart, who was the subject of a sex scandal. Swaggart was caught with a prostitute in New Orleans and of particular importance is that the evidence for his 'way-ward behaviour' was provided by a photograph of him with a prostitute. Four stories reported this event. The photographs form a topic in this example. Marvin Gorman, a preacher who had been denounced by Swaggart, hired a private detective to follow Swaggart:

> Swaggart, the gumshoe said, was with a prostitute in a seedy motel room on the outskirts of New Orleans ... Gorman confronted him. Swaggart pleaded for mercy ... promised he would confess his sins to the church authorities. But he didn't, and after four months, Gorman took the private eye's photographs to the elders of the Assembly of God Church.

In this story (GREAT BALLS OF FIRE, *Observer*, 28.2.88, p. 11), the reader has to wait until the fifth paragraph to find out that the private detective had taken photographs.

Other stories (in the Irish press) detailed Swaggart's response following the revelation. The issue of investigation by his church is made redundant by the references to Gorman's actions;

... *pictures of the evangelist with an alleged prostitute in a motel* as evidence of his charges (Sin was no mistake, says retiring TV evangelist, *Irish Times*, 23.2.88, emphasis added).

The evangelist, who turned his preaching into a multi-million dollar world-wide ministry, said in the confession that he had sinned against God ... Although Mr. Swaggart did not elaborate, he was reported to have been *photographed leaving a New Orleans hotel with a prostitute* ...Several sources have indicated that a defrocked rival evangelist, the Rev. Martin Gorman, whom Mr. Swaggart helped oust from the Assemblies of God for sexual misconduct, gave the church officials photographs of Mr. Swaggart and a prostitute leaving the hotel. Another former television evangelist ... claimed evidence of Mr. Swaggart's involvement with prostitutes had 'lain dormant since last October' (TV evangelist in sex scandal agrees to 'rehabilitation', *Irish Times*, 24.2.88, emphasis added).

Further coverage of this story is from a review of radio programmes (Tom Widger's radio week, Hal lay loo yah! Rapture me up). In this review of a radio programme on the Swaggart scandal, Widger says that

What makes Mr. Swaggart's fall ... all the more shameful is that not alone is he a mere fornicator – *he was photographed entering a house of ill repute with a prostitute* – but he is also a hypocrite (*Sunday Tribune*, 28.2.88, emphasis added).

Swaggart's 'fall' was evidenced, not only by private detective's observational report, but by the photographs of him (variously) entering or leaving a motel/hotel/house of ill repute. The photograph provides valid or strong evidence (Goffman, 1979, p. 14) that its model had been in a certain place, doing a certain thing and in association with certain others. Barthes provides an example of this, with its attendant consequences when he recounts the event in which a US senator was forced out of office following the publication of a 'trick' photograph, in which two photographs were juxtapositioned so that it 'looked' as if the US senator was in deep conversation with a well known communist (1977, p. 20). The public outcry demonstrates the ways in which photographs are accepted as evidence and also the ways in which the production of images is concealed.

Denial of 'knowing' someone, as Goffman (1979) noted, cannot be sustained in the face of pictures which show a person chatting to a person he claims not to know. In fact, Goffman avers, on occasion in courts, claims as to what occurred may find better support through photographs.

A caught photograph of persons in action, into which category the photographs of Swaggart and the prostitute fall, can, Goffman states, provide all the evidence that one needs that a particular event ... very likely did occur (1979, p. 20). The stories of Swaggart's activities also underline how the reading of a photograph parallels the reading of 'live scenes': the photograph is a 'freeze-frame' of a sequence of action from a concatenated sequence of events: Swaggart's entry into and exit from (depending on which story one reads) a motel/hotel/house of ill repute with an (alleged) prostitute is one part in the action sequence of prostitution. (Of course, the inclusion of 'with a prostitute' in each of the stories serves to clarify what 'a house of ill repute' is, why he should be going into or coming out of a motel or hotel, it formulates activity.) There is no direct reference to the exchange of money for sexual services.

Sexual acts are mentioned however in the GREAT BALLS OF FIRE story (*Observer*, 28.2.88), in a caption attached to a photograph of a woman, whom the caption identifies as Debra Murphree: 'Told by Swaggart to pose in porno positions'. A larger photograph 'shows' Swaggart visibly distraught and is placed to the right of 'the prostitute's' photograph (see above). The reading of these photographs could set up a sequence: Murphree, who is not distraught, is the causative agent leading to Swaggart's display of distress. The use of a sequence of photographs is discussed below, suffice to note that it allows complex ideas to be introduced. A third photograph is included in this story, that of 'Swaggart's cousin Jerry Lee Lewis and his child bride' (caption).

7.14 Action sequences and synoptic visions: Photographs 'of' prostitution

One of the most problematic features of the phenomenon of prostitution, a feature evident in all of the frameworks of prostitution, relates to definitional conundrums. I have discussed this earlier (Chapters Two and Three, cf. Appendix I) and wish here to simply note that there is a consensus that prostitution is the exchange of money for sexual services. This is the act of prostitution. This study has been oriented to uncovering how this act is written about in the stories and more centrally how the key player, the prostitute, is recognised and identified as a prostitute, given that the act of exchange of money, either prior to or after sexual activities, is not a subject of press discourse.[12]

The act of prostitution is a two part act involving the giving of sexual services [on the part of the prostitute] and the giving of money [on the part of the client]. However, it is not, as I have suggested, prostitution itself which is the subject of attention (particularly in relation to legislative measures against prostitution), but rather the activities of loitering and soliciting which have been the focus of attention. In an apt example of this, Andrieu-Sanz & Vasquez-Anton's opening statement to their paper on the social organisation of prostitution in Bilbao, Spain, is that

> Whenever prostitution is discussed in everyday situations the stereotype of sleazy night-life is evoked, as if prostitutes spent all their time slinking along walls wearing mini-skirts and cloying perfume (1989, p. 70).

The act of exchange is not what is at issue in the press stories, in contrast to the feminist discourses of prostitution in which this exchange is made central. Rather, the act itself is not discussed but its documentary evidences are – the presence of the prostitute in her mini-skirt, slinking along walls. Hence, as I have been arguing, the act of prostitution is 'read' by way of predictive acts of loitering (especially) and soliciting. The newspaper stories of prostitution thus parallel those of the legal discourses of prostitution, namely, the concern with presence and with loitering and soliciting as standing for the act of prostitution. To reiterate, in the legal framework, prostitution (in Britain and Ireland) is not itself illegal; it is the related acts of loitering and soliciting which are criminalised. These points are of relevance when we turn to consider one aspect of the photographs. Specifically, drawing upon Gagnon and Simon (1974), I am concerned with how the 'script' of prostitution involves a sequence of actions, from the activity of loitering and soliciting to the payment and provision of sexual services. Hence, prostitution is, as I suggested (above), a dyadic act, comprising a two part structure encompassing a four part action sequence:

[– predictive acts –]   [– prostitution –]
Loitering –> Soliciting –> Payment <—> Sexual Services

This action sequence is important because I want to suggest that the newspaper coverage of prostitution makes the predictive acts equivalent to, and interchangeable with, prostitution. Goffman (1979, p. 10) argues that photography omits temporal sequence and everything else except static visual displays. The photographs of prostitutes 'caught' standing are photographs of loitering, yet these photographs make what is one sequence in the prostitution script stand for the others. In this sense Goffman's comments that photography 'condenses' is particularly telling. Of crucial importance in this regard are his comments about caught photographs (by which he means those photographs of a scene in which a camera would have been unlikely), comments which echo those arguments advanced in the preceding chapters:

> Caught pictures can provide valid documents or records, allowing the viewer to make relatively reliable inferences as to what had led up to the activity represented and what was likely to have followed, in the same way, if to a lesser extent, as can an actual viewer of a live scene infer what is going on at the moment of viewing (1979, pp. 13-14).

Caught photographs are then rather like holding a jigsaw piece up against the total or complete picture which comes on the game's box. Extending this metaphor, the photograph is the jigsaw piece and the accompanying caption and written text which is adjacent, above, below or surrounds it, realises the completed picture.

Goffman develops this analysis by introducing the argument that all scenes are representations of 'events' happening:

> Narrative like action is to be read from what is seen, *a before and after* are to be inferred and this location in the *ongoing stream* of activity provides the context (1979, p. 16).

Temporal sequence is interrupted by the photograph. This is unlike a portrait, of which it cannot be said that a scene is in progress. In the latter, Goffman suggests, a subject is featured more than a stream of events. The photographs of prostitutes can be divided into those which are 'portraits' [mug shots, head and shoulder shots] in which the subject is 'the prostitute' and those photographs which are 'photographs', that is they extract a sequence from the composite script. They are not about the prostitute proper but about prostitution. The *Hot Press* illustration is particularly instructive in this latter regard: the fishnet stocking-ed legs between which the viewer sees an approaching car is not about the subject, that is a particular prostitute, it is about the 'stream of events'. A scene is in progress, most graphically in this case, and the still is one which is about loitering but the *anticipated* solicitation and subsequent act prostitution are evoked[13] (see Appendix III, no. 3).

This illustration activates the script of loitering -> prostitution, it enables a mental concatenation of the different activities. I do not consider this illustration 'ambiguous', indeed, although without a caption, its meaning is, I suggest, non-negotiable.

Goffman, discussing the witnessing of a display which is part of a stream of actions, remarks that in photographic portraiture 'actions are mere representations', and he considers the example of the scientist pictured peering down a microscope (although interestingly, does not ask how it is that we recognise this person as a scientist, as opposed to a visiting politician who performs this activity for a photo call). He suggests that the pictured scene is contrived, it wouldn't be seen in real life, rather it is

> ... something that is *only* to be found as a posing for a picture, having been staged in response to a conception of what would make a colourful, telling photograph, and behind this, a conception of what constitutes the appropriate convention for 'representing' the particular calling ... what one has is ... the sort of activity the model chooses to be identified with, this activity being symbolised, as it were by *a quotation of one of its dramatically telling phases* (1979, p. 19, emphasis in original).

In an accompanying footnote, Goffman refers to a 'synoptic view', an evocative turn of phrase, which signals how a scene can be a telescopic vision of some larger activity sequence to which it belongs and which it signals.

Further, Goffman suggests that photographs can also be used to provide documentation or an instance-record of the sort of behavioural practice which can be illustrated pictorially. At the risk of labouring the points made above, I want to suggest that a photograph of a man handing a woman money, in this consumer society, would be too ambiguous. The absence of money as a sign of prostitution, and the preponderance of images of women standing in the street, loitering, suggest that the issue of availability is central to the imagery: a sort of 'available for hire' signal. It is this that is the real issue in prostitution, not the act of prostitution per se, but the availability of women who can be identified as available for the provision of sexual services. The implications of this are discussed below. The instance-record is evidence, evidence that an instance of the practice *did* occur as pictured on the occasion of the picture taking. This issue of the validity of the photograph is discussed below, but Goffman's related comments are of relevance here. He suggests calling

> ... such a picture an *instantiation* ... [recording] an instance of a practice, instantiates it, is necessarily a good illustration of it ....For any photograph which merely illustrates a behavioural practice must also provide not merely an instance record of the illustrative practice but an instance itself (1979, p. 20).

The action sequence of prostitution includes, for street prostitution, the activities of loitering and soliciting. It is on these activities that the press stories and the photographs which visualise the claims in the stories

211

regarding evidence of prostitution concentrate. The appearance, place and time (night) are all present in these photographs. The short skirts, the street or deserted places and night-time prepare the viewer for the 'action' in the photograph, that is loitering.

The 'leaning into car window' is, I suggest, a conventionalised 'sign' of the prostitute and the repetition of this image is found both in the data set and in the extra materials collected (see Appendix III, no. 2). A further 'sign', or rather evidence that the photograph testifies to, that a woman is a prostitute is the image of her standing alone in a dark street.

The conventionalised 'sign' of prostitution/of the prostitute is contentious in the face of arguments about the lack of markers to identify a woman as a prostitute in these post-modern times. But one interesting feature of the additional data collected, specifically from an Irish tabloid, *The Star* (and one from the *Irish Independent* in the data set) were of photographs of *models* of prostitutes. These photographs suggest that a recognised 'pose' of the prostitute exists, a pose which includes both appearance and place and time. The poses are formulaic, they are 'hyper-ritualised', in Goffman's (1979) words. These photographs were almost identical to photograph number 2 (Appendix III).

Again, to refer back to Goffman in relation to the issue posed, his work on advertisements is particularly suggestive in relation to the current issue:

> what the advertisement is concerned to depict is not particular individuals already known, *but rather an activity which would be recognisable were we to see it performed in real life by persons not known to us personally* (1979, p. 19, emphasis added).

Thus, the photographs show social types, examples of categories of persons. And further in relation to caught photographs:

> ... when one establishes that a picture of something really is of the subject it portrays, it is very hard to avoid thinking that one has established something beyond this, namely, something about the event's currency, typicality, commonness ... and so forth (1979, p. 20).

He points out that no matter how posed or 'artificial' a picture is, it is likely to contain elements that record instances of real things. The photographs relevant to these points are intentionally choreographed to be unambiguous about matters that in uncontrived scenes may well be uninforming (Goffman, 1979, p. 23).

7.15 Photographing the subject of prostitution

> … A photograph should include everything appertaining to its subject and relevant to its purpose. If this cannot be done with one picture, then others must be taken in order that the whole subject is covered … (Tagg, 1988, p. 95).

How could the whole subject of prostitution be covered? What would a collection of photographs of prostitution contain? As noted, the action sequence of prostitution covered in news pictures focuses on the loitering and soliciting activities, the activities are, in Goffman's suggestive words, 'bereft of their longitudinal view' (1979, p. 22). The maximum number of photographs in any one story in the data set is three. However, in 1989 the *Sunday Correspondent* featured a photojournalistic story, LIVING ON THE STREETS (17.12.89, pp. 12-17) which included 11 photographs (see note 2). This story provides an opportunity to consider how the subject of [street] prostitution could be fully covered. I will briefly describe the different photographs, without referring to the main written story, before moving to comment.

Photograph 1 (p. 12) is of a woman lying in bed with a little boy beside her. The caption identifies who she is and directs attention to the book she is reading – its subject matter is AIDS.

Photograph 2 (p. 13) is of what initially looks like a traffic jam, it is at night and the car headlights illuminate the scene. Three women can be made out, in the background of the photograph, one is at the door of a car. The caption, 'Prostitutes working a busy street in Manhattan', directs us to 'find' the prostitutes in this scene and to identify them as such.

The third, fourth and fifth photographs are all on one page with captions to each located at the top right of the page. We see a woman standing on a street corner, one standing against a wall and one leaning into a car – the captions identify all these women as prostitutes. All are at night and their location is not marked, other than being on the street. The different views of prostitution are pictured here: street corner, 'lolling' against a brick wall, leaning into a car.

Two more photographs are positioned opposite to these (p. 15) which feature a woman leaning out of what we are told (by the caption) is a police van. Photograph 7 is very dark and a figure can be discerned with difficulty. The figure's proximity to the front of what looks like a truck makes the location look like a service park but on closer inspection, the location seems to be beside a toll bridge.

Photographs 8, 9, and 10 are of a man, identified as a pimp, the contents of a handbag which foregrounds condoms (perhaps an elliptical reference to AIDS) and a woman walking down the street. The first two are taken at night, the last in day light, but it is dawn. The final photograph is of a person at the top of a stairs, this is Misty and her son going to bed.

The photo-montage seems to be following Misty's day, a 'day in the life of Misty, the prostitute' type of sequence, where the women photographed can stand for Misty, also a prostitute. The inclusion of AIDS, condoms, a pimp, a woman in a police van, and scenes from night to early morning work to construct the subject of prostitution. The photographs, with the accompanying text work to construct the boundaries of prostitution – other aspects of the lives of women 'like' Misty are not shown, the one domestic scene is photograph 1, in which she is pictured with her son. Again, the photographs of prostitutes stand for prostitution, the photographs of women standing on the streets are part of the wider action sequence of prostitution.

The street is the 'setting' for prostitution. The woman in the police van, who has been arrested, represents an interruption of this sequence. The sartorial appearance of the women, of the short skirts and varying degrees of undress work with the caption identification, to identify them as prostitutes. The caption directs our viewing of the photographs. One aspect of these photographs is the absence of other people in the photographs – there are no other women in these photographs. Men, however, are present, explicitly as the pimp and the client, but also indirectly, as men in cars. These women seem to exist in an extra-ordinary world and presence in that world is evidence of intent to prostitute.

7.16 Historically and culturally specific visions

Gagnon & Simon (1974) argue that the cultural and historical specificity of different forms of prostitution needs to be considered. This is often ignored, for example, Roberts (1993) argues that ancient temple prostitution is an antecedent of current forms of prostitution and that both can be considered as prostitution as it is understood in contemporary society. An interesting visual example of the attempt to stabilise the image of prostitution in cultural terms is in the *Marie Claire* article about prostitution legislation world-wide. The photograph accompanying this information digest is of two women who, in Britain and Ireland at least, are in conventional (street) prostitutes' poses (i.e., lounging against a wall, dressed in tight fitting, short dresses and wearing high heels). The photograph works, I suggest, to present prostitution and its public form as similar world wide, when in fact, its organisation in Thailand and public display is dissimilar to that in the UK (cf. Cohen 1987).

In considering the role of clothing as an identificatory marker of a woman's sexual-occupational or deviant status (depending upon the framework employed), the historical and cultural specificity of signs/clothing was discussed. Identifying the prostitute has not remained constant, the signs have not remained legible. Marjorie Garber (1993) provides an instance of this: prior to World War 1, boys wore pink and girls blue, a reversal of what is contemporarily, in Western industrialised societies the 'norm'. She notes that what is so particularly fascinating about this detail is 'the fact that it reversed a binarism – that it disconcerted not only feelings of tradition, continuity and naturalness (rather than arbitrariness) of association, but also a way of reading' (1993, p. 2). Roberts (1993) includes photographs of prostitutes in her work on the history of prostitution and these photographs testify to how 'prostitutes' clothes' have not remained constant throughout history; indeed, without the caption these women could be anyone, that is, there is no immediate recognition of them as prostitutes by contemporary viewers.

Prostitution and the public forms of prostitution do not occur in a vacuum; for example the changing legal situation, the shifting social and cultural meaning of clothing and relatedly, the understanding of what 'prostitutes' clothes' are, impact upon the public display of prostitution. The photographs from the core data 'bank' did not provide any evidence of this, indeed the photographs could be said to be only providing us with a snapshot picture of imagery of prostitution in a narrow time period and little sense of the differing cultural and legal contexts within which prostitution, or rather, loitering and soliciting occurs. However, major legislative changes occurred, as noted in Chapter Two, in the Irish Republic vis-à-vis prostitution in 1993. The newspaper stories collected over the 1993-1995 period are, particularly over 1994, concerned with the state process of drafting the new legislation, and its effects upon the women working as prostitutes were constantly reported. A story, with accompanying photographs appeared in the *Cork Examiner* which explicitly focuses attention onto the context of public displays of prostitution (YOU CAN EARN UP TO £300 A DAY TAX FREE, 14.11.94).

The story, with multiple headlines, is about the investigative journalistic efforts of Ailin Quinlan who sets up an interview with a worker from a massage parlour and includes a report from the Cork Gardaí (police) dealing with a possible increase in the numbers of brothels operating in the city. The legislation, which enables the Garda to direct a suspected prostitute to leave the street may be leading to a decline in street prostitution and an concomitant increase in brothel prostitution. This of course was one of the results of the Criminal Law Amendment Act 1885 which has been documented by Walkowitz (1980, 1981). The caption: 'The world's oldest profession … fast becoming *a view from the past* on Cork streets as the vice underworld finds new way to disguise prostitution' raises issues of masking behaviours so that identifying a prostitute on the basis of what I have suggested is a conventional sign of prostitution (or rather evidence of intent to prostitute), namely a woman leaning into a car window, at night, on the streets, is related to the legislative context.

The identification of prostitutes is not immediate in cultural terms either. An example of this is found in an *Irish Times* story (THOUSANDS OF YOUNG GIRLS ARE PROSTITUTES, 2.8.95, p. 10, World News) about 'working girls' in Bangladesh (see note 2). In the story, Zana, a 30 year old prostitute, is reported as saying that they are

> … not allowed to wear shoes when they go shopping in another town. About 5,000 girls are working at Kandupatti, … Some wear western styled bra-tops but most wear saris. They wear silver speckled face powder, red and pink lipstick on their eyelids and decorate their foreheads with gold stars and black spots.

The photograph, captioned 'A young prostitute …' indicates the relevance of Goffman's (1959) comments about the decoding capacity of audiences. It pictures a young woman holding hands with a man. She is dressed in a sari. A Westerner, specifically an Irish person, who had not been to Bangladesh, nor knew of the position of women in this society, would not necessarily 'see' or read this photograph as being one of a prostitute.

7.17 Conclusion

This chapter has aimed to draw together some of the points made in the previous chapters dealing with appearance, place and time and the use of these in establishing the sexual and/or occupational identity of women. It has been particularly concerned to point to the neglected aspect of news pictures in analyses of newspaper coverage of different issues. It is necessarily selective and has focused attention to the specific areas which are of relevance to me. A central argument was that in viewing photographs we use the same procedures to identify 'what is going on' as we automatically use as viewers of 'live scenes'; we use the location, the time and the appearance of the photographed individuals to make inferences about what the photograph is about, who the subject of the photograph is. Loitering and soliciting, as one lot of actions in the dyadic structure of prostitution, are taken as prostitution in both the written stories and the photographs. This reading is validated by captions, headlines and the text of the story proper in which the identification 'prostitute' is given.

As this chapter suggests, the visual imagery of prostitution is an important aspect of press discourses on prostitution and its neglect means that analyses are somewhat partial. The relevance of Garfinkel's (1967) and Goffman's (1979) work to the analysis of news photographs/ pictures has been demonstrated and points to the work that is done by the newspaper reader in interpreting 'what the picture is about'. Goffman's (1979) distinction between two subjects 'of' photographs is particularly relevant in the photographs of prostitution; both the prostitute and the scene of prostitution are captured in these photographs. As with the written descriptions of prostitutes, appearance, place and time provide the basis for inferring evidence of intent to prostitute.

Notes

1   As I noted in the introduction, the time span over which this study was undertaken involved periods in which I undertook other research work and while the fields of study were unrelated, common concerns cropped up. Taking an example from research into young people's knowledge, beliefs and attitudes about HIV/AIDS, a notable feature of respondents' concerns was their explicit desire to see a person with AIDS. Mere verbal description was not enough, for them the reality of HIV infection was only to be evidenced in their visually experiencing the infected person. Simon Watney (1987) has focused upon media representations of people with HIV/AIDS but surprisingly, given the acknowledged importance of the visual in everyday life, does not analyse media images of PLWAs in television programmes or in the tabloid newspapers.

2   The selected photographs (including one illustration) are reproduced in Appendix III. Whilst the analysis is based upon all of the news photographs and sketches accompanying the news reports, difficulties obtaining copyright clearance for some of the news pictures resulted in only two of the pictures from the core data set being reproduced here. Some of the sections, namely, 7.15,

'Photographing the subject of prostitution', and 7.16, 'Historically and culturally specific visions', are based on two (referenced) newspaper articles. The photographs are unavailable and so my descriptions (or verbalisations) of the photographs will have to guide the reader. This is clearly not an ideal situation, but it is the preferred option, given the neglect, by previous writers, of press photography.

3 Barthes (1977) discusses this aspect of photography extensively – the photograph testifies to someone having really been at the scene.

4 Fairclough later refers to photographs/images when he analyses a radio interview between Margaret Thatcher and a BBC reporter. He refers to how Thatcher takes up a particular subject position in the talk, and refers to how the reader (as analyst) should consider MT's appearance 'in photographs of her you have seen' (1989, p. 183). However, he does not go on to consider intertextuality, to consider how the listeners of a radio programme will have seen Thatcher on television, in press reports, in magazines. In short he unproblematically brings into the analysis of a radio programme images which readers will have (or be expected to have) seen of the then Prime Minister.

5 A preliminary note is required in respect of 'images'. Image has been used in a variety of ways; for example, Viney in her analysis of images of illness, defines images as individuals' 'representations of illness-related events which include not only ideas but feelings, attitudes and beliefs. Images involve meanings which people have developed through their efforts to understand what is happening to them' (1989, p. 9). Heidensohn (1985, p. 85) defines images as 'form, semblance, counterpart' (OED). Image is also defined [Chambers] as a representation in the mind, especially of a visible object. The preceding analysis has pointed to this former meaning of images. However, in referring to images in this chapter, I am concerned with visual icons, that is, the photographic image.

6 The photographs referred to are listed (1-3) in Appendix III and are referenced accordingly.

7 See Holland et al. (1986, p. 3) for a discussion of the impact of semiology on photographic analysis.

8 This 'of' distinction is an analyst's construct, not a journalistic distinction.

9 It is perhaps apposite to note at this point that the analysis of the photographs is not in-depth, attempting to 'decode' each element

in the photographs. Nor am I going to describe the selected photographs in terms of for example, 'we see a woman standing there' mode, which is Fairclough's (1989) analytic approach, unless I am making a particular point about reading.

10   An example of a photograph without text is the advertising campaign the pop group Hot House Flowers initiated in Dublin in the late 1980s. Poster size photographs of well known Dublin 'characters' appeared all over the city for a number of weeks. Certainly, looking at these posters, there were no clues as to what they were 'about' other than (as a Dubliner) recognising the people photographed. It was only later that text was added to these images (literally, as the text was pasted over the posters) – the word was 'People', the title of the group's new album. This seems to be an increasingly popular advertising strategy (Smithwicks beer had a similar campaign). This example displays a delayed solution to the 'puzzle'.

11   It may be that there are legal restrictions on photographing clients.

12   Bloor & McKeganey (1990) have discussed the differing modes of operation regarding female and male prostitutes obtaining money; the former tend to, at least in Edinburgh, get the money before providing sexual services, whereas the latter group do not tend to ask for the money up-front, waiting until after the sexual activity. This has been related to issues of control and ability to negotiate.

13   This image appeared in *Hot Press* (March 1986, pp. 10-13), as part of a four page special issue on 'sex for sale'. The image was accompanied by a rider in which the editor (Niall Stokes) referred to the contentious nature of the images which were produced to accompany the various stories. This rider is of interest given the readings that this illustration evoked.

> This accompanying full colour illustration divided opinion most drastically. Originally conceived as a potential front cover, David [Rooney] saw it as working off the stereotype [sic] male sexual fantasy: this is what the client thinks he wants, but any notion of 'eroticism' is completely negated by the sinister presence of the cruising car – it reads as an extension of the male phallus depicted in a truly despicable light. But that was just one reading. There were women who thought the image worked, There were men who were extremely hostile to it – and vice versa. The consensus was that it shouldn't run. To take the risk of in any way compounding the problem of violence towards women by using a highly-charged yet ambiguous image on the cover of *Hot*

Press would be wrong. From an editorial point of view, it was a lesson in how fraught the issue is – and in how differently images can be interpreted by people who share the same basic convictions on feminism (p. 13).

8 The contextual web: Finding the connections

8.1 Introduction

British and Irish press stories of prostitution are, it is suggested, read as 'recognisably correct' stories. This recognition is produced over the course of reading and is based upon the unequivocal descriptions of 'prostitutes' on the basis of appearance, place and time of presence. This chapter attempts to answer the 'so what?' question that all research, and particularly, I would suggest, textual analysis, has to face. This question moves me from the local context of the press as a specific discourse site to the wider context of asymmetrical gender relations. It is an attempt to consider how the local process of textual discursivity produces and reproduces (or sustains) the wider social processes. Such an aim may seem to be incompatible with ethnomethodology, or indeed with Goffman's sociology. However, I will suggest that it is not, rather I move beyond the local context of the texts to situate them. My reason for adopting ethnomethodology was to deal with a problem relating to the analysis of the data, not a wholesale adoption of ethnomethodological theories of social life.

In moving from a focus on the corpus of press stories on prostitution to the wider context in which they are produced and circulated, I want to sketch out what Sue Fisher (1986) has termed 'the contextual web'. The 'web' I want to consider is co-existing discourses, for example, magazine articles on fashion and on personal safety, previous research on sexual violence against women, and in turn, a wider discourse of provocation. I want to suggest that (given that inferences of intent to prostitute are made in regard to appearance, specifically sartorial appearance, time and place of presence) perceived evidence of intent is provocative, meaning that it brings about a recognition of intent to prostitute. And, more importantly, to suggest that as prostitution is about sexual availability (in the sense of being available to men for sexual activities in return for monetary payment), appearance, place and time of presence are deemed to signal 'sexual availability'. In moving from a consideration of the texts on women who prostitute to all women, I am following the directive of the International Committee on Prostitutes Rights as expressed in the Draft Statement on Prostitution and Feminism (1986), namely that analyses of prostitution link the condition of prostitutes to that of all women.

The contextual web has been a central concern for discourse analysts, for example, Fowler comments that the difficulty is not in describing the linguistic structure of texts ... but in relating textual structure to social theory and to social context (1985, p. 75), for feminists and, of course, for both quantitative and qualitative researchers. In relation to the news media, van Dijk (1988, p. 28) notes that complex theoretical and empirical picture. He suggests the following context (or series of links):

> news reports <-> news structures <-> cognitive process and representations ... (scripts, attitudes, ideologies) <-> news production as social interaction (this includes the process of news gathering) <-> inter-group interactions between journalists and other groups <-> internal organisational routines and so on of the news organisation <-> external goals and interests of the news organisation and a private or public corporation <-> institutional relationship between the media institutions and other institutions <-> the historical and cultural position of the media institution and its relations with other institutions (1988, p. 28).

John Thompson (1990) has suggested a similar model of linkages in his proposals regarding the methodological approach to the study of news discourse. His model includes three phases of analysis: firstly, a socio-historical analysis which locates the social and historical conditions of the production, circulation and reception of symbolic forms; secondly, a formal linguistic discourse analysis of individual texts (which means, Thompson says, studying symbolic forms [newspaper stories] as complex symbolic constructions which display an articulated structure).[1] If this analysis is done on its own, it produces a misleading and abstract exercise, disconnected from social historical conditions and oblivious to what is being expressed by the symbolic forms whose structure it seeks to unveil. Thirdly, the interpretation of symbolic forms, a creative construction of possible meaning. This model is within a wider theoretical model of the analysis of ideology. I finish this study still having problems with Thompson's argument about creative explication of possible meaning: my aim in this thesis is to attempt to do more than be simply creative. It is to pose suggestive links which may be further investigated in further empirical analysis.[2]

Fisher, remarking upon a similar multi-phase research scheme established by Duster (1981), suggests that for a single researcher

> This is rather a larger order. Collective work or the combination of studies across settings, perspectives and methodologies are required to create a broader vision than single efforts can provide (1986, p. 168).

I agree with Fisher and for that reason consider that my choice of 'secondary sources', such as feminist work on rape is justified. My approach differs from that proposed by van Dijk (1988) and Thompson (1990) as I am going to focus upon inter-discursive context (as I have already done to a limited extent in my considerations of the different discourses on prostitution) and then consider the issue of the 'micro-macro'.

8.2   Inter-discursive relations

My initial approach to the data, although abandoned as a specific method, was not without gain: Michel Pecheux's approach to discourse proposes that every discourse is constructed out of what he terms the preconstructed and the enunciated, and discourse structure can be analysed in terms of the relations between these, as articulated in the relative clause. The preconstructed refers that which relates to a previous external construction in opposition to what is constructed by the utterance, that is enunciation (1982, p. 64). His model of discourse is based upon the view (also expressed in Foucauldian discourse analysis) that 'every discourse is subject to the intrusion of other discourses into itself' (Frow, 1986, p. 4). Pecheux was concerned with the constitution of subject positions in discourse and was, as such, not of relevance to the current project. However, his points about the preconstructed sensitised me to the ways in which a constant process of traversing of press discourses by other discourses was occurring, indeed this can be demonstrated by a datum from the data set. In a *Guardian* story, headlined 'HOT BLONDE' PLEADS NYMPHOMANIA AS TOWN QUAKES AT KISS-AND-TELL LIST (9.9.1991):

S1   A Florida woman accused of prostitution is a nymphomaniac with uncontrollable desires who needs sex as therapy, a court in Fort Lauderdale has been told.

This opening sentence articulates assumptions from the psycho-pathological discourse in which prostitution is 'caused' by uncontrollable urges; that there is an underlying clinical basis for this behaviour. Later in the article, this is disputed (S16) but the story ends by citing the defence lawyer who insisted that it was an addiction like any other (S18). It is not only that discourses are constantly traversing, being articulated with other discourses but that readers, over their course of reading will draw upon other discourses in making sense of the presumed sense of the text, and indeed in rejecting or resisting the 'preferred meaning'. van Dijk's work on cognitive processing (1985) is concerned with this, as indeed is the ethnomethodological and Goffmanian approach to social life, in the forms of 'typifications' and expectations from past experiences with scenes.

Coward and Ellis have referred to intertextuality, the relation between texts (here termed inter-discursivity) as a 'controlled process of echoing, of recalling' (1977, p. 51). The structuralist conceptualisation of language is evident in Foucault's argument that 'The meaning of a statement would be defined not by the treasure of intentions that it might contain … but by the difference that articulates it upon other real or possible statements, which are *contemporary to it or to which it is opposed in the linear series of time*' (1975, p. xvii). This comment points to the linkages between past 'statements' (here simplistically understood as discourses) and those in circulation contemporaneously.

Theories of intertextuality suggest then that any one text is necessarily read in relationship to others, and that a range of textual knowledges is brought to bear on it. The relations, as Fiske points out, do not take the form of specific allusions from one text to another and there is no need for readers to be familiar with specific or the same texts to read intertextually. Fiske provides as an example, Madonna's *Material Girl*, suggesting that the intertextuality is not between this song (and video) and Marilyn Monroe in the film *Gentlemen Prefer Blondes*. Rather he suggests, the intertextual relation is between the culture's 'image bank' of the sexy blonde star (1987, p. 108). Hence Madonna's song realises its meaning intertextuality by drawing on all texts that contribute to and draw upon 'the blonde' in our culture. Intertextual knowledges thus pre-orient the reader to exploit polysemy (in this case in television programmes) by activating the text in certain ways.[3] Drawing upon Barthes, he comments that 'reality' is not accessible, all we can know is the culture's representation of reality (p.115). Hence, in our readings of prostitution and related activities we make sense by reference to what we have read before, and indeed, what we have seen before. In the review of

Lyn: a story of prostitution (Madden & Levine, 1987) the deprivation of women who work in prostitution was central (LYN'S GROUP IS THE MOST DEPRIVED OF ALL, *Irish Times*, 5.10.87). The involuntary nature of the activity was one reading of the book which drew upon variants of feminist and Christian moralist discourses and these knowledges structured the public discourse of prostitution around that time.[4]

One simple approach to considering how texts are read has been to consider the context of their reading. This context starts on the newspaper pages. One example of juxtapositioning the data set is in the case of a story about prostitution in Holland, VICE: DUTCH EURO MOVE (*Irish Independent*, 25.2.89) which is placed above a second story about sexual harassment. This story (MINI-SKIRT STORM) is about a judge who

... suggested that his victim may have been asking for trouble ... said Maria Lopez's short skirt may have partly provoked the offence ... said 'Such economy of cloth is more provocative than a skirt with a few more centimetres' ... He could not resist the temptation (ibid.).

Another way of considering intertextuality is by considering those press stories which are tagged onto the bottom of 'proper' stories (that is stories with a headline). One example of this is in PROSTITUTES WITH HIV 'SHOULD GET SICK PAY' (*Independent*, 11.6.91). This reports a researcher's recommendation that prostitutes infected with HIV should receive sick pay and maintenance. The 'tagged on' story is about the High Court's approval of compensation payments to haemophiliacs 'infected with the Aids virus (sic) ... during NHS treatment.' This addition may produce a reading of 'innocent' – 'guilty', with prostitutes seen to have been culpable and the haemophiliacs 'innocent', a distinction which is well established and available to readers.

Other modes of inter-discursivity are less evident. I want to suggest, in relation to clothing, place and time, that women's magazines are one source of meanings and knowledges about the world and that these are tacit knowledges which are invoked in the readings of stories of prostitution. Pratt, in his study of pornography and everyday life, has suggested that 'soft-porn' magazines *contribute* to the general discourse in which sexual relationships are structured and formed and which promotes the belief that social reality should bear a correspondence to the episodes in the magazines (1986, p. 76).

A woman whose husband called her a 'tart' tried to disclaim the validity of the designation by saying that 'this is crazy because I don't wear much make-up' (*Essentials*, 1989). 'Tart' is used interchangeably with prostitute, but it is also part of what Lees (1986) has termed a 'vocabulary of abuse'. Further, excessive make-up is seen as a 'sign' of a prostitute. The problem solver (Suzie) tells the woman to 'explain how and why he is *misinterpreting* the situation' (emphasis added). Women have, in this discourse, to account for their appearance.

Looks (September, 1989) ran a feature article, which is commonly available in different women's magazines, WHAT DO BOYS THINK ABOUT THE WAY WE DRESS?, stating that 'Like it or not your looks are the first pieces of information people "read" about you. They're the front line so make sure they're delivering the right message to the world'. Tarde (in Corrigan, 1988, p. 34) suggested that while clothing and other appearances will accurately translate their general social and personal state, one can never be sure with women or children: men's appearances are to be taken on trust, women's are not. Hence, as Corrigan notes, Tarde's approach was to suggest that women and children may not know how to treat clothed appearance responsibly, where responsibility entails accurate portrayal of social state.

This is not the message in the *Looks* article, nor indeed in other magazine articles about fashion for women, rather the message is that women are responsible for their self-presentation. They are responsible for 'getting it right'. One of the clothed women is presented as a 'vamp' and the boys comment on what they think about her clothes. One (Justin, from Manchester) said, 'She looks a bit of a tart'. From a problem page in a national Irish newspaper a young woman writes to complain that 'I'm 16 and all my friends are wearing short skirts and tops and ... my father ... says I look like a tart' (*Sunday Independent*, 6.8.95). 'Patricia' (the problem solver) responds: 'What parents are always worried about is that teenagers might send out the wrong signals, without knowing it ... Girls can end up in trouble with unwanted attention from men because of the way they dress'. Women's dress is provocative.

Another writer on the what men think about women's clothes, states that 'The short-skirted executive was a case in point. She dresses like a tart, they said to themselves, so she should be treated as one. But tarts only dress like tarts within the language of the day' (*Cosmopolitan*, May, 1995). Of course, dressing 'like a prostitute' does not remain the same over time, but the point is that these different discourses, from problem pages in newspapers to women's magazines, all instruct women on how not to appear as a prostitute. These articles make reference, either directly or obliquely, to the possibility and the consequences of *misinterpretation*.[5]

In Peter Sutcliffe's trial, referred to in Chapter One, a central issue in determining his state of mind had as one aspect his misidentification of women as prostitutes. Michael Havers on the prosecution team stated that

Your story would have gone straight down the drain if you had to say to the doctors that six of them were not prostitutes.

And a Dr. Miline, one of the psychiatrists called by the defence team, stated that he did not believe that Sutcliffe was simulating mental illness. Responding to a question about the diagnoses of paranoid schizophrenia, he continued:

... the way he might behave ... The way he may misinterpret people's behaviour ... I use this [misinterpretation of behaviours] in particular relating to his confusion at times to identify absolutely and with certainty who were and who were not his victims – that is prostitutes (Boulos, 1983, p. 30)

Sutcliffe's madness then hinged upon his confusion as to who was a prostitute. With this, the assumption is expressed that it is possible, that a sane person would be able to identify, and identify unequivocally, who is a prostitute. Sutcliffe was convicted of murder, not manslaughter, that is the jury did not believe that he was suffering from mental illness at the time of the killings. His methods of identification were perhaps heard as 'recognisably correct' (cf. Chapter Six).

8.2.1 Inter-discursivity: The discourse of rape

Walby, Hay and Soothill (1983), considering the social construction of rape in the UK national press, focus upon two main categories (which contain sub-categories); 'loss of control' and 'victim provocation'. It is the latter category which is of relevance for current purposes. 'Victim provocation' comprises two sub-categories:

Sexual provocation:
(i)   clothing;
(ii)   previous sexual history;
(iii)   drink (victim);
(iv)   familiar with rapist.
and
Spatial:
(i)   woman enters man's space, e.g., his home;
(ii)   public space, e.g., street;
(iii)   hitching;
(iv)   other (Walby et al., 1983).

These two categories with their sub-items (clothing, public space) are clearly of relevance to this study given the specific attention of the press discourses to appearance, of which clothing is a sub-category, and place, in particular the public street. The two key categories of loss of control and victim provocation accounted for nearly 100% of their sample of 330 reports. Provocation means that the raped woman was primarily or at least partially responsible for provoking the attack (1983, p. 90). Provocation has two forms, spatial (where she places herself) and what she wears. Walby et al. remark that

... the notion of victim provoked rape is ... peculiar ... [it] implies that the victim did not consent to intercourse, so why should she provoke it? ... The situation appears to be that some people may think that the woman *deserved* to be raped because of her sexual conduct (ibid., emphasis in original).

While Walby et al. note Smart and Smart's (1978) argument that the spatial location of rape, especially the streets, is central to reports on rape, the data for Walby et al.'s study do not suggest this centrality of space in relation to press reports. They note Smart and Smart's argument that the reports are a form of social control of women in deterring them from free movement in public spaces.

I do not advance this argument, rather I would suggest that the identification of women in specific places (and times) as 'sexually available for hire', i.e. as prostitutes, works to determine the terms on which women are present in public places (McRobbie, cited in Lees, 1986, has also argued this). What the above suggests, quite crucially for my purposes, is that a range of discourses (here confined to the press, but also evident in other feminist-sociological analyses of interaction, e.g., Lees, 1986) which are concerned with women's presence in the social world are concerned with appearance and place (and by implication time, given that social time is relevant to the identification of places, as demonstrated in Chapter Six). Thus, it is not only in the British and Irish press discourses of prostitution that appearance, place and time are used to categorise women as 'prostitutes', appearance and place are also used in press discourses of rape to construct women as provocateurs, as agents who bring about reactions to themselves.

8.3   Social control in social context

When the analysis phase was initially concluded, I understood that the newspaper stories were articulating rules about how not to be identified as 'a prostitute'; these rules related to appearance, especially clothed appearance, time of presence and the location of presence. However, as noted in Chapter Six, this was prior to my understanding of the function of the descriptions and place and time formulations, namely, the warranting, the providing of evidence of intent, of this presence. Ethnomethodology suggests that rules are not fixed and immutable; rather they are indexical and further that the invocation of rules on any particular occasion is bound to that occasion; for example, if there is a 'No Smoking' sign in an auditorium, this rule is not attended to if a magician, as part of her/his act lights up a cigarette. A further extension to this indexicality of rules is, I would suggest, the gender of the person doing the behaviour that is being assessed by observers. Would appearance, place of presence and time of presence be reported in relation to male prostitutes?

The content analysis indicated that there were six stories in the data set in which male prostitution was mentioned. Place was a consideration in these stories (for example in the *Irish Times*, 30.1.89). They refer to how specific places in the city are 'for men'. Time is not mentioned. Appearance was mentioned in two of the stories, once in relation to rent-boys in drag ('just like us' (the women)), a second described the clothes an ex-rent boy wore. However, that appearance is not routinely reported about men is evident in a story from outside the data set (see note).[6]

It is only at this point, having moved from the texts themselves to the relations between texts, that I can, legitimately, move to consider the broader context. In introducing the argument (Chapter Six) about evidence of intent to prostitute produced (by the reader interacting with the text) through the descriptions of appearance, place and time, I noted that this was one function of the descriptions. However, this function fulfils a textual 'task'. I want here to attempt to consider the wider context in which the production and reception of these texts occurs, a consideration which is necessarily limited given space constraints, but one which is vital in specifying the wider import of the stories of prostitution.

The context is one characterised by asymmetrical gender relations between men and women, a context in which women experience oppression in their everyday lives. In providing 'evidence' of this I refer the reader to the volumes of feminist (in particular) work on healthcare (Davis, 1988), sexual harassment (Herbert, 1989; Halson, 1992), the more general theme of violence against women (Cameron and Frazer, 1987; Kelly, 1988; Bart and Moran, 1993) and the constraints experienced by women in their everyday lives (cf. Lees, 1986, 1989). This is the context in which the newspaper stories are produced and read. And it is to this context that I am looking in considering the wider function of the newspaper stories of prostitution. My main argument in this respect is that the discourses of prostitution have material effects; they constrain women's freedom.

Herbert (1989) describes a range of what she terms 'female controlling practices'. She comments that women are *taught* to avoid danger, that is perceived danger, as Stanko (1993) has pointed out (1989, p. 147). However, Herbert does not, unlike Lees (1986), describe *how* women are 'taught'. I would consider that the press discourses on prostitution provide an 'education' to both male and female readers. She simply comments that strategies include women staying at home and wearing decent and respectable clothes.

Lees (1986) focuses upon discourse in considering the oppression of women. Effectively she demonstrates that the 'rules of application' for the category 'slag' are variable, that any young woman can be categorised as a 'slag' with its negative effects. Women's sexual reputation is considered to reflect her 'worth'. My approach bears a similarity to that of Lees – she looks at how the category 'slag' is actually used rather than attempting to define it. She suggests that the

> ... key to an understanding of the power exercised over the girls by the language of sexuality lies in the hidden or unstated assumptions of the discourse in which they participate (1986, p. 28).

The unstated assumptions, the 'ineffable' as Garfinkel termed them (1967), are those background, taken-for-granted, common-sensical notions about femininity, about respectability. One theorist who has considered the social control of women, Greer Litton Fox (1977), suggests that one of the main forms of social control in Western societies is a form of control embodied in value constructs such as 'nice-girl'. 'Niceness' is always achieved, an ongoing process occurring in every social situation a women enters or participates in. She proposes that a woman's presence, destination and mode of traverse are all assessed in terms of their 'fit' with 'niceness', for example, the 'come-on' line 'what's a nice girl like you doing in a place like this?' suggests that there are certain places where 'nice girls' are not found. There are also consequences of being in 'not nice places', namely that women are culpable for attacks on themselves. This geographical limitation, as considered by Herbert (above), is linked to temporal restrictions which also operate. The newspaper stories are providing information not only about women who prostitute but also about the ecology of urban centres (in particular), about the places where, upon entering a woman is evidencing (to observers) an intent.

8.4 Social control: The role of the press

Walby et al. (1983) argue that the press reports present an image of rape which is far removed from 'reality'. They move on from a reference of this discrepancy to note that

> Regrettably ... we must conclude that we are increasingly being encouraged to take on the definitions which are provided so stridently by the media. The bringing together of media images and reality is a pernicious process, for it is rarely the case that the media recognise the inaccuracies of their images and hasten to correct any misinterpretations (1983, p. 95).

In contradistinction to their approach which sets the official statistics on rape and the sociological accounts of rape alongside the press discourses in order to determine how the latter match up to the presumed reality of the former, I have conceptualised the different discourses as having the same status as the press discourses. There is no 'reality' out there which is reflected in the press accounts, rather, they actively construct a reality and combine with other discourses to form a hegemonic dominance, a dominance which is not given but constantly maintained. Journalists draw upon pre-existing knowledge, knowledge which is articulated in different discourses of prostitution. Common-sense knowledge, that which every competent member of society possesses and which has been informed by legal, medical, sociological and other discourses, is central to press discourse and the commonsense articulated in the press discourses relates to the notion that women can be readily identified as 'prostitutes' (cf. Aggleton and Homans, 1987; Giddens, 1989).

8.5 Evidence: Some final comments

Goode and Troiden (1974, p. 23) arguing that every form of deviant behaviour is an exaggerated case of conventional behaviour, ask what kinds of acts must a woman perform in order to be defined as a prostitute; how long does she have to be 'in the life' before we all – herself included – decide that she is magically granted the status of *being* a prostitute? The data in this study suggest that 'being' a prostitute is assessed by observers on the basis of appearance and place and time of appearance, rather than, for example, knowledge of legal status (of 'known prostitute').

Parent-Duchatelet, a physician in 19th century France, had a dream about the ready identification of 'prostitutes', a vision in which the troublesome lack of correspondence between appearance and reality, between the correct identification of a prostitute and misidentification is removed:

> We will have arrived at the limit of perfection and of the possible ... if we arrange it so that men, and in particular those who are looking for [prostitutes] can distinguish them from honest women (cited in Clarke, 1987, p. 109).

The press discourses of prostitution in which the descriptions of appearance, place and time are used, both in combination and singly, articulate this dream. But it is a dream which is not 'targeted' only at men, it is also of relevance to women. It is common-sense knowledge that evidence of intent to prostitute, to be sexually available, is inferred on the basis of those three dimensions of a scene. Women, if they are not to be misidentified, must ensure that their presence is not provocative, i.e. that it does not give rise to a formulation of the intent of their presence.

8.6 Concluding remarks

Stories of prostitution in the British and Irish press are read as 'recognisably' stories of prostitution via the use of appearance, place and time descriptions. These descriptions work to produce a reading of the story as unequivocally about prostitutes or scenes of prostitution and further, they are used to infer evidence of intent to prostitute. This has been the pivotal concern of my thesis which has moved from a wide focus (representations of prostitutes in newspaper texts and a content analysis of key categories in the data) to a narrow one (that of how are categorisations of women as prostitutes produced) and expanded again to consider the links between and across a range of texts and the wider context within which such reports are to be considered. In this respect I have tried to, in a very general manner, link the local (the newspaper texts) to the global context of their production and reception.

The emergence of the research question, following initial attempts to analyse the stories, led me to ethnomethodology, with its concern with the production of social life and the role of description in that process. I did not accept all of the elements of ethnomethodology, using it in an instrumental manner, and would be criticised on that basis by ethnomethodological 'purists'. In addition, I was especially concerned with the ethnomethodological strand which is concerned with practical, everyday reasoning, not with the more formalist ethnomethodological work on conversation structure. This strand displays affinities with the work of Erving Goffman, and his observations about the organisation of social life were used to interpret the function of appearance, place and time in the stories of prostitution.

The interpretative approach to the analysis of the texts may be criticised from the point of view of formal discourse analysis which explicates textual structure, and relatedly, the identification of discursive conflict. It may be argued that this aspect should have been the topic of this study. To these criticisms my defence is that these were precisely my aims when I set out to investigate the discourses of prostitution in the press. I consider that this defence is crucial precisely because of the problems I encountered in my initial attempts to analyse the stories using a formal method of analysis. The method which was ultimately forged enabled me to 'unearth' a critical feature of the texts, a feature which is present across different topics and different newspapers in the two countries (Britain and Ireland). In addition, the work of the ethnomethodologists and of Goffman provided a framework within which to analyse the newspaper photographs which were given a far more central place in the analysis than is usually the case in studies of press discourses. The validity of the method stands in relation to the findings yielded by its use.

As with all research, this inquiry does not close the subjects of the representations of prostitutes in the British and Irish press. It does not claim to constitute the 'last word' on the subject, only to have identified a general process occurring across the different texts. As stated previously, the current effort is best conceptualised as a piece in a larger puzzle. Various future areas of investigation were suggested over the course of the study.

As I remarked in Chapter Six, the emergence of the question of 'evidence of intent to prostitute' led me to consider the ways in which law enforcement agents identify 'prostitutes'. The interview with the solicitor indicated that not only were appearance, place and time used by journalists to warrant the category 'prostitute' (and infer evidence of intent) but are also used by police officers in their verbalisations of how they suspected, in Sacks' (1972) terms, the assembly of a crime. Further, systematic collection of data on courtroom interaction would provide valuable data on this aspect.

In Chapter Three I described the rationale behind the selection of the broadsheet over the tabloid press. I also included in the circulation figures the average annual totals for leading UK and Irish tabloids, averages which far outstrip the circulation figures of individual broadsheets. I accepted Hollway's (1981) argument that the arguments made à propos of patterns discernible in broadsheet press coverage will stand for tabloid press coverage. However, in retrospect, this acceptance is open to dispute and I would suggest that this argument has the status of a hypothesis rather than as something proven. Further research on the descriptions of prostitutes in the tabloid press is therefore a viable proposal.

I have, albeit in a terse manner, related the findings from the data to wider issues of asymmetrical gender relations. Male prostitution has only briefly been mentioned throughout this thesis and seems to be an obvious area for further research, particularly given the changing legal situation in respect of homosexuality and, in Ireland, the recent legislative changes to sexual offences legislation (Criminal Law (Sexual Offences) Act 1993) to include men as prostitutes (although as noted, a legal category of 'known prostitute' no longer exists).

A wider comparative study could be conducted to test arguments made in this study. Some data from Australian press reports (1991-1992) exhibited a similar concern with appearance, place and time as that detailed in the present study. A detailed study of the Australian press, particularly across different States/Territories with their differing legislation on prostitution, may provide data on variation in descriptions according to legal context.

The analysis of the photographs could form the basis of a separate study. Here I was concerned to focus upon the two types of photographs, those of 'the prostitute' and those of 'the scene of prostitution'. In addition, I focused briefly upon the reading process, on the interaction between captions, headlines and photographs. A wider study of press photographs, with more detailed 'decoding', could be the basis of a further study.[7]

Finally, as the 'zooming in' analytic strategy demanded, I was forced to abandon other dimensions of the press stories. The content analysis procedure reported in Chapter Three was necessarily abridged and further research could be carried out in relation to each of the categories with a more focused tracking (or genealogy) of discourses as the objective of the analysis. This would enable a more precise mapping of the discourses of prostitution as outlined in Chapter Two.

As a final note, Roberts has already produced a vision of the future:

When any woman can walk the streets at night, on her own, dressed as she pleases, without running the risk of being branded a whore, arrested for streetwalking, or raped and *then* branded a whore, we will know that the theory of women's liberation from male violence has been translated into fact (1993, p. 358).

In this future, the words of Peter Sutcliffe, 'But I knew she was a prostitute', would require more than imputations of intent to prostitute on the basis of appearance, time and place to make sense.

Notes

1   I use the notion of articulation to refer both to production of speech/writing and 'linkage' (cf. Fiske, 1987).

2   My approach, as has been detailed, has been to start with formal discourse analysis, move to a more interpretative approach which has its origins in the ethnomethodological work on practical reasoning and on the production of social life and to remain 'within the text' before moving outside to wider social contexts.

3   Fiske distinguishes between vertical and horizontal intertextuality; for current purposes, such detail is not required.

4   I was particularly interested in the lack of references in the press review of the book to the references, in the book, to how Lyn felt that what she was doing 'suited her'. This 'voluntaristic' discourse, articulated in the prostitutes' discourse, was absent from the reviews of the book.

5   Misidentification of women who are not available for prostitution as those who are, can work the other way: An article, collected in the course of a data checking procedure from the McCarthy *CD ROM Index* (1995) told of how a bank manager (Manser) 'will be remembered, particularly for the occasion in New York when he mistook a prostitute for a journalist and was half way through dinner with her when he realised the error' (MANSER SETS UP ON THE LEFT BANK, *Daily Telegraph*, 5.1.95). Such 'errors' do not invalidate the thesis advanced here, rather they indicate how appearance is not reliable. I consider that the discourses of prostitution are suggesting that they are reliable, a utopian approach but one which, as Corrigan (1988) demonstrated, could hardly be otherwise if social life is to function smoothly. We live in an interpretative utopia (p. 259).

6   The example was found in a murder story. It describes the accused 'Mr Patrick Gillane was wearing a light-blue patterned short-sleeved shirt open to the waist showing a black vest underneath. His brother was dressed in an open-neck shirt with the sleeves rolled up'. (HUSBAND CHARGED WITH MURDER ROLE, *Irish Times*, 3.7.95).

The inclusion of detailed dress descriptions, so common in the stories of prostitution in relation to women, is here unusual. No comparable reports were found by me in the course of 'everyday' as opposed to 'analysis' reading over the course of this study.

7 I did not refer to what may be a 'function' of press photographs of 'prostitutes', namely their titillating function. This would tie in with the economic aspect of the newspaper industry. I did not find these photographs 'titillating', although perhaps heterosexual men would find them so.

Appendix I

Definitions in the
discourses of prostitution

Davis (1937): Prostitution is a contractual relation in which (sociological) services are provided and traded; in commercial coitus both parties use sex for an end not socially functional.

Glover (1943) (*psycho-pathological*): Prostitution exhibits regressive characteristics, it represents a primitive phase in sexual development. It is a kind of sexual backwardness.

Benjamin & Masters (1964) (*sociological*): Prostitution is a cash transaction. The prostitute defines herself when she decides to have sexual intercourse with a person, not her husband, who offers her money for engaging in intercourse.

Gagnon & Simon (1974) (*sociological*): Prostitution is the exchange of sexual access on a relatively indiscriminate level for monetary reward that is specifically for the act itself.

Rosenblum (1974) (*feminist*): Prostitution is emotionally indifferent promiscuity.

'J' in Millett (1975) (*practitioner*): Prostitution is not just a commercial transaction: the customer buys the prostitute's loss of free speech and humiliation.

Wild (1978) (*sociological*): Prostitution is most accurately viewed as a service occupation – an occupation in which a service is offered for a negotiable fee – and can be analysed along the same lines as other service-oriented occupations ... Prostitution is more than the sale of sex – it is sale of an illusion ... it involves the sale of sexuality and impersonal conduct.

Gannon (1979) (*feminist*): Prostitution involves the explicit sale of a prostitute's sexuality. It is a social institution in which women are economically and sexually exploited by men.

Goldstein (1979) (*criminological*): Prostitution is non-marital sexual service for material gain.

Walkowitz (1980) (*feminist*): Prostitution [is] an occupation – one that involves casual sexual encounters with men for cash payment.

Perkins & Bennett (1985) (*practitioner*): Prostitution is a business transaction understood as such by the parties involved and in the nature of a short-term contract in which one or more people pay an agreed price to one or more other people for helping them attain sexual gratification by various methods.

Day (1989) (*anthropological*): Acts of prostitution may be defined as the exchange of sexual services for money or goods between two or more people.

Gossop et al. (1994) (*epidemiological*): A form of prostitution is the provision of sex in return for drugs.

Barry (1995) (*feminist*): Prostitution is female sexual slavery.

Appendix II

Listing of newspaper stories of prostitution in the British and Irish press: 1987 - 1991

Those newspaper articles with accompanying photographs, illustrations and/or sketches are indicated by an asterisk (*). The photographs specifically referred to in Chapter Seven are presented in bold type.

1987
UK press
SOHO GIRLS PONDER NEW OFFENSIVE, *Observer*, 14.6.87
THE DANGEROUS IRONIES OF SAFE SEX, *Independent*, 3.8.87
RISKS WOMEN FACE, *Observer*, 1.1.87
WAR ON VICE GIRLS, *South London Press*, 6.3.87*

Irish press
MAN MUST PAY £400 TO INJURED PROSTITUTE, *Irish Times*, 13.1.87
ARCHER PAID – PROSTITUTE, *Irish Times*, 11.07.87*
ARCHER – AN ACCESSIBLE FIGURE, *Irish Times*, 25.7.87*
ARCHER AWARDED £1/2M AFTER WINNING LIBEL CASE, *Irish Times*, 25.7.87
COGHLAN COMMUTED FROM ROCHDALE TO LONDON, *Irish Times*, 25.7.87
LYN'S GROUP IS THE MOST DEPRIVED OF ALL, *Irish Times*, 5.10.87
DUBLIN'S VAGRANT BOYS DRIVEN TO PROSTITUTION, *Irish Times*, 5.10.87
ONE WOMAN'S ESCAPE FROM THE SAVAGERY OF DUBLIN'S STREETS, *Irish Times*, 7.10.87*
PROSTITUTE FIGHTS TEST-TUBE BABY BAN, *Irish Times*, 21.10.87
CHILDREN FOR SALE, *Irish Independent*, 16.12.87*
EXPOSED – THE REAL WORLD OF DUBLIN'S BRUTAL PIMPS, *Evening Press*, 7.10.87*
PROSTITUTE WITH AIDS 'A WALKING TIME BOMB', *Evening Press*, 12.12.87
JEFFREY BORES MONICA SILLY, *Sunday Independent*, 27.9.87
AIDS RIFE AMONG DUBLIN VICE GIRLS!, *Sunday World*, 22.2.87

1988

UK press

GIRLS OF THE REEPERBAHN FIND GROWING DEARTH OF CUSTOMERS, *Guardian*, 3.4.88*

THE RENT BOY DAVID, *Guardian*, 5.11.88*

PROSTITUTES' PENSION 'WOULD CUT AIDS', *Independent*, 11.1.88

LYN'S GAME PLAN FOR SAFE SEX, *Observer*, 28 .2. 88*

GREAT BALLS OF FIRE, *Observer*, 28.2.88*

Irish press

SEX EXPENSES, *Irish Times*, 28.1.88

SIN WAS NO MISTAKE, SAYS RETIRING TV EVANGELIST, *Irish Times*, 23.2.88

TV EVANGELIST IN SEX SCANDAL AGREES TO 'REHABILITATION', *Irish Times*, 24.2.88

GARDAÍ INVESTIGATE PROSTITUTION REPORT, *Irish Times*, 3.3.88

WOMAN TELLS COURT OF ALLEGED RAPE, *Irish Times*, 3.3.88

ALLEGED RAPE VICTIM 'BRUISED, UNSTEADY', *Irish Times*, 5.3.88

ALLEGED RAPE VICTIM WAS PROSTITUTE, SAYS WITNESS, *Irish Times*, 8.3.88

TWO DUBLIN TRAVELLERS FOUND GUILTY OF RAPE, *Irish Times*, 9.3.88

MEN LIKELY TO BE CHARGED IN TIPP 'CHILD SEX SCANDAL', *Sunday Tribune*, 7.2.88

'CHILD PROSTITUTE', *Sunday Tribune*, 7.2.88

'DIFFICULT' GIRLS, *Sunday Tribune*, 14.2. 88

YOUNG GIRLS' COURTROOM ORDEAL IN CLARE SEX CASE, *Sunday Tribune*, 28.2.88

HAL LAY LOO YAH: RAPTURE ME UP, *Sunday Tribune*, 28.2.88

OH! DADDY, *Sunday Tribune*, 29.5.88

1989

UK press

THAILAND TOURISTS DRUG SCARE, *Guardian*, 20.11.89

ALL IN THE BEST POSSIBLE TASTE, *Guardian*, 20.11.89*

DSS RULES 'FAILING YOUNG OFFENDERS', *Guardian*, 21.11.89

BLESSED BE THE MEEK FOR THEY MAY GET A MISTRIAL, *Observer*, 3.9.89*

KEELER AND SON, *Daily Mail*, 3.3.89*

CECIL'S GIRL IN DRUG SET BACK, *Mail on Sunday*, 5.11.89*

DOUBLE LIFE OF A HORSEY SET CALL GIRL, *Sunday Mirror*, 13.8.89*

THE AIDS TIME BOMB, *Sunday Mirror*, 13.8.89*

Irish press

TWILIGHT WORLD OF PROSTITUTION, *Irish Times*, 30.1.89*

A LOOK AT THE LEGAL SITUATION, *Irish Times*, 30.1.89

IN RETURN FOR A PLACE TO STAY, *Irish Times*, 30.1.89*

I'M REALLY CAREFUL WITH CLIENTS, *Irish Times*, 30.1.89

When prostitution is just another job, *Irish Times*, 17.4.89*
Vice: Dutch Euro move, *Irish Independent*, 25.2.89
The best days of our lives can be among the worst, *Sunday Tribune*, 24.12.89

1990
UK press
Miss Whiplash shows her metal over taxman's morals, *Guardian*, 16.5.90*
Brothel keeper loses tax appeal, *Guardian*, 19.5.90
Prostitution held to be a taxable trade, *Guardian*, 6.6.90
Curbing crawlers on redlight night-shift, *Guardian*, 9.7.90*
Clients fleeced by clip and run rip-off, *Guardian*, 9.7.90
Hotel booking scam leaves frustrated punter stranded, *Guardian*, 9.7.90
Streets apart, *Guardian*, 13.7.90*
Tender living carers, *Guardian*, 7.11.90
Prisoner plotted to have detective killed, *Guardian*, 13.11.90
Admirer sent Ripper bikini photograph, *Guardian*, 12.12.90
Yorkshire Ripper 'believed he was humane killer', *Independent*, 8.12.90
Wendy, victim of low life in sordid square mile, *Sunday Telegraph*, 9.12.90*
Guess who's coming to the erotic dinner, *Observer*, 25.11.90*

Irish press
An Irishman's diary, *Irish Times*, 23.1.90
Reform prostitution law: TD, *Irish Independent*, 9.8.90
No-job girls 'turn to vice', *Irish Independent*, 10.8.90

1991
UK press
Body of prostitute, 15, 'killed by pimp' found eight years later, *Guardian*, 22.1.91
'Hot blonde' pleads nymphomania as town quakes at kiss-and-tell list, *Guardian*, 9.9.91
Prostitutes warned after body identified, *Independent*, 9.1.91
Prostitutes with HIV 'should get sick pay', *Independent*, 11.6.91
Killing leads to calls for new laws on prostitution, *Independent*, 20.8.91
The girls next door are bonkers, *Independent*, 10.9.91
Polls find majority support 'discreet' legal brothels, *Independent*, 11.9.91
Legal brothels would be quieter, *Independent*, 13.9.91
Anger at leniency for rapist who agreed to wear condom, *The Times*, 12.4.91
Rapist gets reduced jail sentence for attack on prostitute, *Daily Telegraph*, 1.8.91*

CLEAN UP YOUR ACT, PRIVATE MEMBERS, *Observer*, 23.6.91*
WORKING GIRLS WIN RIGHT TO CARRY ON AT EUROPE'S RED LIGHTS, *Observer*, 10.2.91
LAMONT LODGER MAKES HER EXCUSES – AND STAYS, *Sunday Telegraph*, 21.4.91*
ATTACK ON CALL GIRL REVEALS AWFUL TRUTH TO HER FAMILY, *Sunday Times*, 18.8.91*

Irish press

PROSTITUTES AND THE LIVES THEY LEAD, *Irish Times*, 11.3.91*
'SEX ATTACK' ON PROSTITUTE, *Irish Independent*, 5.2.91
KEEPING A FAMILY BY DAY AND A BROTHEL BY NIGHT, *Irish Press*, 16.10.91*
ATTACKS ON BROTHEL POLITICIAN 'WRONG', *Irish Press*, 25.10.91*

An additional illustration used in the analysis of press photography (Chapter Seven) accompanied the following article:
SEX FOR SALE, *Hot Press*, 12.3.87

Appendix III

Appendix II

Newspaper photographs

Whilst the analysis is based upon all photographs, illustrations and sketches which accompanied the newspaper reports on prostitution, I have only reproduced two here, with an additional illustration which appeared in a magazine article on prostitution. There were difficulties experienced obtaining copyright permission; for example, the *Irish Times* does not grant copyright clearance for photographs which show faces. Newspaper titles no longer in existence made contacting photographers for copyright clearance impossible; in other cases, photographers were simply untraceable. The selected photographs are considered by me as exemplars in respect of the arguments made in Chapter Seven. The reader must therefore 'take on trust' that they are typical, an unfortunate result of the difficulties encountered but one which is unavoidable. (Of course, the reader may refer to the newspapers which are, after all, publicly available.)

Three pictures are reproduced here, in consecutive order:

1. ALL IN THE BEST POSSIBLE TASTE, *Guardian*, 20.11.89
   No caption.

2. CURBING CRAWLERS ON REDLIGHT NIGHT-SHIFT, *Guardian*, 9.7.90
   Caption: Fair game ... A woman talks to a prospective client in Mayfair, London, a favourite haunt of kerb crawlers and prostitutes.

3. SEX FOR SALE, *Hot Press*, 12.3.87
   No caption.

JAMES STRACHAN

Bibliography

Adam, B. (1990), *Time and Social Theory*, Polity Press: Cambridge.

Aggleton, P. and Homans, H. (1987), *Educating About AIDS*, NHS Training Authority.

Albert, E. (1982), 'Ethnomethodology: The audience that "knows" the speech, "discovers" it', *Studies in Communications*, Vol. 2, pp. 91-110.

Alcoff, L. (1988), 'Cultural feminism versus post-structuralism: the identity crisis in feminist theory', *Signs: Journal of Women in Culture and Society*, Vol. 13 (31).

Allen, J. (1986), 'Evidence and silence', in Pateman, C. and Gross, E. (eds), *Feminist Challenges*, Allen & Unwin, London.

Althusser, L. (1971), 'Ideology and ideological state apparatuses' in *Lenin and Philosophy and Other Essays*, trans. D. Brewster, NLB, London.

Anderson, D. & Sharrock, W.W. (1979), 'Biasing the news: technical issues in "media studies"', *Sociology*, Vol. 13.

Andrieu-Sanz, R. and Vasquez-Anton, K. (1989), 'Young prostitutes in Bilbao: a description and interpretation' in Cain, M. (ed.), *Growing Up Good*, Sage, London.

Ang, I. (1990), 'Culture and communication: Towards an ethnographic critique of media consumption in the transnational media system', *European Journal of Communication*, Vol. 5 (2-3), pp. 239-260.

Anon. (1989), 'AIDS: Prevention, policies and prostitutes', *The Lancet*, May, pp. 1111-1113.

Atkinson, J.M. (1982), *Discovering Suicide: Studies in the Social Organisation of Sudden Death*, 2nd ed., Macmillan Press Ltd, London.

Atkinson, J.M. (1990), 'Ethnomethodological approaches to socio-legal studies' in Coulter, J. (ed.), op. cit.

Atkinson, M. and Boles, J. (1977), 'Prostitution as an Ecology of Confidence Games: The Scripted Behaviour of Prostitutes and Vice Officers', in Byrant, C. (ed.), *Sexual Deviancy in Social Context*, pp. 219-231, New York, New Viewpoints.

Atkinson, J.M. and Heritage, J. (1984), *Structures of Social Action: Studies in Conversation*, University Press, Cambridge.

Bailey, K. (1987), *Methods of Social Research*, The Free Press, New York.

Bakhtin, M. (1981), 'Forms of time and the chronotope in the novel' in Holquist, M. (ed.), *The Dialogic Imagination*, trans. C. Emerson & M. Holquist, University of Texas Press, Austin.

Bardsley, B. (1987), *Flowers in Hell: An Investigation into Women and Crime*, Pandora, London.

Barthes, R. (1977), *Image–Music–Text*, trans. S. Heath, Fontana Paperbacks, London.

Barthes, R. (1985), *The Fashion System*, trans. M. Ward and R. Howard, Jonathan Cape, London.

Bauman, Z. (1990), *Thinking Sociologically*, Basil Blackwell, Oxford.

deBeauvoir, S. (1953), *The Second Sex*, London, Jonathan Cape Limited.

Becker, H. (1981), *Exploring Society Photographically*, University Press, Chicago.

Becker, H. (1986), *Writing for Social Scientists*, University of Chicago Press, London.

Bell, A. (1991), *The Language of the News Media*, Basil Blackwell, Oxford.

Bell, L. (ed.), (1987), *Good Girls/Bad Girls: Sex Trade Workers and Feminists Face to Face*, The Women's Press, Ontario.

Benjamin, H. and Masters, R. (1964), *The Prostitute in Society*, Julian Press Inc., New York.

Bentz, Malhotra, V. and Mayes, P. (1993), *Women's Power and Roles as Portrayed in Visual Images of Women in the Arts and Mass Media*, Edwin Meller Press, New York.

Berger, P. and Luckmann, T. (1966), *The Social Construction of Reality*, Penguin Books, Middlesex.

Billig, M. (1988), 'Methodology and scholarship in understanding ideological explanation' in Antaki, C. (ed.), *Analysing Everyday Explanation*, pp. 199-215, Sage, London.

Blum, A. and McHugh, P. (1971), 'The Social Ascription of Motives', *American Sociological Review*, Vol. 36 (February), pp. 98-109.

Boffin, T. and Gupta, S. (1990), *Ecstatic Antibodies: Resisting the AIDS Mythology*, Rivers Oram Press, London.

Boulos, B. (1983), The Yorkshire Ripper: A case study of 'the Sutcliffe Papers', Stanley, L. (ed.), *Department of Sociology Occasional Paper* (11), Manchester University, Manchester.

Bourdieu, P. (1990), 'Time Perspectives of the Kabyle' in Hassard, J. (ed.), op. cit., pp. 219-237.

Boyle, C. and Noonan, S. (1987), 'Gender neutrality, prostitution and pornography', in Bell, L. (ed.), *Good Girls/Bad Girls*, pp. 37-47, The Women's Press, Ontario.

Brandt, A. (1988), 'AIDS and metaphor: Towards the social meaning of epidemic disease', *Social Research*, Vol. 53, No. 3, pp. 413-432.

British Parliamentary Papers (1866), *Reports from Select Committees on the Contagious Diseases Bill and Act* (1866), Irish University Press, Dublin.

Brown, G. and Yule, G. (1983), *Discourse Analysis*, Cambridge University Press, Cambridge.

Bullough, V., Elcano, B., Deacon, M., and Bullough, B. (eds) (1977), *A Bibliography of Prostitution*, Garland, New York.

Butcher, H., Coward, R., Evaristi, M., Garber, J., Harrison, R. and Winship, J. (1974), *Images of Women in the Media*, Centre for Contemporary Cultural Studies Occasional Paper, CCCS, Birmingham.

Cameron, D. and Frazer, E. (1987), *The Lust to Kill: A Feminist Investigation of Sexual Murder*, Polity Press, Cambridge.

Caughie, J. (ed.) (1981), *Theories of Authorship: A Reader*, Routledge & Kegan Paul, London.

Central Statistics Office (1995), *Annual Abstract of Statistics*, HMSO, London.

Central Statistics Office (1995), *Social Trends*, HMSO, London.

Charlston, P. (1992), *Criminal Law: Cases and Materials*, Butterworth, Dublin.

Cicourel, A. (1964), *Method and Measurement in Sociology*, The Free Press, New York.

Clarke, T.J. (1985), *The Painting of Modern Life*, Alfred A. Knopf, New York.

Clarkson, C.M., & Keating, H.M. (1994), *Criminal Law: Texts and Materials*, 3rd edition, Sweet & Maxwell Ltd., London.

Cohen, B. (1980), *Deviant Street Networks: Prostitution in New York City*, D.C. Heath, Canada.

Cohen, E. (1987), 'Sensuality and venality in Bangkok: The dynamics of cross-cultural mapping of prostitution', *Deviant Behaviour*, Vol. 8, No. 3, pp. 223-234.

259

Cohen, S. (1985), *Visions of Social Control: Crime, Punishment and Classification*, Polity & Blackwell, Oxford.

Cohen, S. (1987), *Folk Devils and Moral Panics: The Creation of Mods and Rockers*, Basil Blackwell, Oxford.

Cohen, S. and Young, J. (eds), (1973), *The Manufacture of News: Deviance, Social Problems and the Mass Media*, Sage, London.

Connell, R. (1987), *Gender and Power: Society, the Person and Sexual Politics*, Polity Press, Cambridge.

Corrigan, P. (1988), *Back-stage Dressing: Clothing and the Urban Family*, unpublished PhD thesis, Department of Sociology, University of Dublin.

Corsaro, W. (1985), 'Sociological approaches to discourse analysis' in van Dijk, T. (ed.), *Handbook of Discourse Analysis: Volume 1 Disciplines of Discourse*, pp. 167-190, Academic Press, London.

Coulter, J. (1990), *Ethnomethodological Sociology*, Edward Elgar, Hants.

Coulthard, M. (1977), *An Introduction to Discourse Analysis*, Longman, London.

Coward, R. and Ellis, J. (1977), *Language and Materialism*, Routledge & Kegan Paul, London.

Crites, L. (ed.) (1980), *The Female Offender*, D.C. Heath & Co., Hants.

Cuff, E.C., Payne, G.C.F., Francis, D.W., Hustler, D.E. and Sharrock, W.W. (eds.) (1979), *Perspectives in Sociology*, George Allen & Unwin Ltd., London.

Curran, J. (1990), 'The new revisionism in mass communication research: A reappraisal', *European Journal of Communication*, Vol. 5, No. 2-3.

Dáil Éireann (1980), *Bunreacht na hÉireann (Constitution of Ireland)*, 1st ed. 1937, Government Publications, Dublin.

Davis, H. (1991), 'Media research: whose agenda?' in J. Eldridge (ed.), *Getting the Message: News, Truth and Power* (Glasgow Media Group), Routledge, London.

Davis, K. (1937), 'The Sociology of Prostitution', *American Journal of Sociology*, Vol. 746, pp. 744-755.

Davis, K. (1988), *Power under the Microscope*, Foris Publications, Dortrecht.

Davis, N. (1971), 'The prostitute – developing a deviant identity', in Helsin, J. (ed.), *Studies in the Sociology of Sex*, Meredith Corporation, New York.

Day, S. (1989), 'Prostitute Women and AIDS: anthropology', *AIDS*, Vol. 2, pp. 421-428.

Delacoste, F. and Alexander, P. (eds) (1988), *Sex Work: Writings by Women in the Sex Industry*, Virago Press, London.

Ditton, J. (1980), 'A bibliographic exegesis of Goffman's sociology', in Ditton, J. (ed.), *The View From Goffman*, The Macmillan Press Ltd., London.

Ditton, J. & Duffy, J. (1983), 'Bias in the newspaper reporting of crime news', *British Journal of Criminology*, Vol. 23, No. 2, pp. 159-162.

Dominelli, L. (1986), 'The power of the powerless: prostitution and the reinforcement of submissive femininity', *The Sociological Review*, February, pp. 65-92.

Douglas, J. (ed.) (1971), *Understanding Everyday Life: Towards the Reconstruction of Sociological Knowledge*, Routledge & Kegan Paul, London.

Drew, P. and Wooton, A. (1988), *Erving Goffman: Exploring the Interaction Order*, Polity Press, Cambridge.

Edwards, S. (1987), 'Prostitutes: Victims of Law, Social Policy and Organised Crime', in Carlen, P. and Worrall, A. (eds), *Gender, Crime and Justice*, pp. 43-56, Open University Press, Milton Keynes.

Edwards, S. (1990), 'Violence against women: feminism and the law', in Gelsthorpe, L. and Morris, A. (eds), *Feminist Perspectives in Criminology*, Open University Press, Buckingham.

Edwards, S. (1993), 'Selling the body, keeping the soul: sexuality, power, the theories and realities of prostitution' in Scott, S. and Morgan, D. (eds), *Body Matters*, Falmer Press, London.

Eisenstein, H. (1988), *Contemporary Feminist Thought*, Allen & Unwin Pty. Ltd., Sydney.

Elias, N. (1992), *Time: An Essay*, Basil Blackwell, Oxford.

Enck, G.E. and Preston, J.D. (1988), 'Counterfeit Intimacy: A dramaturgical analysis of an erotic performance', *Deviant Behaviour*, Vol. 9, No. 4, pp.369-81.

English Collective of Prostitutes. (1988), *Prostitute Women and AIDS: Resisting the Virus of Oppression*, ECP, London.

Ericson, R.V., Baranek, P.M. and Chan, J.B.L. (1987), *Visualising Deviance: A Study of News Organisation*, Open University Press, Milton Keynes.

Evans, H. (1978), *Book Pictures on a Page: Photojournalism, Graphics and Picture Editing*, Heinemann, London.

Fairclough, N. (1985), 'Critical and Descriptive Goals in Discourse Analysis', *Journal of Pragmatics*, Vol. 9, pp. 739-763.

Fairclough, N. (1989), *Language and Power*, Longman, Harlow.

Finnegan, F. (1979), *Poverty and Prostitution: A study of Victorian prostitutes in York*, Cambridge University Press, Cambridge.

Fisher, J. (1987), 'Objects of fetishism', in Parker, R. and Pollock, G. (eds), *Framing Feminism: Art and the Women's Movement 1970-1985*, Pandora, London.

Fisher, S. (1986), *In the Patient's Best Interest: Women and the Politics of Medical Decisions*, Rutgers University Press, New Jersey.

Fiske, J. (1987), *Television Culture*, Methuen & Co. Ltd, London.

Forsyth, C. and Fournet, L. (1987), 'A typology of office harlots: mistresses, party girls, and career climbers', *Deviant Behaviour*, Vol. 8, pp. 319-328.

Foucault, M. (1975), *The Birth of the Clinic*, trans. A.M. Sheridan Smith, Vintage Books, New York.

Foucault, M. (1976), *The History of Sexuality*, trans. R. Hurley, Penguin Books Ltd., Middlesex, 1981.

Fowler, R. (1985), 'Power', in van Dijk, T. (ed.), *Handbook of Discourse Analysis*, Academic Press, London.

Fowler, R. (1991), *Language in the News: Discourse and Ideology in the Press*, Routledge, London.

Fox, G.L. (1988), '"Nice girl": social control of women through a value construct', *Signs: Journal of Women in Culture and Society*, Vol. 2, No. 4.

Freund, E. (1987), *The Return of the Reader: Reader-Response Criticism*, Methuen, London.

Frow, J. (1986), *Formal Method in Discourse Analysis*, unpublished manuscript, Department of Linguistics, University of Queensland.

Gagnon, J. and Simon, W. (1973), *Sexual Conduct: The Social Sources of Human Sexuality*, Hutchinson and Co. Ltd., London.

Gannon, I. and Gannon, J. (1980), *Prostitution: The Oldest Male Crime*, Jig Publications, Dublin.

Garber, M. (1993), *Vested Interests: Cross Dressing and Cultural Anxiety*, Penguin, London.

Garber, M., Matlcok, J. and Walkowitz, R. (1993), *Media Spectacles*, Routledge, London.

Garfinkel, H. (1967), *Studies in Ethnomethodology*, Englewood Cliffs, New Jersey.

Garfinkel, H. (1972), 'Studies of routine grounds of everyday activities', in Sudnow, D. (ed.), *Studies in Social Interaction*, pp. 1-30, The Free Press, New York.

Garfinkel, H. and Sacks, H. (1970), 'On formal structures of practical actions', in McKinney, J. and Tiryakian, E. (eds), *Theoretical Sociology: Perspectives and Developments*, Meredith Corporation, New York.

Giddens, A. (1976), *New Rules of Sociological Method*, Hutchinson, London.

Giddens, A. (1989), *Sociology*, Polity Press, Cambridge.

Glaser, B. and Strauss, A. (1968), *The Discovery of Grounded Theory: Strategies for Qualitative Research*, Weidenfeld and Nicolson, London.

Glasgow University Media Group. (1976), *Bad News*, Routledge & Kegan Paul, London.

Glover, E. (1943), 'The psycho-pathology of prostitution', lecture to the International Bureau for the Suppression of Traffic in Women and Children, published in Glover, E. (ed.), *The Roots of Crime*, International Universities, New York, 1961.

Goffman, E. (1959), *The Presentation of the Self in Everyday Life*, Penguin Books Ltd., London.

Goffman, E. (1961), 'Role distance', in *Encounters: Two Studies in the Sociology of Interaction*, pp. 73-134, Penguin Books Ltd., Middlesex.

Goffman, E. (1963), 'The symptomatic significance of situational improprieties', in *Behaviour in Public Places: Notes on the Social Organisation of Gatherings*, pp. 216-241, The Free Press, New York.

Goffman, E. (1963), *Stigma*, Englewood Cliffs, New Jersey.

Goffman, E. (1965), 'Attitudes and rationalisations regarding body exposure', in Roach, M.E. and Eicher, J.B. (eds), *Dress, Adornment and the Social Order*, pp. 50-52, Wiley & Sons Inc., New York.

Goffman, E. (1965), 'Identity Kits', in Roach, M.E. and Eicher, J.B. (eds), op. cit., pp. 246-7.

Goffman, E. (1967), 'Where the action is', in *Interaction Ritual: Essays on Face to Face Behaviour*, The Penguin Press, London.

Goffman, E. (1971), *Relations in Public Places*, The Penguin Press, London.

Goffman, E. (1979), *Gender Advertisements*, The Macmillan Press, London.

Goffman, E. (1981), *Forms of Talk*, Basil Blackwell, Oxford.

Golding, P. and Elliott, P. (1979), *Making the News*, Longman Group Ltd., London.

Goldman, E. (1979), *Red Emma Speaks: The Selected Speeches and Writings of the Anarchist and Feminist*, A.K. Shulman (ed.), Wildwood House Ltd., London.

Goldstein, P. (1979), *Prostitution and Drugs*, Lexington Books, Lexington, MA.

Good, E. and Troiden, R. (eds) (1974), *Sexual Deviance and Sexual Deviants*, William Morrow & Co. Inc., New York.

Gossop, J. et al. (1994), 'Female prostitution and drug taking practices in South London', *Addiction*, Vol. 4.

Hall, S., Hobson, D., Lowe, A. and Willis, P. (eds) (1980), *Culture, Media, Language*, Hutchinson, London.

Halson, J. (1992), *Sexual Harassment, Oppression and Resistance: A feminist ethnography of some young people from Henry James School*, unpublished PhD dissertation, Department of Sociology, University of Warwick.

Hansen, K.V. (1987), 'Feminist conceptions of public and private: a critical analysis', *Berkeley Journal of Sociology*, Vol. XXXII, pp. 105-128.

Harris, Z. (1952a), 'Discourse analysis', *Language*, Vol. 28, No. 1, pp. 1-30.

Harris, Z. (1952b), 'Discourse analysis: A sample text', *Language*, Vol. 28, No. 4, pp. 474-494.

Hartley, J. (1992), *The Politics of Pictures: The Creation of the Public in the Age of Popular Media*, Routledge, London.

Hassard, J. (ed.) (1990), *The Sociology of Time*, The Macmillan Press Ltd., London.

Hebdige, D. (1979), *Subculture – The Meaning of Style*, Methuen and Co. Ltd., London.

Heft, M. (1980), 'Hustling for rights' in Crites, L. (ed.), op. cit.

Heidensohn, F. (1985), *Women and Crime*, Macmillan, Basingstoke.

Henderson, S. (1990), 'Women and HIV / AIDS', *Update*, April.

Henley, N. (1977), *Body Politics: Power, Sex and Non-verbal Communication*, Simon & Schuster, New York.

Herbert, C. (1989), *Talking of Silence: The Sexual Harassment of Schoolgirls*, Falmer Press, Bristol.

Heritage, J. (1984), *Garfinkel and Ethnomethodology*, Polity Press, Cambridge.

Hodder, I. (1994), 'The interpretation of documents and material culture', in Denzin, N. and Lincoln, Y. (eds), *Handbook of Qualitative Research*, pp. 393-402, Sage, London.

Hodge, B. (1989), 'Discourse in time: Some notes on method', in Torode, B. (ed.), op. cit., pp. 93-112.

Holland, P. (1992), *What is a Child? Popular Images of Children*, Virago, London.

Holland, P., Spence, J. and Watney, S. (eds) (1986) *Photography/Politics: Two*, London, Comedia.

Hollway, W. (1981), '"I just wanted to kill a woman": the Ripper and male sexuality', *Feminist Review*, No. 9.

Home Office. (1957), *Report of the Committee on Homosexual Offences and Prostitution* (Wolfenden Report), HMSO, London.

Horton, M. and Aggleton, P. (1990), 'Perverts, Inverts and Experts: the Cultural Production of an AIDS Research Paradigm' in Aggleton, P., Davis, P. and Hart, G. (eds), *AIDS: Social Practices, Social Representations*, pp. 74-100, Falmer Press, London.

International Committee for Prostitutes' Rights. (1986), *Draft Statement on Prostitution and Feminism*, released at the Second World Whores Congress, Brussels, October.

Jaget, C. (1980), *Prostitutes: Our Life*, Falling Wall Press, Bristol.

Jalbert, P. (1973), 'Some constructs for analysing news', in Davis, H. and Walton, P. (eds), *Language, Image, Media*, Basil Blackwell Ltd, Oxford.

Jalbert, P. (1995), 'Critique and analysis in media studies: Media criticism as practical action', *Discourse and Society*, Vol. 6, No. 1, pp. 7-26, Sage, London.

James, J. (1978), 'The prostitute as victim', in Chapman, J. and Gates, M. (eds), *The Victimisation of Women*, pp. 175-199, Sage, London.

James, J. (1980), 'Motivations for entrance into prostitution', in Crites, L. (ed.), *The Female Offender*, pp. 177-205, D.C. Heath and Co., Hants.

Jefferson, G. (ed.) (1992), *Harvey Sacks: Lectures on Conversation*, Vols. 1 & 2, introduced by E. Schegloff, Blackwell, Oxford.

Jones, C. (1986), 'Prostitution and the ruling class in eighteenth-century Montpellier', *History Workshop*, pp. 6-28.

Kalin, T. (1990), 'Flesh histories', *Views*, Boston University, Boston.

Kane, E. (1983), *Doing Your Own Research*, Marion Boyars, London.

Keith, M. and Pile, S. (1993), *Place and the Politics of Identity*, Routledge, London.

Kelly, L. (1988), *Surviving Sexual Violence*, Polity Press in association with Basil Blackwell Ltd, Oxford.

Kessler, K. and McKenna, W. (1978), *Gender: An Ethnomethodological Approach*, John Wiley & Sons Inc., New York.

Kinnell, H. (1989), *Prostitutes, their Clients and Risks of HIV Infection in Birmingham*, District Health Authority Occasional Paper, Birmingham.

Kirk, J. and Miller, M. (1896), *Reliability and Validity in Qualitative Research*, Sage, London.

Kitzinger, J. and Miller, D. (1992), '"African AIDS": The media and audience beliefs', in Aggleton, P., Davies, P. and Hart, G. (eds), *AIDS: Rights, Risk and Reason*, pp. 28-52, Falmer Press, London.

Kress, G. (1985), 'Ideological structures in discourse' in van Dijk, T. (ed.), *Handbook of Discourse Analysis*, Vol. 4, pp. 27-41, Academic Press, London.

Krippendorf, K. (1980), *Content Analysis: An Introduction to its Methodology*, Sage, London.

Lauer, R.H. (1986), *Social Problems and the Quality of Life*, WCB, Iowa.

Lees, S. (1986), *Losing Out: Sexuality and Adolescent Girls*, Hutchinson Group Ltd., London.

Lees, S. (1989), 'Learning to love: sexual reputation, morality and the social control of girls', in Cain, M. (ed.), *Growing Up Good: Policing the Behaviour of Girls in Europe*, Sage Publications Ltd., London.

Levine, J. and Madden, L. (1987), *Lyn: A Story of Prostitution*, Attic Press, Dublin.

Lichtenberg, J. (1991), 'In defence of objectivity', in Curran, J. and Gurevitch, M. (eds), *Mass Media and Society*, pp. 216-231, Edward Arnold, London.

Lupton, D. (1994), *Moral Threats and Dangerous Desires: AIDS in the News Media*, Francis and Taylor, London.

Lury, C. (1982), *An Ethnography of an Ethnography: Reading Sociology*, Department of Sociology Occasional Paper (9), Manchester University, Manchester.

McHoul, A.W. (1982), *Telling How Texts Talk: Essays on Reading and Ethnomethodology*, Routledge and Kegan Paul, London.

McHugh, P. (1968), *Defining the Situation: The Organisation of Meaning in Social Interaction*, Bobbs-Merrill, Indianapolis.

McHugh, P. (1970), 'A common sense perception of deviance', in Dretzel, H. (ed.), *Recent Sociology: Patterns of Communicative Behaviour*, The Macmillan Co., New York.

McIntosh, M. (1978), 'Who needs prostitutes? The ideology of male sexual needs', in Smart, C. & Smart, B. (eds), *Women, Sexuality and Social Control*, Routledge and Kegan Paul, London.

McKeganey, N. and Smith, B. (1980), 'Reading and writing as collaborative production: some comments on Anderson's and Sharrock's "Biasing the news"', *Sociology*, Vol. 14, pp. 615-621.

McLeod, E. (1982), *Women Working: Prostitutes Now*, Croom Helm Ltd., London.

McRobbie, A. (1982), 'The problem of feminist research: between talk, text and action', *Feminist Review*, Vol. 12, pp. 46-56.

McRobbie, A. (ed.) (1989), *Zootsuits and Second Hand Dresses: An Anthropology of Fashion and Music*, Macmillan Education Ltd., London.

Maio, K. (1988), *Feminists in the Dark: Reviewing the Movies*, The Crossing Press, California.

de Marley, D. (1986), *Working Dress: A History of Occupational Clothing*, BT Batsford Ltd., London.

Marshall, C. & Rossman, G. (1995), *Designing Qualitative Research*, second edition, Sage Publications Ltd., London.

Marshall, S. (1990), 'Picturing deviancy', in Boffin, T. and Gupta, S. (eds), *Ecstatic Antibodies: Resisting the AIDS Mythology*, Rivers Oram Press, London.

266

Martins, H. (1974), 'Time and theory in sociology' in Rex, J. (ed.), *Approaches to Sociology: An Introduction to Major Trends in British Sociology*, pp. 246-293, Routledge & Kegan Paul, London.

Martins, H. (1993), *Knowledge and Power: Essays in Honour of John Rex*, I.B. Tauris & Co. Ltd., London.

Maynard, D. (1984), *Inside Plea Bargaining*, Plenum Press, New York.

Meyrowitz, J. (1985), *No Sense of Place: The Impact of Electronic Media on Social Behaviour*, Oxford University Press Inc., New York.

Millett, K. (1970), *Sexual Politics*, Hart-Davis, London.

Millett, K. (1975), *The Prostitution Papers*, Avon, New York.

Mills, C. Wright. (1959), *The Sociological Imagination*, Oxford University Press, New York.

Milne, K. (1987), 'Sex and the soaps', *New Society*, 10 April.

Moore, W.E. (1963), *Man, Time and Society*, John Wiley & Sons, New York.

Morgan, D. and Scott, S. (eds) (1993), *Body Matters*, Falmer Press, London.

Morley, D. (1993), 'Active audience theory: pendulums and pitfalls', *Journal of Communication*, Vol. 43, No. 4, pp. 255-261.

Murdock, G. (1980), 'Misrepresenting media sociology – a reply to Anderson and Sharrock', *Sociology*, Vol. 14, pp. 457-468.

Nead, L. (1984), 'The pure and the fallen', *Times Higher Education Supplement*, 28.12.84, p. 9.

Nead, L. (1988), *Myths of Sexuality: Representations of Women in Victorian Britain*, Basil Blackwell, London.

Nestle, J. (1988), 'Lesbians and prostitutes: A historical sisterhood', in Delacoste, F. and Alexander, P (eds), *Sex Work: Writings by Women in the Sex Industry*, pp. 2231-247, Virago Press, London.

O'Neill, M. (1992), 'Prostitution, ideology and the structuration of gender relations: Towards a critical feminist praxis', presented at the British Sociological Annual Conference.

Orwell, G. (1933), *Down and Out in London*, Penguin, London.

Pateman, C. (1988), *The Sexual Contract*, Oxford, Polity Press in association with Basil Blackwell Ltd., Cambridge.

Pecheux, M. (1982), *Language, Semantics and Ideology*, first ed. 1975, Macmillan, London.

Perkins, R. (1989), 'Wicked women or working girls: The prostitute on the silver screen', *Media Information Australia*, No. 51, February.

Perkins, R. (1991), *Working Girls: Prostitutes, their Life and Social Control*, Australian Institute of Criminology, Canberra.

Perkins, R., Lovejoy, F. and Marina (1990), '"Protecting the community": Prostitutes and public health legislation in the age of AIDS', *Criminology Australia*, pp. 6-8, October/November.

Pheterson, G. (1988), 'The social consequences of unchastity', in Delacoste, F. and Alexander, P. (eds), op. cit.

Plummer, K. (ed.) (1981), *The Making of the Modern Homosexual*, Hutchinson & Co. Ltd., London.

Pollner, M. (1987), *Mundane Reason: Reality in Everyday and Sociological Discourse*, University Press, Cambridge.

Potter, J. and Wetherell, M. (1987), *Discourse and Social Psychology: Beyond Attitudes and Behaviour*, Sage Publications, London.

Psathas, G. (ed.) (1979), *Everyday Language: Studies in Ethnomethodology*, Irvingon Publishers Inc., New York.

Radway, J. (1984), *Reading the Romance: Women, Patriarchy and Popular Literature*, University of North Carolina Press.

Radway, J. (1986), 'Identifying ideological seams: mass culture, analytical method and cultural practice', *Communication*, Vol. 9, pp. 95-119.

Riberio, A. (1986), *Dress and Morality*, BT Batsford, London.

Richardson, K. and Corner, J. (1986), 'Reading reception: mediation and transparency in viewers' accounts of a TV programme', *Media, Culture and Society*, Vol. 8, pp. 485-508, Sage.

Roberts, N. (1993), *Whores in History: Prostitution in Western Society*, Grafton, London.

Rock, P. (1973), *Deviant Behaviour*, Hutchinson, London.

Rolph, C.H. (1954), *Women of the Streets: A Sociological Study of the Common Prostitute*, Secker & Warburg, London.

Root, J. (1984), *Images of Women: Sexuality*, Pandora Press, London.

Rosenblum, K. (1975), 'Female deviance and the female sex role: a preliminary investigation', *British Journal of Sociology*, Vol. 26, pp. 169-185.

Ross, M.W. and Ryan, L. (1995), 'The little deaths: Perceptions of HIV, sexuality and quality of life in gay men', *Journal of Psychology and Human Sexuality*, Vol. 7, No. 1/2, pp. 1-20.

Rustin, M. (1993), 'Ethnomethodology', in Morgan, D. and Stanley, L. (eds), *Debates in Sociology*, Manchester University Press, Manchester.

Ryan, L. (1987), 'Representations of Prostitutes: An interpretative approach to the analysis of media texts', unpublished Senior Sophister dissertation, Department of Sociology, Trinity College, Dublin.

Sacks, H. (1963), 'Sociological description', *Berkeley Journal of Sociology*, Vol. 8, pp. 1-16.

Sacks, H. (1970), *Spring Lectures 1970*, unpublished ms, University of California.

Sacks, H. (1972), 'Notes on Police Assessment of Moral Character', in Sudnow, D. (ed.), op. cit., pp. 280-293.

Sacks, H. (1974), 'On the analysability of stories by children', in Turner, R. (ed.), *Ethnomethodology: Selected Readings*, pp. 216-232, Penguin, Harmondsworth.

Sacks, H. (1976), 'The search for help: no-one to turn to' in Schneidman, E. (ed.), *Essays in Self-Destruction*, pp. 203-223, Science House, New York.

Sacks, H. (1978), 'Some technical considerations of a dirty joke', in Schenkein, J. (ed.), *Studies in the Organisation of Conversational Interaction*, pp. 250-269, Academic Press Inc. Ltd., London.

Sacks, H. (1979), 'Hot Rodder: a revolutionary category', in Psathas, G. (ed.), *Everyday Language: Studies in Ethnomethodology*, pp. 7-14, Irvington Publications Inc., New York.

Sacks, H. (1984), 'Notes on Methodology', in Atkinson, J.M. and Heritage, J. (eds), *Structures of Social Action: Studies in Conversation Analysis*, Cambridge University Press, Cambridge.

Sacks, H., Schegloff, E. and Jefferson, G. (1974), 'A simplest systematics for the organisation of turn-taking in conversation', *Language*, No. 50, pp. 696-735.

Schegloff, E. (1972), 'Notes on a conversational practice: formulating place', in Sudnow, D. (ed.), *Studies in Social Interaction*, pp. 75-118, The Free Press, New York.

Schegloff, E. (1982), 'Discourse as interactional achievement', in Tannen, D. (ed.), *Georgetown University Round Table on Languages and Linguistics*, pp. 71-93, Georgetown University Press, Washington DC.

Schegloff, E. (1988), 'Goffman and the analysis of conversation', in Drew, P. and Wooton, A. (eds), *Erving Goffman: Exploring the Interaction Order*, pp. 88-135, Polity Press, Cambridge.

Schenkein, J. (1979), 'The Radio Raiders Story', in Psathas, G. (ed.), *Everyday Language: Studies in Ethnomethodology*, pp. 187-210, Irvington Publisher, New York.

Schur, E. (1980), *The Politics of Deviance: Stigma Contests and the Uses of Power*, New Jersey, Prentice Hall Inc.

Sharrock, W.W. and Anderson, D. (1982), 'The persistent evasion of technical problems in media studies: a reply to Murdock and McKegney and Smith', *Sociology*, Vol. 16, pp. 108-115.

Silver, R. (1993), *The Girl in Scarlet Heels*, Century, London.

Silverman, D. (1985), *Qualitative Methodology and Sociology*, Gower, Hants.

Silverman, D. (1993), *Interpreting Qualitative Data: Methods for Analysing Talk, Text and Interaction*, Sage, London.

Silverman, D. (1993), 'The machinery of interaction: Remaking social science', *The Sociological Review*, pp. 731-752, Blackwell, Oxford.

Smart, C. (1976), *Women, Crime and Criminology: A Feminist Critique*, Routledge & Kegan Paul Ltd., London.

Smart, C. and Smart, B. (eds) (1978), *Women, Sexuality and Social Control*, Routledge and Kegan Paul, London.

Smith, J.C., and Hogan, B. (1992), *Criminal Law*, 7th edition, Butterworth Limited, Dublin.

Sorokin, P. and Merton, R. (1937/1991), 'Social time: A methodological and functional analysis', in Hassard, J. (ed.), op. cit.

Stanko, E. (1993), '"Ordinary fear": women, violence and personal property', in Bart, P. and Moran, E. (eds), *Violence against Women: The Bloody Footprints*, Sage, London.

Sweetman, R. (1979), *On Our Backs: Sexual Attitudes in a Changing Ireland*, Pan Books, London.

Tagg, J. (1988), *The Burden of Representation: Essays on Photographies and Histories*, Macmillan Education Ltd., London.

ten Have, P. (1985), 'Contrastive analysis of interview talk', in Hak, T., Haafkens, J. and Nijhoff, G. (eds), *Working Papers on Discourse and Conversational Analysis*, (Konteksten series no. 5), Erasmus University, Institute for Preventive and Social Psychiatry, Rotterdam.

Tesch, R. (1990), *Qualitative Research: Analysis Types and Software Tools*, Falmer Press, Hampshire.

Thompson, J. (1984), *Studies in the Theory of Ideology*, Polity, Cambridge.

Thompson, J. (1987), 'Language and ideology: a framework for analysis', *Sociological Review*, Vol. 35, No. 3.

Thompson, J. (1988), 'Mass communication and modern culture: contribution to a critical theory of ideology', *Sociology*, Vol. 22, No. 3.

Thompson, J. (1990), *Ideology and Modern Culture: Critical Social Theory in the Era of Mass Communication*, Polity, Cambridge.

Torode, B. (1987), 'AIDS in Africa and British media "bias"', paper presented to the Discourse Analysis Workshop, University of Bradford.

Torode, B. (ed.) (1989), *Text and Talk as Social Practice*, Foris Publications, Dortrecht.

Trades Union Congress. (1984), *Images of Inequality*, Trades Union Congress, London.

Travers, A. (1994), 'Destigmatising the stigma of self in Garfinkel's and Goffman's accounts of normal appearances', *Philosophy of the Social Sciences*, Vol. 24, No. 1, pp. 5-40, Sage Publications Inc., CA.

Tuchman, G. (1991), 'Media institutions: Qualitative methods in the study of news', in Jensen, K.B. and Jankowski, N.W. (eds), *Handbook of Qualitative Methodologies for Mass Communications Research*, Routledge, London.

Turner, B. (1984), *The Body and Society: Explorations in Social Theory*, Basil Blackwell, Oxford.

Turner, G. (1990), *British Cultural Studies: An Introduction*, Unwin Hyman Ltd., London.

Turner, R. (1971), 'Words, utterance and activities', in Douglas, J. (ed.), op. cit.

Turnstall, J. (1983), *The Media in Britain*, Constable & Co., London.

van Dijk, T.A. (ed.) (1985), *Discourse and Communication: New Approaches to the Analysis of Mass Media Discourse and Communication*, Walter de Gruyter & Co., Berlin.

van Dijk, T.A. (1988), *News Analysis: Case Studies of International and National News in the Press*, Lawrence Erlbaum Associates Inc., New Jersey.

van Maanen, J. (1988), *Tales of the Field: On Writing Ethnography*, The University of Chicago Press, London.

van Zoonen, L. (1991), 'Feminist perspectives on media' in Curran, J. and Gurevitch, M. (eds), *Mass Media and Society*, Edward Arnold, London.

Viney, L. (1989), *Images of Illness*, Robert Krieger, Florida.

Walby, S., Hay, A. and Soothill, K. (1983), 'The social construction of rape', *Theory, Culture and Society*, Vol. 2, No. 1.

Walkowitz, J. (1980), *Prostitution and Victorian Society: Women, Class and the State*, University Press, Cambridge.

Walkowitz, J. (1980), 'The politics of prostitution', *Signs: Journal of Women in Culture and Society*, Vol. 6, No. 1, pp. 123-135.

Walkowitz, J. (1981), 'Male vice and female virtue: feminism and the politics of prostitution in nineteenth-century Britain' in O'Brien, M. (ed.), *The Politics of Reproduction*, pp. 419-434, Routledge & Kegan Paul, London.

Waters, E. (1989), 'Restructuring the "woman question": Perestroika and prostitution', *Feminist Review*, No. 33.

Watney, S. (1987), *Policing Desire: Pornography, AIDS and the Media*, Methuen, London.

Watson, G. and Seiler, R.M. (eds) (1992), *Text in Context: Contributions to Ethnomethodology*, Sage, London.

Weedon, C. (1987), *Feminist Practice and Post-Structuralist Theory*, Basil Blackwell, Oxford.

Weeks, J. (1979), *Coming Out: Homosexual Politics in Britain, from the Nineteenth Century to the Present*, Quartet Books, London.

Wild, P. (1978), 'Working Girls: a case study of job satisfaction', paper presented at the Pacific Sociological Association Conference, Washington.

Wilson, E. (1983), *What Is To Be Done About Violence Against Women?*, Penguin, Middlesex.

Wilson, E. (1991), *The Sphinx in the City*, Virago, London.

Wittgenstein, L. (1953), *Philosophical Investigations*, Basil Blackwell, Oxford.

Wolf, N. (1991), *The Beauty Myth*, Vintage, London.

Zerubavel, E. (1979), *Patterns of Time in Hospital Life*, University of Chicago Press, London.

Legislation

1956 Street Offences Act, Ch. 57 (UK).
1982 Criminal Justice Act, Ch. 48 (UK).
1985 Sexual Offences Act, Ch. 44 (UK).
1993 Criminal Law (Sexual Offences) Act, No. 20 (Ireland).